C-4112   CAREER EXAMINATION SERIES

This is your
PASSBOOK for...

Postal Electronic/ Maintenance/ Mechanic Exam (955)

Test Preparation Study Guide
Questions & Answers

NATIONAL LEARNING CORPORATION®

COPYRIGHT NOTICE

This book is SOLELY intended for, is sold ONLY to, and its use is RESTRICTED to individual, bona fide applicants or candidates who qualify by virtue of having seriously filed applications for appropriate license, certificate, professional and/or promotional advancement, higher school matriculation, scholarship, or other legitimate requirements of education and/or governmental authorities.

This book is NOT intended for use, class instruction, tutoring, training, duplication, copying, reprinting, excerption, or adaptation, etc., by:

1) Other publishers
2) Proprietors and/or Instructors of "Coaching" and/or Preparatory Courses
3) Personnel and/or Training Divisions of commercial, industrial, and governmental organizations
4) Schools, colleges, or universities and/or their departments and staffs, including teachers and other personnel
5) Testing Agencies or Bureaus
6) Study groups which seek by the purchase of a single volume to copy and/or duplicate and/or adapt this material for use by the group as a whole without having purchased individual volumes for each of the members of the group
7) Et al.

Such persons would be in violation of appropriate Federal and State statutes.

PROVISION OF LICENSING AGREEMENTS – Recognized educational, commercial, industrial, and governmental institutions and organizations, and others legitimately engaged in educational pursuits, including training, testing, and measurement activities, may address request for a licensing agreement to the copyright owners, who will determine whether, and under what conditions, including fees and charges, the materials in this book may be used them. In other words, a licensing facility exists for the legitimate use of the material in this book on other than an individual basis. However, it is asseverated and affirmed here that the material in this book CANNOT be used without the receipt of the express permission of such a licensing agreement from the Publishers. Inquiries re licensing should be addressed to the company, attention rights and permissions department.

All rights reserved, including the right of reproduction in whole or in part, in any form or by any means, electronic or mechanical, including photocopying, recording, or by any information storage and retrieval system, without permission in writing from the Publisher.

Copyright © 2024 by
National Learning Corporation

212 Michael Drive, Syosset, NY 11791
(516) 921-8888 • www.passbooks.com
E-mail: info@passbooks.com

PUBLISHED IN THE UNITED STATES OF AMERICA

PASSBOOK® SERIES

THE *PASSBOOK® SERIES* has been created to prepare applicants and candidates for the ultimate academic battlefield – the examination room.

At some time in our lives, each and every one of us may be required to take an examination – for validation, matriculation, admission, qualification, registration, certification, or licensure.

Based on the assumption that every applicant or candidate has met the basic formal educational standards, has taken the required number of courses, and read the necessary texts, the *PASSBOOK® SERIES* furnishes the one special preparation which may assure passing with confidence, instead of failing with insecurity. Examination questions – together with answers – are furnished as the basic vehicle for study so that the mysteries of the examination and its compounding difficulties may be eliminated or diminished by a sure method.

This book is meant to help you pass your examination provided that you qualify and are serious in your objective.

The entire field is reviewed through the huge store of content information which is succinctly presented through a provocative and challenging approach – the question-and-answer method.

A climate of success is established by furnishing the correct answers at the end of each test.

You soon learn to recognize types of questions, forms of questions, and patterns of questioning. You may even begin to anticipate expected outcomes.

You perceive that many questions are repeated or adapted so that you can gain acute insights, which may enable you to score many sure points.

You learn how to confront new questions, or types of questions, and to attack them confidently and work out the correct answers.

You note objectives and emphases, and recognize pitfalls and dangers, so that you may make positive educational adjustments.

Moreover, you are kept fully informed in relation to new concepts, methods, practices, and directions in the field.

You discover that you are actually taking the examination all the time: you are preparing for the examination by "taking" an examination, not by reading extraneous and/or supererogatory textbooks.

In short, this PASSBOOK®, used directedly, should be an important factor in helping you to pass your test.

POSTAL ELECTRONIC / MAINTENANCE / MECHANIC EXAM

Sample Questions

Examination 955 – Postal Electronic / Maintenance / Mechanic

The purpose of this booklet is to illustrate the types of questions that will be used in Test 955. The samples will also show how the questions in the test are to be answered.

Test 955 measures knowledge, skills, and abilities (KSAs) used by a variety of maintenance positions. Exhibit A lists the actual KSAs that are measured. However, not all KSAs that are measured in this test are scored for every position. The qualification standard for each position lists the KSAs required for the position. Only those questions that measure KSAs required for the position(s) for which you are applying will be scored for the position(s).

The suggested answers to each question are lettered A, B, C, etc. Select the BEST answer and make a heavy pencil mark in the corresponding space on the Sample Answer Sheet. Each mark must be dense black. Each mark must cover more than half the space and must not extend into neighboring spaces. If the answer to Sample 1 is B, you would mark the Sample Answer Sheet like this:

Test consists of Personal Inventory, General Aptitude and Spatial Relations sections. Subject areas to be tested are listed on the following page.

STUDY CAREFULLY BEFORE YOU GO THE EXAMINATION ROOM

(1) **Knowledge of basic mechanics** refers to the theory of operation, terminology, usage, and characteristics of basic mechanical principles as they apply to such things as gears, pulleys, cams, pawls, power transmissions, linkages, fasteners, chains, sprockets, and belts; and including hoisting, rigging, roping, pneumatics, and hydraulic devices.

(2) **Knowledge of basic electricity** refer to the theory, terminology, usage, and characteristics of basic electrical principles such as Ohm's Law, Kirchoff's Law, and magnetism, as they apply to such things as AC-DC circuitry and hardware, relays, switches, and circuit breakers.

(3) **Knowledge of basic electronics** refers to the theory, terminology, usage, and characteristics of basic electronic principles concerning such things as solid state devices, vacuum tubes, coils, capacitors, resistors, and basic logic circuitry.

(4) **Knowledge of digital electronics** refers to the terminology, characteristics, symbology, and operation of digital components as used in such things as logic gates, registers, adders, counters, memories, encoders and decoders.

(5) **Knowledge of safety procedures and equipment** refers to the knowledge of industrial hazards (e.g., mechanical, chemical, electrical, electronic) and procedures and techniques established to avoid injuries to self and others such as lock-out devices, protective clothing, and waste disposal techniques.

(6) **Knowledge of basic computer concepts** refers to the terminology, usage, and characteristics of digital memory storage/processing devices such as internal memory, input-output peripherals, and familiarity with programming concepts.

(19) **Ability to perform basic mathematical computations** refers to the ability to perform basic calculations such as addition, subtraction, multiplication and division with whole numbers, fractions and decimals.

(20) **Ability to perform more complex mathematics** refers to the ability to perform calculations such as basic algebra, geometry, scientific notation, and number conversions, as applied to mechanical, electrical and electronic applications.

(21) **Ability to apply theoretical knowledge to practical applications** refers to mechanical, electrical and electronic maintenance applications such as inspection, troubleshooting equipment repair and modification, preventive maintenance, and installation of electrical equipment.

(22) **Ability to detect patterns** refers to the ability to observe and analyze qualitative factors such as number progressions, spatial relationships, and auditory and visual patterns. This includes combining information and determining how a given set of numbers, objects, or sounds are related to each other.

(23) **Ability to use written reference materials** refers to the ability to locate, read, and comprehend text material such as handbooks, manuals, bulletins, directives, checklists and route sheets.

(26) **Ability to follow instructions** refers to the ability comprehend and execute written and oral instructions such as work orders, checklists, route sheets, and verbal directions and instructions.

(31) <u>Ability to use hand tools</u> refers to knowledge of, and proficiency with, various hand tools. This ability involves the safe and efficient use and maintenance of such tools as screwdrivers, wrenches, hammers, pliers, chisels, punches, taps, dies, rules, gauges, and alignment tools.

(35) <u>Ability to use technical drawings</u> refers to the ability to read and comprehend technical materials such as diagrams, schematics, flow charts, and blueprints.

(36) <u>Ability to use test equipment</u> refers to the knowledge of, and proficiency with, various types of mechanical, electrical and electronic test equipment such as VOMS, oscilloscopes, circuit tracers, amprobes, and tachometers.

(37) <u>Ability to solder</u> refers to the knowledge of, and ability to safely and effectively apply, the appropriate soldering techniques.

Job Description

Maintenance positions require highly skilled and experienced individuals. All applicants must meet the knowledge, skills, and abilities requirements listed.
Maintenance duties require prolonged standing, walking, climbing, bending, reaching, and stooping. Employees must lift and carry heavy objects on level surfaces, on ladders, and/or on stairways. For positions requiring driving, applicants must have a valid state driver's license, a safe driving record, and at least two years of documented driving experience.

Electronic Technician -- Performs the full range of diagnostic, preventive maintenance, alignment and calibration, and overhaul tasks, on both hardware and software on a variety of mail processing, customer service, and building equipment and systems, applying advanced technical knowledge to solve complex problems.

1. The primary function of a take-up pulley in a belt conveyor is to

   A) carry the belt on the return trip.
   B) track the belt.
   C) maintain proper belt tension.
   D) change the direction of the belt.

2. Which device is used to transfer power and rotary mechanical motion from one shaft to another?

   A) Bearing
   B) Lever
   C) Idler roller
   D) Gear
   E) Bushing

3. Which of the following circuits is shown in Figure III-A-22?

   A) Series circuit
   B) Parallel circuit
   C) Series, parallel circuit
   D) Solid state circuit
   E) None of the above

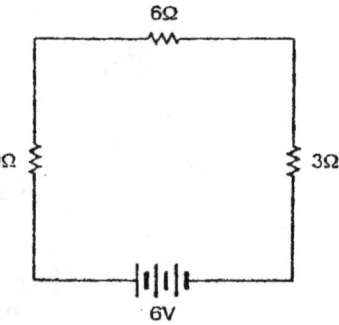

Figure III-A-22

4. A circuit has two resistors of equal value in series. The voltage and current in the circuit are 20 volts and 2 amps respectively. What is the value of EACH resistor?

   A) 5 ohms
   B) 10 ohms
   C) 20 ohms
   D) Not enough information given

5. What is the total net capacitance of two 60-farad capacitors connected in series?

   A) 30 farads
   B) 60 farads
   C) 90 farads
   D) 120 farads
   E) 360 farads

6. Select the Boolean equation that matches the circuit diagram in Figure 79-4-17B.

   A) Z = AB+CD+EF
   B) Z = (A+B) (C+D) (E+F)
   C) Z = A+B+C+D+EF
   D) Z = ABCD (E+F)

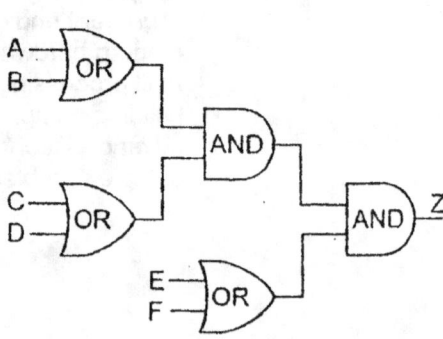

FIGURE 79-4-17B

7. If two 30-mH inductors are connected in series, what is the total net inductance of the combination?

   A) 15 mH
   B) 20 mH
   C) 30 mH
   D) 45 mH
   E) 60 mH

8. In pure binary the decimal number 6 would be expressed as

   A) 001
   B) 011
   C) 110
   D) 111

9. In Figure 75-8-11, which of the following scores will be printed?

   A) All scores > 90 and < 60
   B) All scores < 90
   C) All scores $\leq$ 90 and $\geq$ 60
   D) All scores < 60

10. Crowbars, light bulbs and vacuum bags are to be stored in the cabinet shown in Figure 75-25-1. Considering the balance of weight, what would be the safest arrangement?

    A) Top Drawer – Crowbars
       Middle Drawer - Light Bulbs
       Bottom Drawer - Vacuum bags
    B) Top Drawer – Crowbars
       Middle Drawer - Vacuum bags
       Bottom Drawer - Light Bulbs
    C) Top Drawer - Vacuum Bags
       Middle Drawer – Crowbars
       Bottom Drawer - Light Bulbs
    D) Top Drawer - Vacuum Bags
       Middle Drawer - Light Bulbs
       Bottom Drawer - Crowbars
    E) Top Drawer - Light Bulbs
       Middle Drawer - Vacuum Bags
       Bottom Drawer - Crowbars

11. Which is most appropriate for pulling a heavy load?

    A) Electric lift
    B) Fork lift
    C) Tow Conveyor
    D) Dolly
    E) Pallet truck

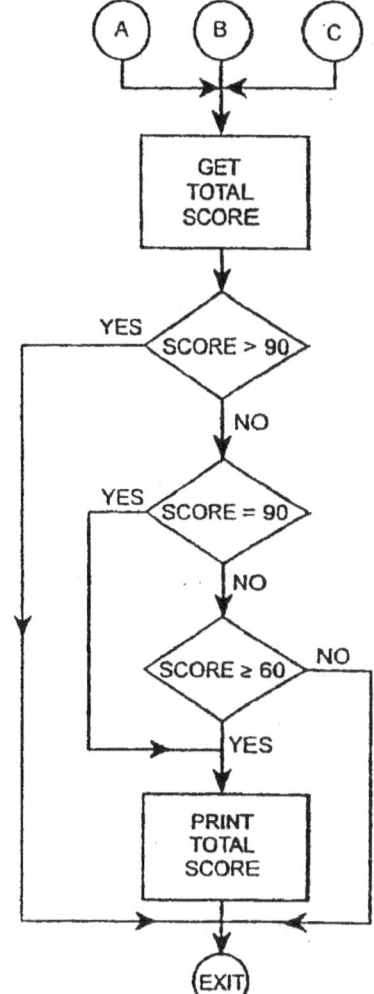

Figure 75-8-11

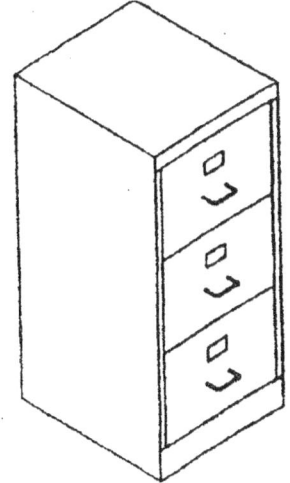

Figure 75-25-1

12. The electrical circuit term "open circuit" refers to a closed loop being opened. When an ohmmeter is connected into this type of circuit, one can expect the meter to

    A) read infinity.
    B) read infinity and slowly return to ZERO.
    C) read ZERO.
    D) read ZERO and slowly return to infinity.
    E) None of the above

13. Contaminants have caused bearings to fail prematurely. Which pair of the items listed below should be kept away from bearings?

    A) Dirt and oil
    B) Grease and water
    C) Oil and grease
    D) Dirt and moisture
    E) Water and oil

14. In order to operate a breast drill, which direction should you turn it?

    A) Clockwise
    B) Counterclockwise
    C) Up and down
    D) Back and forth
    E) Right, then left

15. Which is the correct tool for tightening or loosening a water pipe?

    A) Slip joint pliers
    B) Household pliers
    C) Monkey wrench
    D) Water pump pliers
    E) Pipe wrench

16. What is one purpose of a chuck key?

    A) Open doors
    B) Remove drill bits
    C) Remove screws
    D) Remove set screws
    E) Unlock chucks

17. When smoke is generated as a result of using a portable electric drill for cutting holes into a piece of angle iron, one should

    A) use a fire watch.
    B) cease the drilling operation.
    C) use an exhaust fan to remove smoke.
    D) use a prescribed coolant solution to reduce friction.
    E) call the Fire Department.

18. The primary purpose of soldering is to

    A) melt solder to a molten state.
    B) heat metal parts to the right temperature to be joined.
    C) join metal parts by melting the parts.
    D) harden metal.
    E) join metal parts.

19. Which of the following statements is correct of a soldering gun?

    A) Tip is not replaceable
    B) Cannot be used in cramped places
    C) Heats only when trigger is pressed
    D) Not rated by the number of watts they use
    E) Has no light

20. What unit of measurement is read on a dial torque wrench?

    A) Pounds
    B) Inches
    C) Centimeters
    D) Foot-pounds
    E) Degrees

21. Which instrument is used to test insulation breakdown of a conductor?

    A) Ohmmeter
    B) Ammeter
    C) Megger
    D) Wheatstone bridge
    E) Voltmeter

22. 1/2 of 1/4 =

   A) 1/12
   B) 1/8
   C) 1/4
   D) 1/2
   E) 8

23. 2.6 - .5 =

   A) 2.0
   B) 2.1
   C) 3.1
   D) 3.3
   E) None of the above

24. Simplify the following expression in terms of amps:

   563×10^{-6}

   A) 563,000,000 amps
   B) 563,000 amps
   C) .563 amps
   D) .000563 amps
   E) .000000563 amps

25. Solve the power equation

   $P = I^2 R$ for R

   A) $R = EI$
   B) $R = I^2 P$
   C) $R = PI$
   D) $R = P/I^2$
   E) $R = E/I$

26. The product of 3 kilo ohms times 3 micro ohms is

   A) 6×10^{-9} ohms
   B) 6×10^{-3} ohms
   C) 9×10^{3} ohms
   D) 9×10^{-6} ohms
   E) 9×10^{-3} ohms

In sample question 27 below, select the statement which is most nearly correct according to the paragraph.

"Prior to 1870, a conveyor that made use of rollers was developed for transporting clay. This construction substituted rolling friction at the idler bearing points for the sliding friction of the slider bed. A primitive type of troughing belt conveyor was developed about the same time for the handling of grain. This design was improved during the latter part of the century when the troughing idler was developed."

27. According to the above paragraph, which of the following statements is most nearly correct?

   A) The troughing belt conveyor was developed about 1870 to handle clay and grain.

   B) Rolling friction construction was replaced by sliding friction construction prior to 1870.

   C) In the late nineteenth century, conveyors were improved with the development of the troughing idler.

   D) The troughing idler, a significant design improvement for conveyors, was developed in the early nineteenth century.

   E) Conveyor belts were invented and developed in the 1800's.

For sample question 28 below, select from the drawings of objects on the right labeled A, B, C, and D, the one that would have the TOP, FRONT, and RIGHT views shown in the drawing at the left

28.

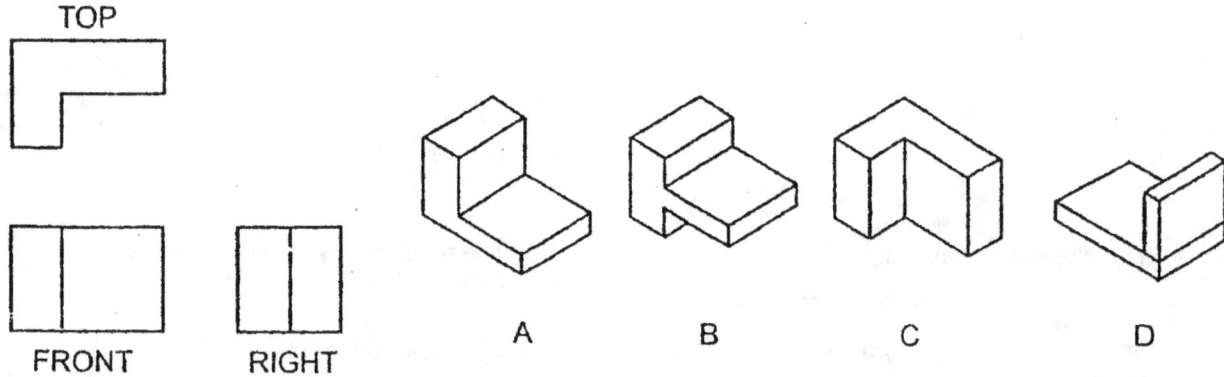

In sample question 29 below, there is, on the left, a drawing of a flat piece of paper and, on the right, four figures labeled A, B, C, and D. When the paper is bent on the dotted lines it will form one of the figures on the right. Decide which alternative can be formed from the flat piece.

29.

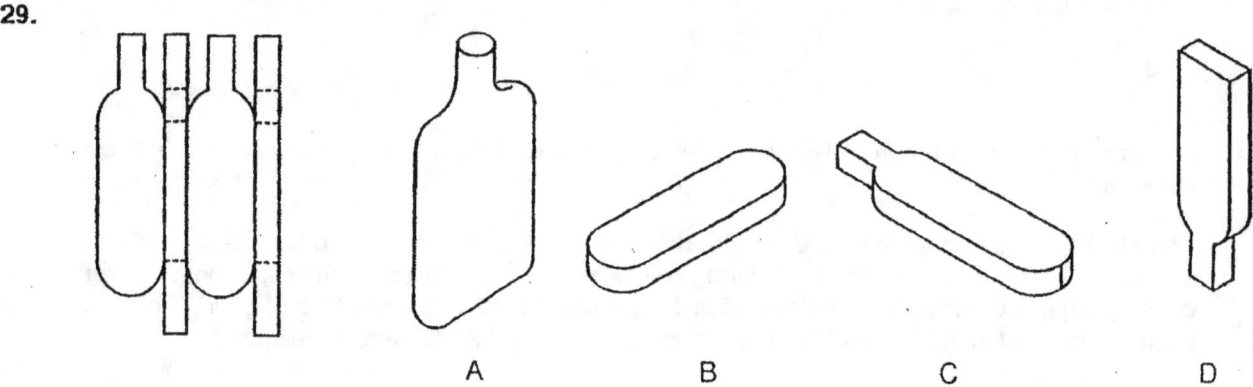

In each of the sample questions below, look at the symbols in the first two boxes. Something about the three symbols in the first box makes them alike; something about the two symbols in the other box with the question mark makes them alike. Look for some characteristic that is common to all symbols in the same box, yet makes them different from the symbols in the other box. Among the five answer choices, find the symbol that can best be substituted for the question mark, because it is <u>like</u> the symbols in the second box, and, <u>for the same reason</u> different from those in the first box.

30.

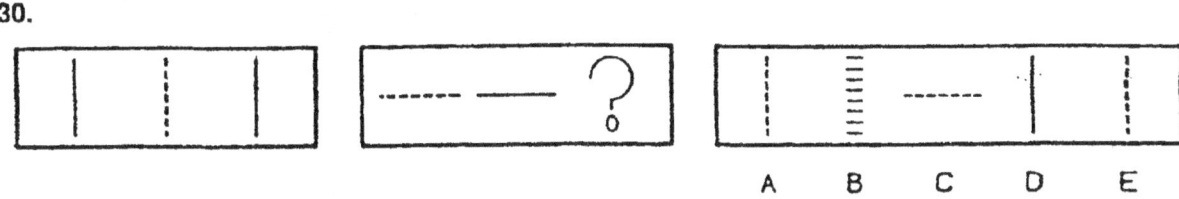

In sample question 30 above, all the symbols in the first box are vertical lines. The second box has two lines, one broken and one solid. Their <u>likeness</u> to each other consists in their being horizontal; and their being horizontal makes them <u>different</u> from the vertical lines in the other box. The answer must be the only one of the five lettered choices that is a horizontal line, either broken or solid. NOTE: There is not supposed to be a series or progression in these symbol questions. If you look for a progression in the first box and the second box, you will be wasting time. Remember, look for a <u>likeness</u> within each box and a <u>difference</u> between the two boxes.

Now do sample questions 31 and 32.

31.

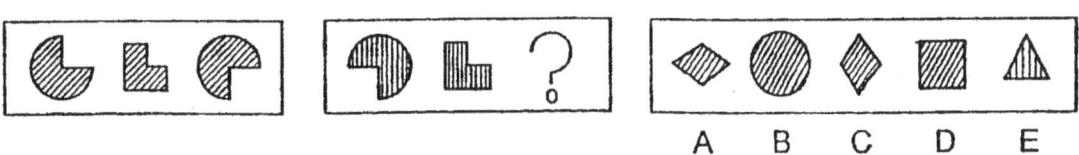

32.

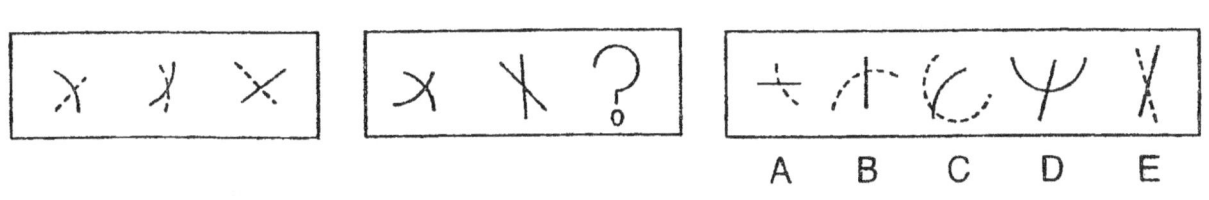

33. In Figure 3-8-6, what is the measurement of Dimension F? Drawing is not actual size.

   A)   1 3/4 inches
   B)   2 1/4 inches
   C)   2 1/2 inches
   D)   3 3/4 inches
   E)   None of the above

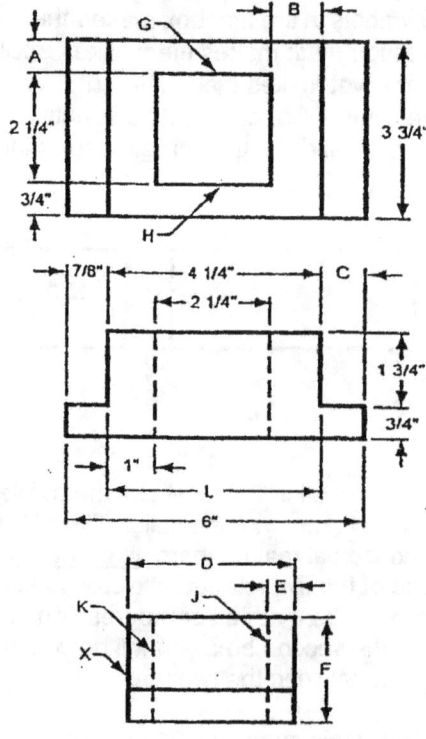

34. In Figure 160-57, what is the current flow through R_3 when:

   V = 50 volts

   R_1 = 25 ohms

   R_2 = 25 ohms

   R3 = 50 ohms

   R_4 = 50 ohms

   R_5 = 50 ohms

   and the current through the entire circuit totals one amp?

   A)   0.5 amp
   B)   5.0 amps
   C)   5.0 milliamps
   D)   50.0 milliamps
   E)   None of the above

Figure 3-8-6

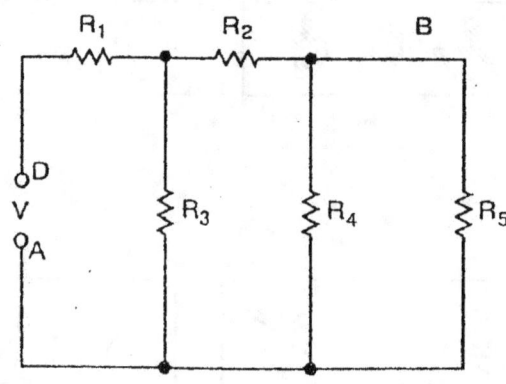

Figure 160-57

Correct Answers to Sample Questions – Part II

1. C
2. D
3. A
4. A
5. A
6. B
7. E
8. C
9. C
10. E
11. E
12. A
13. D
14. A
15. E
16. B
17. D
18. E
19. C
20. D
21. C
22. B
23. B
24. D
25. D
26. E
27. C
28. C
29. C
30. C
31. E
32. D
33. C
34. A

HOW TO TAKE A TEST

I. YOU MUST PASS AN EXAMINATION

A. *WHAT EVERY CANDIDATE SHOULD KNOW*

Examination applicants often ask us for help in preparing for the written test. What can I study in advance? What kinds of questions will be asked? How will the test be given? How will the papers be graded?

As an applicant for a civil service examination, you may be wondering about some of these things. Our purpose here is to suggest effective methods of advance study and to describe civil service examinations.

Your chances for success on this examination can be increased if you know how to prepare. Those "pre-examination jitters" can be reduced if you know what to expect. You can even experience an adventure in good citizenship if you know why civil service exams are given.

B. *WHY ARE CIVIL SERVICE EXAMINATIONS GIVEN?*

Civil service examinations are important to you in two ways. As a citizen, you want public jobs filled by employees who know how to do their work. As a job seeker, you want a fair chance to compete for that job on an equal footing with other candidates. The best-known means of accomplishing this two-fold goal is the competitive examination.

Exams are widely publicized throughout the nation. They may be administered for jobs in federal, state, city, municipal, town or village governments or agencies.

Any citizen may apply, with some limitations, such as the age or residence of applicants. Your experience and education may be reviewed to see whether you meet the requirements for the particular examination. When these requirements exist, they are reasonable and applied consistently to all applicants. Thus, a competitive examination may cause you some uneasiness now, but it is your privilege and safeguard.

C. *HOW ARE CIVIL SERVICE EXAMS DEVELOPED?*

Examinations are carefully written by trained technicians who are specialists in the field known as "psychological measurement," in consultation with recognized authorities in the field of work that the test will cover. These experts recommend the subject matter areas or skills to be tested; only those knowledges or skills important to your success on the job are included. The most reliable books and source materials available are used as references. Together, the experts and technicians judge the difficulty level of the questions.

Test technicians know how to phrase questions so that the problem is clearly stated. Their ethics do not permit "trick" or "catch" questions. Questions may have been tried out on sample groups, or subjected to statistical analysis, to determine their usefulness.

Written tests are often used in combination with performance tests, ratings of training and experience, and oral interviews. All of these measures combine to form the best-known means of finding the right person for the right job.

II. HOW TO PASS THE WRITTEN TEST

A. NATURE OF THE EXAMINATION

To prepare intelligently for civil service examinations, you should know how they differ from school examinations you have taken. In school you were assigned certain definite pages to read or subjects to cover. The examination questions were quite detailed and usually emphasized memory. Civil service exams, on the other hand, try to discover your present ability to perform the duties of a position, plus your potentiality to learn these duties. In other words, a civil service exam attempts to predict how successful you will be. Questions cover such a broad area that they cannot be as minute and detailed as school exam questions.

In the public service similar kinds of work, or positions, are grouped together in one "class." This process is known as *position-classification*. All the positions in a class are paid according to the salary range for that class. One class title covers all of these positions, and they are all tested by the same examination.

B. FOUR BASIC STEPS

1) Study the announcement

How, then, can you know what subjects to study? Our best answer is: "Learn as much as possible about the class of positions for which you've applied." The exam will test the knowledge, skills and abilities needed to do the work.

Your most valuable source of information about the position you want is the official exam announcement. This announcement lists the training and experience qualifications. Check these standards and apply only if you come reasonably close to meeting them.

The brief description of the position in the examination announcement offers some clues to the subjects which will be tested. Think about the job itself. Review the duties in your mind. Can you perform them, or are there some in which you are rusty? Fill in the blank spots in your preparation.

Many jurisdictions preview the written test in the exam announcement by including a section called "Knowledge and Abilities Required," "Scope of the Examination," or some similar heading. Here you will find out specifically what fields will be tested.

2) Review your own background

Once you learn in general what the position is all about, and what you need to know to do the work, ask yourself which subjects you already know fairly well and which need improvement. You may wonder whether to concentrate on improving your strong areas or on building some background in your fields of weakness. When the announcement has specified "some knowledge" or "considerable knowledge," or has used adjectives like "beginning principles of…" or "advanced … methods," you can get a clue as to the number and difficulty of questions to be asked in any given field. More questions, and hence broader coverage, would be included for those subjects which are more important in the work. Now weigh your strengths and weaknesses against the job requirements and prepare accordingly.

3) Determine the level of the position

Another way to tell how intensively you should prepare is to understand the level of the job for which you are applying. Is it the entering level? In other words, is this the position in which beginners in a field of work are hired? Or is it an intermediate or advanced level? Sometimes this is indicated by such words as "Junior" or "Senior" in the class title. Other jurisdictions use Roman numerals to designate the level – Clerk I, Clerk II, for example. The word "Supervisor" sometimes appears in the title. If the level is not indicated by the title, check the description of duties. Will you be working under very close supervision, or will you have responsibility for independent decisions in this work?

4) Choose appropriate study materials

Now that you know the subjects to be examined and the relative amount of each subject to be covered, you can choose suitable study materials. For beginning level jobs, or even advanced ones, if you have a pronounced weakness in some aspect of your training, read a modern, standard textbook in that field. Be sure it is up to date and has general coverage. Such books are normally available at your library, and the librarian will be glad to help you locate one. For entry-level positions, questions of appropriate difficulty are chosen -- neither highly advanced questions, nor those too simple. Such questions require careful thought but not advanced training.

If the position for which you are applying is technical or advanced, you will read more advanced, specialized material. If you are already familiar with the basic principles of your field, elementary textbooks would waste your time. Concentrate on advanced textbooks and technical periodicals. Think through the concepts and review difficult problems in your field.

These are all general sources. You can get more ideas on your own initiative, following these leads. For example, training manuals and publications of the government agency which employs workers in your field can be useful, particularly for technical and professional positions. A letter or visit to the government department involved may result in more specific study suggestions, and certainly will provide you with a more definite idea of the exact nature of the position you are seeking.

III. KINDS OF TESTS

Tests are used for purposes other than measuring knowledge and ability to perform specified duties. For some positions, it is equally important to test ability to make adjustments to new situations or to profit from training. In others, basic mental abilities not dependent on information are essential. Questions which test these things may not appear as pertinent to the duties of the position as those which test for knowledge and information. Yet they are often highly important parts of a fair examination. For very general questions, it is almost impossible to help you direct your study efforts. What we can do is to point out some of the more common of these general abilities needed in public service positions and describe some typical questions.

1) General information

Broad, general information has been found useful for predicting job success in some kinds of work. This is tested in a variety of ways, from vocabulary lists to questions about current events. Basic background in some field of work, such as sociology or economics, may be sampled in a group of questions. Often these are principles which have become familiar to most persons through exposure rather than through formal training. It is difficult to advise you how to study for these questions; being alert to the world around you is our best suggestion.

2) Verbal ability

An example of an ability needed in many positions is verbal or language ability. Verbal ability is, in brief, the ability to use and understand words. Vocabulary and grammar tests are typical measures of this ability. Reading comprehension or paragraph interpretation questions are common in many kinds of civil service tests. You are given a paragraph of written material and asked to find its central meaning.

3) Numerical ability

Number skills can be tested by the familiar arithmetic problem, by checking paired lists of numbers to see which are alike and which are different, or by interpreting charts and graphs. In the latter test, a graph may be printed in the test booklet which you are asked to use as the basis for answering questions.

4) Observation

A popular test for law-enforcement positions is the observation test. A picture is shown to you for several minutes, then taken away. Questions about the picture test your ability to observe both details and larger elements.

5) Following directions

In many positions in the public service, the employee must be able to carry out written instructions dependably and accurately. You may be given a chart with several columns, each column listing a variety of information. The questions require you to carry out directions involving the information given in the chart.

6) Skills and aptitudes

Performance tests effectively measure some manual skills and aptitudes. When the skill is one in which you are trained, such as typing or shorthand, you can practice. These tests are often very much like those given in business school or high school courses. For many of the other skills and aptitudes, however, no short-time preparation can be made. Skills and abilities natural to you or that you have developed throughout your lifetime are being tested.

Many of the general questions just described provide all the data needed to answer the questions and ask you to use your reasoning ability to find the answers. Your best preparation for these tests, as well as for tests of facts and ideas, is to be at your physical and mental best. You, no doubt, have your own methods of getting into an exam-taking mood and keeping "in shape." The next section lists some ideas on this subject.

IV. KINDS OF QUESTIONS

Only rarely is the "essay" question, which you answer in narrative form, used in civil service tests. Civil service tests are usually of the short-answer type. Full instructions for answering these questions will be given to you at the examination. But in case this is your first experience with short-answer questions and separate answer sheets, here is what you need to know:

1) Multiple-choice Questions

Most popular of the short-answer questions is the "multiple choice" or "best answer" question. It can be used, for example, to test for factual knowledge, ability to solve problems or judgment in meeting situations found at work.

A multiple-choice question is normally one of three types—
- It can begin with an incomplete statement followed by several possible endings. You are to find the one ending which *best* completes the statement, although some of the others may not be entirely wrong.
- It can also be a complete statement in the form of a question which is answered by choosing one of the statements listed.

- It can be in the form of a problem – again you select the best answer.

Here is an example of a multiple-choice question with a discussion which should give you some clues as to the method for choosing the right answer:

When an employee has a complaint about his assignment, the action which will *best* help him overcome his difficulty is to
    A. discuss his difficulty with his coworkers
    B. take the problem to the head of the organization
    C. take the problem to the person who gave him the assignment
    D. say nothing to anyone about his complaint

In answering this question, you should study each of the choices to find which is best. Consider choice "A" – Certainly an employee may discuss his complaint with fellow employees, but no change or improvement can result, and the complaint remains unresolved. Choice "B" is a poor choice since the head of the organization probably does not know what assignment you have been given, and taking your problem to him is known as "going over the head" of the supervisor. The supervisor, or person who made the assignment, is the person who can clarify it or correct any injustice. Choice "C" is, therefore, correct. To say nothing, as in choice "D," is unwise. Supervisors have and interest in knowing the problems employees are facing, and the employee is seeking a solution to his problem.

2) True/False Questions

The "true/false" or "right/wrong" form of question is sometimes used. Here a complete statement is given. Your job is to decide whether the statement is right or wrong.

SAMPLE: A roaming cell-phone call to a nearby city costs less than a non-roaming call to a distant city.

This statement is wrong, or false, since roaming calls are more expensive.

This is not a complete list of all possible question forms, although most of the others are variations of these common types. You will always get complete directions for answering questions. Be sure you understand *how* to mark your answers – ask questions until you do.

V. RECORDING YOUR ANSWERS

Computer terminals are used more and more today for many different kinds of exams.

For an examination with very few applicants, you may be told to record your answers in the test booklet itself. Separate answer sheets are much more common. If this separate answer sheet is to be scored by machine – and this is often the case – it is highly important that you mark your answers correctly in order to get credit.

An electronic scoring machine is often used in civil service offices because of the speed with which papers can be scored. Machine-scored answer sheets must be marked with a pencil, which will be given to you. This pencil has a high graphite content which responds to the electronic scoring machine. As a matter of fact, stray dots may register as answers, so do not let your pencil rest on the answer sheet while you are pondering the correct answer. Also, if your pencil lead breaks or is otherwise defective, ask for another.

Since the answer sheet will be dropped in a slot in the scoring machine, be careful not to bend the corners or get the paper crumpled.

The answer sheet normally has five vertical columns of numbers, with 30 numbers to a column. These numbers correspond to the question numbers in your test booklet. After each number, going across the page are four or five pairs of dotted lines. These short dotted lines have small letters or numbers above them. The first two pairs may also have a "T" or "F" above the letters. This indicates that the first two pairs only are to be used if the questions are of the true-false type. If the questions are multiple choice, disregard the "T" and "F" and pay attention only to the small letters or numbers.

Answer your questions in the manner of the sample that follows:

32. The largest city in the United States is
    A. Washington, D.C.
    B. New York City
    C. Chicago
    D. Detroit
    E. San Francisco

1) Choose the answer you think is best. (New York City is the largest, so "B" is correct.)
2) Find the row of dotted lines numbered the same as the question you are answering. (Find row number 32)
3) Find the pair of dotted lines corresponding to the answer. (Find the pair of lines under the mark "B.")
4) Make a solid black mark between the dotted lines.

VI. BEFORE THE TEST

Common sense will help you find procedures to follow to get ready for an examination. Too many of us, however, overlook these sensible measures. Indeed, nervousness and fatigue have been found to be the most serious reasons why applicants fail to do their best on civil service tests. Here is a list of reminders:

- Begin your preparation early – Don't wait until the last minute to go scurrying around for books and materials or to find out what the position is all about.
- Prepare continuously – An hour a night for a week is better than an all-night cram session. This has been definitely established. What is more, a night a week for a month will return better dividends than crowding your study into a shorter period of time.
- Locate the place of the exam – You have been sent a notice telling you when and where to report for the examination. If the location is in a different town or otherwise unfamiliar to you, it would be well to inquire the best route and learn something about the building.
- Relax the night before the test – Allow your mind to rest. Do not study at all that night. Plan some mild recreation or diversion; then go to bed early and get a good night's sleep.
- Get up early enough to make a leisurely trip to the place for the test – This way unforeseen events, traffic snarls, unfamiliar buildings, etc. will not upset you.
- Dress comfortably – A written test is not a fashion show. You will be known by number and not by name, so wear something comfortable.

- Leave excess paraphernalia at home – Shopping bags and odd bundles will get in your way. You need bring only the items mentioned in the official notice you received; usually everything you need is provided. Do not bring reference books to the exam. They will only confuse those last minutes and be taken away from you when in the test room.
- Arrive somewhat ahead of time – If because of transportation schedules you must get there very early, bring a newspaper or magazine to take your mind off yourself while waiting.
- Locate the examination room – When you have found the proper room, you will be directed to the seat or part of the room where you will sit. Sometimes you are given a sheet of instructions to read while you are waiting. Do not fill out any forms until you are told to do so; just read them and be prepared.
- Relax and prepare to listen to the instructions
- If you have any physical problem that may keep you from doing your best, be sure to tell the test administrator. If you are sick or in poor health, you really cannot do your best on the exam. You can come back and take the test some other time.

VII. AT THE TEST

The day of the test is here and you have the test booklet in your hand. The temptation to get going is very strong. Caution! There is more to success than knowing the right answers. You must know how to identify your papers and understand variations in the type of short-answer question used in this particular examination. Follow these suggestions for maximum results from your efforts:

1) Cooperate with the monitor

The test administrator has a duty to create a situation in which you can be as much at ease as possible. He will give instructions, tell you when to begin, check to see that you are marking your answer sheet correctly, and so on. He is not there to guard you, although he will see that your competitors do not take unfair advantage. He wants to help you do your best.

2) Listen to all instructions

Don't jump the gun! Wait until you understand all directions. In most civil service tests you get more time than you need to answer the questions. So don't be in a hurry. Read each word of instructions until you clearly understand the meaning. Study the examples, listen to all announcements and follow directions. Ask questions if you do not understand what to do.

3) Identify your papers

Civil service exams are usually identified by number only. You will be assigned a number; you must not put your name on your test papers. Be sure to copy your number correctly. Since more than one exam may be given, copy your exact examination title.

4) Plan your time

Unless you are told that a test is a "speed" or "rate of work" test, speed itself is usually not important. Time enough to answer all the questions will be provided, but this does not mean that you have all day. An overall time limit has been set. Divide the total time (in minutes) by the number of questions to determine the approximate time you have for each question.

5) **Do not linger over difficult questions**

If you come across a difficult question, mark it with a paper clip (useful to have along) and come back to it when you have been through the booklet. One caution if you do this – be sure to skip a number on your answer sheet as well. Check often to be sure that you have not lost your place and that you are marking in the row numbered the same as the question you are answering.

6) **Read the questions**

Be sure you know what the question asks! Many capable people are unsuccessful because they failed to *read* the questions correctly.

7) **Answer all questions**

Unless you have been instructed that a penalty will be deducted for incorrect answers, it is better to guess than to omit a question.

8) **Speed tests**

It is often better NOT to guess on speed tests. It has been found that on timed tests people are tempted to spend the last few seconds before time is called in marking answers at random – without even reading them – in the hope of picking up a few extra points. To discourage this practice, the instructions may warn you that your score will be "corrected" for guessing. That is, a penalty will be applied. The incorrect answers will be deducted from the correct ones, or some other penalty formula will be used.

9) **Review your answers**

If you finish before time is called, go back to the questions you guessed or omitted to give them further thought. Review other answers if you have time.

10) **Return your test materials**

If you are ready to leave before others have finished or time is called, take ALL your materials to the monitor and leave quietly. Never take any test material with you. The monitor can discover whose papers are not complete, and taking a test booklet may be grounds for disqualification.

VIII. EXAMINATION TECHNIQUES

1) Read the general instructions carefully. These are usually printed on the first page of the exam booklet. As a rule, these instructions refer to the timing of the examination; the fact that you should not start work until the signal and must stop work at a signal, etc. If there are any *special* instructions, such as a choice of questions to be answered, make sure that you note this instruction carefully.

2) When you are ready to start work on the examination, that is as soon as the signal has been given, read the instructions to each question booklet, underline any key words or phrases, such as *least, best, outline, describe* and the like. In this way you will tend to answer as requested rather than discover on reviewing your paper that you *listed without describing*, that you selected the *worst* choice rather than the *best* choice, etc.

3) If the examination is of the objective or multiple-choice type – that is, each question will also give a series of possible answers: A, B, C or D, and you are called upon to select the best answer and write the letter next to that answer on your answer paper – it is advisable to start answering each question in turn. There may be anywhere from 50 to 100 such questions in the three or four hours allotted and you can see how much time would be taken if you read through all the questions before beginning to answer any. Furthermore, if you come across a question or group of questions which you know would be difficult to answer, it would undoubtedly affect your handling of all the other questions.

4) If the examination is of the essay type and contains but a few questions, it is a moot point as to whether you should read all the questions before starting to answer any one. Of course, if you are given a choice – say five out of seven and the like – then it is essential to read all the questions so you can eliminate the two that are most difficult. If, however, you are asked to answer all the questions, there may be danger in trying to answer the easiest one first because you may find that you will spend too much time on it. The best technique is to answer the first question, then proceed to the second, etc.

5) Time your answers. Before the exam begins, write down the time it started, then add the time allowed for the examination and write down the time it must be completed, then divide the time available somewhat as follows:
    - If 3-1/2 hours are allowed, that would be 210 minutes. If you have 80 objective-type questions, that would be an average of 2-1/2 minutes per question. Allow yourself no more than 2 minutes per question, or a total of 160 minutes, which will permit about 50 minutes to review.
    - If for the time allotment of 210 minutes there are 7 essay questions to answer, that would average about 30 minutes a question. Give yourself only 25 minutes per question so that you have about 35 minutes to review.

6) The most important instruction is to *read each question* and make sure you know what is wanted. The second most important instruction is to *time yourself properly* so that you answer every question. The third most important instruction is to *answer every question*. Guess if you have to but include something for each question. Remember that you will receive no credit for a blank and will probably receive some credit if you write something in answer to an essay question. If you guess a letter – say "B" for a multiple-choice question – you may have guessed right. If you leave a blank as an answer to a multiple-choice question, the examiners may respect your feelings but it will not add a point to your score. Some exams may penalize you for wrong answers, so in such cases *only*, you may not want to guess unless you have some basis for your answer.

7) Suggestions
    a. Objective-type questions
        1. Examine the question booklet for proper sequence of pages and questions
        2. Read all instructions carefully
        3. Skip any question which seems too difficult; return to it after all other questions have been answered
        4. Apportion your time properly; do not spend too much time on any single question or group of questions

5. Note and underline key words – *all, most, fewest, least, best, worst, same, opposite*, etc.
6. Pay particular attention to negatives
7. Note unusual option, e.g., unduly long, short, complex, different or similar in content to the body of the question
8. Observe the use of "hedging" words – *probably, may, most likely*, etc.
9. Make sure that your answer is put next to the same number as the question
10. Do not second-guess unless you have good reason to believe the second answer is definitely more correct
11. Cross out original answer if you decide another answer is more accurate; do not erase until you are ready to hand your paper in
12. Answer all questions; guess unless instructed otherwise
13. Leave time for review

b. Essay questions
1. Read each question carefully
2. Determine exactly what is wanted. Underline key words or phrases.
3. Decide on outline or paragraph answer
4. Include many different points and elements unless asked to develop any one or two points or elements
5. Show impartiality by giving pros and cons unless directed to select one side only
6. Make and write down any assumptions you find necessary to answer the questions
7. Watch your English, grammar, punctuation and choice of words
8. Time your answers; don't crowd material

8) Answering the essay question

Most essay questions can be answered by framing the specific response around several key words or ideas. Here are a few such key words or ideas:

M's: manpower, materials, methods, money, management
P's: purpose, program, policy, plan, procedure, practice, problems, pitfalls, personnel, public relations

a. Six basic steps in handling problems:
1. Preliminary plan and background development
2. Collect information, data and facts
3. Analyze and interpret information, data and facts
4. Analyze and develop solutions as well as make recommendations
5. Prepare report and sell recommendations
6. Install recommendations and follow up effectiveness

b. Pitfalls to avoid
1. *Taking things for granted* – A statement of the situation does not necessarily imply that each of the elements is necessarily true; for example, a complaint may be invalid and biased so that all that can be taken for granted is that a complaint has been registered

2. *Considering only one side of a situation* – Wherever possible, indicate several alternatives and then point out the reasons you selected the best one
3. *Failing to indicate follow up* – Whenever your answer indicates action on your part, make certain that you will take proper follow-up action to see how successful your recommendations, procedures or actions turn out to be
4. *Taking too long in answering any single question* – Remember to time your answers properly

IX. AFTER THE TEST

Scoring procedures differ in detail among civil service jurisdictions although the general principles are the same. Whether the papers are hand-scored or graded by machine we have described, they are nearly always graded by number. That is, the person who marks the paper knows only the number – never the name – of the applicant. Not until all the papers have been graded will they be matched with names. If other tests, such as training and experience or oral interview ratings have been given, scores will be combined. Different parts of the examination usually have different weights. For example, the written test might count 60 percent of the final grade, and a rating of training and experience 40 percent. In many jurisdictions, veterans will have a certain number of points added to their grades.

After the final grade has been determined, the names are placed in grade order and an eligible list is established. There are various methods for resolving ties between those who get the same final grade – probably the most common is to place first the name of the person whose application was received first. Job offers are made from the eligible list in the order the names appear on it. You will be notified of your grade and your rank as soon as all these computations have been made. This will be done as rapidly as possible.

People who are found to meet the requirements in the announcement are called "eligibles." Their names are put on a list of eligible candidates. An eligible's chances of getting a job depend on how high he stands on this list and how fast agencies are filling jobs from the list.

When a job is to be filled from a list of eligibles, the agency asks for the names of people on the list of eligibles for that job. When the civil service commission receives this request, it sends to the agency the names of the three people highest on this list. Or, if the job to be filled has specialized requirements, the office sends the agency the names of the top three persons who meet these requirements from the general list.

The appointing officer makes a choice from among the three people whose names were sent to him. If the selected person accepts the appointment, the names of the others are put back on the list to be considered for future openings.

That is the rule in hiring from all kinds of eligible lists, whether they are for typist, carpenter, chemist, or something else. For every vacancy, the appointing officer has his choice of any one of the top three eligibles on the list. This explains why the person whose name is on top of the list sometimes does not get an appointment when some of the persons lower on the list do. If the appointing officer chooses the second or third eligible, the No. 1 eligible does not get a job at once, but stays on the list until he is appointed or the list is terminated.

X. HOW TO PASS THE INTERVIEW TEST

The examination for which you applied requires an oral interview test. You have already taken the written test and you are now being called for the interview test – the final part of the formal examination.

You may think that it is not possible to prepare for an interview test and that there are no procedures to follow during an interview. Our purpose is to point out some things you can do in advance that will help you and some good rules to follow and pitfalls to avoid while you are being interviewed.

What is an interview supposed to test?

The written examination is designed to test the technical knowledge and competence of the candidate; the oral is designed to evaluate intangible qualities, not readily measured otherwise, and to establish a list showing the relative fitness of each candidate – as measured against his competitors – for the position sought. Scoring is not on the basis of "right" and "wrong," but on a sliding scale of values ranging from "not passable" to "outstanding." As a matter of fact, it is possible to achieve a relatively low score without a single "incorrect" answer because of evident weakness in the qualities being measured.

Occasionally, an examination may consist entirely of an oral test – either an individual or a group oral. In such cases, information is sought concerning the technical knowledges and abilities of the candidate, since there has been no written examination for this purpose. More commonly, however, an oral test is used to supplement a written examination.

Who conducts interviews?

The composition of oral boards varies among different jurisdictions. In nearly all, a representative of the personnel department serves as chairman. One of the members of the board may be a representative of the department in which the candidate would work. In some cases, "outside experts" are used, and, frequently, a businessman or some other representative of the general public is asked to serve. Labor and management or other special groups may be represented. The aim is to secure the services of experts in the appropriate field.

However the board is composed, it is a good idea (and not at all improper or unethical) to ascertain in advance of the interview who the members are and what groups they represent. When you are introduced to them, you will have some idea of their backgrounds and interests, and at least you will not stutter and stammer over their names.

What should be done before the interview?

While knowledge about the board members is useful and takes some of the surprise element out of the interview, there is other preparation which is more substantive. It *is* possible to prepare for an oral interview – in several ways:

1) Keep a copy of your application and review it carefully before the interview

This may be the only document before the oral board, and the starting point of the interview. Know what education and experience you have listed there, and the sequence and dates of all of it. Sometimes the board will ask you to review the highlights of your experience for them; you should not have to hem and haw doing it.

2) Study the class specification and the examination announcement

Usually, the oral board has one or both of these to guide them. The qualities, characteristics or knowledges required by the position sought are stated in these documents. They offer valuable clues as to the nature of the oral interview. For example, if the job involves supervisory responsibilities, the announcement will usually indicate that knowledge of modern supervisory methods and the qualifications of the candidate as a supervisor will be tested. If so, you can expect such questions, frequently in the form of a hypothetical situation which you are expected to solve. NEVER go into an oral without knowledge of the duties and responsibilities of the job you seek.

3) Think through each qualification required

Try to visualize the kind of questions you would ask if you were a board member. How well could you answer them? Try especially to appraise your own knowledge and background in each area, *measured against the job sought*, and identify any areas in which you are weak. Be critical and realistic – do not flatter yourself.

4) Do some general reading in areas in which you feel you may be weak

For example, if the job involves supervision and your past experience has NOT, some general reading in supervisory methods and practices, particularly in the field of human relations, might be useful. Do NOT study agency procedures or detailed manuals. The oral board will be testing your understanding and capacity, not your memory.

5) Get a good night's sleep and watch your general health and mental attitude

You will want a clear head at the interview. Take care of a cold or any other minor ailment, and of course, no hangovers.

What should be done on the day of the interview?

Now comes the day of the interview itself. Give yourself plenty of time to get there. Plan to arrive somewhat ahead of the scheduled time, particularly if your appointment is in the fore part of the day. If a previous candidate fails to appear, the board might be ready for you a bit early. By early afternoon an oral board is almost invariably behind schedule if there are many candidates, and you may have to wait. Take along a book or magazine to read, or your application to review, but leave any extraneous material in the waiting room when you go in for your interview. In any event, relax and compose yourself.

The matter of dress is important. The board is forming impressions about you – from your experience, your manners, your attitude, and your appearance. Give your personal appearance careful attention. Dress your best, but not your flashiest. Choose conservative, appropriate clothing, and be sure it is immaculate. This is a business interview, and your appearance should indicate that you regard it as such. Besides, being well groomed and properly dressed will help boost your confidence.

Sooner or later, someone will call your name and escort you into the interview room. *This is it.* From here on you are on your own. It is too late for any more preparation. But remember, you asked for this opportunity to prove your fitness, and you are here because your request was granted.

What happens when you go in?

The usual sequence of events will be as follows: The clerk (who is often the board stenographer) will introduce you to the chairman of the oral board, who will introduce you to the other members of the board. Acknowledge the introductions before you sit down. Do not be surprised if you find a microphone facing you or a stenotypist sitting by. Oral interviews are usually recorded in the event of an appeal or other review.

Usually the chairman of the board will open the interview by reviewing the highlights of your education and work experience from your application – primarily for the benefit of the other members of the board, as well as to get the material into the record. Do not interrupt or comment unless there is an error or significant misinterpretation; if that is the case, do not hesitate. But do not quibble about insignificant matters. Also, he will usually ask you some question about your education, experience or your present job – partly to get you to start talking and to establish the interviewing "rapport." He may start the actual questioning, or turn it over to one of the other members. Frequently, each member undertakes the questioning on a particular area, one in which he is perhaps most competent, so you can expect each member to participate in the examination. Because time is limited, you may also expect some rather abrupt switches in the direction the questioning takes, so do not be upset by it. Normally, a board member will not pursue a single line of questioning unless he discovers a particular strength or weakness.

After each member has participated, the chairman will usually ask whether any member has any further questions, then will ask you if you have anything you wish to add. Unless you are expecting this question, it may floor you. Worse, it may start you off on an extended, extemporaneous speech. The board is not usually seeking more information. The question is principally to offer you a last opportunity to present further qualifications or to indicate that you have nothing to add. So, if you feel that a significant qualification or characteristic has been overlooked, it is proper to point it out in a sentence or so. Do not compliment the board on the thoroughness of their examination – they have been sketchy, and you know it. If you wish, merely say, "No thank you, I have nothing further to add." This is a point where you can "talk yourself out" of a good impression or fail to present an important bit of information. Remember, *you close the interview yourself*.

The chairman will then say, "That is all, Mr. _____, thank you." Do not be startled; the interview is over, and quicker than you think. Thank him, gather your belongings and take your leave. Save your sigh of relief for the other side of the door.

How to put your best foot forward

Throughout this entire process, you may feel that the board individually and collectively is trying to pierce your defenses, seek out your hidden weaknesses and embarrass and confuse you. Actually, this is not true. They are obliged to make an appraisal of your qualifications for the job you are seeking, and they want to see you in your best light. Remember, they must interview all candidates and a non-cooperative candidate may become a failure in spite of their best efforts to bring out his qualifications. Here are 15 suggestions that will help you:

1) Be natural – Keep your attitude confident, not cocky

If you are not confident that you can do the job, do not expect the board to be. Do not apologize for your weaknesses, try to bring out your strong points. The board is interested in a positive, not negative, presentation. Cockiness will antagonize any board member and make him wonder if you are covering up a weakness by a false show of strength.

2) Get comfortable, but don't lounge or sprawl

Sit erectly but not stiffly. A careless posture may lead the board to conclude that you are careless in other things, or at least that you are not impressed by the importance of the occasion. Either conclusion is natural, even if incorrect. Do not fuss with your clothing, a pencil or an ashtray. Your hands may occasionally be useful to emphasize a point; do not let them become a point of distraction.

3) Do not wisecrack or make small talk

This is a serious situation, and your attitude should show that you consider it as such. Further, the time of the board is limited – they do not want to waste it, and neither should you.

4) Do not exaggerate your experience or abilities

In the first place, from information in the application or other interviews and sources, the board may know more about you than you think. Secondly, you probably will not get away with it. An experienced board is rather adept at spotting such a situation, so do not take the chance.

5) If you know a board member, do not make a point of it, yet do not hide it

Certainly you are not fooling him, and probably not the other members of the board. Do not try to take advantage of your acquaintanceship – it will probably do you little good.

6) Do not dominate the interview

Let the board do that. They will give you the clues – do not assume that you have to do all the talking. Realize that the board has a number of questions to ask you, and do not try to take up all the interview time by showing off your extensive knowledge of the answer to the first one.

7) Be attentive

You only have 20 minutes or so, and you should keep your attention at its sharpest throughout. When a member is addressing a problem or question to you, give him your undivided attention. Address your reply principally to him, but do not exclude the other board members.

8) Do not interrupt

A board member may be stating a problem for you to analyze. He will ask you a question when the time comes. Let him state the problem, and wait for the question.

9) Make sure you understand the question

Do not try to answer until you are sure what the question is. If it is not clear, restate it in your own words or ask the board member to clarify it for you. However, do not haggle about minor elements.

10) Reply promptly but not hastily

A common entry on oral board rating sheets is "candidate responded readily," or "candidate hesitated in replies." Respond as promptly and quickly as you can, but do not jump to a hasty, ill-considered answer.

11) Do not be peremptory in your answers

A brief answer is proper – but do not fire your answer back. That is a losing game from your point of view. The board member can probably ask questions much faster than you can answer them.

12) Do not try to create the answer you think the board member wants

He is interested in what kind of mind you have and how it works – not in playing games. Furthermore, he can usually spot this practice and will actually grade you down on it.

13) Do not switch sides in your reply merely to agree with a board member

Frequently, a member will take a contrary position merely to draw you out and to see if you are willing and able to defend your point of view. Do not start a debate, yet do not surrender a good position. If a position is worth taking, it is worth defending.

14) Do not be afraid to admit an error in judgment if you are shown to be wrong

The board knows that you are forced to reply without any opportunity for careful consideration. Your answer may be demonstrably wrong. If so, admit it and get on with the interview.

15) Do not dwell at length on your present job

The opening question may relate to your present assignment. Answer the question but do not go into an extended discussion. You are being examined for a *new* job, not your present one. As a matter of fact, try to phrase ALL your answers in terms of the job for which you are being examined.

Basis of Rating

Probably you will forget most of these "do's" and "don'ts" when you walk into the oral interview room. Even remembering them all will not ensure you a passing grade. Perhaps you did not have the qualifications in the first place. But remembering them will help you to put your best foot forward, without treading on the toes of the board members.

Rumor and popular opinion to the contrary notwithstanding, an oral board wants you to make the best appearance possible. They know you are under pressure – but they also want to see how you respond to it as a guide to what your reaction would be under the pressures of the job you seek. They will be influenced by the degree of poise you display, the personal traits you show and the manner in which you respond.

ABOUT THIS BOOK

This book contains tests divided into Examination Sections. Go through each test, answering every question in the margin. We have also attached a sample answer sheet at the back of the book that can be removed and used. At the end of each test look at the answer key and check your answers. On the ones you got wrong, look at the right answer choice and learn. Do not fill in the answers first. Do not memorize the questions and answers, but understand the answer and principles involved. On your test, the questions will likely be different from the samples. Questions are changed and new ones added. If you understand these past questions you should have success with any changes that arise. Tests may consist of several types of questions. We have additional books on each subject should more study be advisable or necessary for you. Finally, the more you study, the better prepared you will be. This book is intended to be the last thing you study before you walk into the examination room. Prior study of relevant texts is also recommended. NLC publishes some of these in our Fundamental Series. Knowledge and good sense are important factors in passing your exam. Good luck also helps. So now study this Passbook, absorb the material contained within and take that knowledge into the examination. Then do your best to pass that exam.

EXAMINATION SECTION

READING COMPREHENSION
UNDERSTANDING AND INTERPRETING
WRITTEN MATERIAL

COMMENTARY

The ability to read and understand written materials—texts, publications, newspapers, orders, directions, expositions—is a skill basic to a functioning democracy and to an efficient business or viable government.

That is why almost all examinations—for beginning, middle, and senior levels—test reading comprehension, directly or indirectly.

The reading test measures how well you understand what you read. This is how it is done: You read a short paragraph and five statements. From the five statements, you choose the one statement, or answer, that is BEST supported by, or best matches, what is said in the paragraph.

SAMPLE QUESTIONS

DIRECTIONS: Each question has five suggested answers, lettered A, B, C, D, and E. Decide which one is the BEST answer. *PRINT THE LETTER OF THE CORRECT ANSWER IN THE SPACE AT THE RIGHT.*

1. The prevention of accidents makes it necessary not only that safety devices be used to guard exposed machinery but also that mechanics be instructed in safety rules which they must follow for their own protection and that the light in the plant be adequate.
   The paragraph BEST supports the statement that industrial accidents
   A. are always avoidable
   B. may be due to ignorance
   C. usually result from inadequate machinery
   D. cannot be entirely overcome
   E. result in damage to machinery

1.____

ANALYSIS

Remember what you have to do:
- First - Read the paragraph
- Second - Decide what the paragraph means
- Third - Read the five suggested answers.
- Fourth - Select the one answer which BEST matches what the paragraph says or is BEST supported by something in the paragraph. (Sometimes you may have to read the paragraph again in order to be sure which suggested answer is best.

This paragraph is talking about three steps that should be taken to prevent industrial accidents
1. Use safety devices on machines
2. Instruct mechanics in safety rules
3. provide adequate lighting

SELECTION

With this in mind, let's look at each suggested answer. Each one starts with "Industrial accidents…"

SUGGESTED ANSWER A
Industrial accidents (A) are always avoidable.
(The paragraph talks about how to avoid accidents, but does not say that accidents are always avoidable.)

SUGGESTED ANSWER B
Industrial accidents (B) may be due to ignorance.
(One of the steps given in the paragraph to prevent accidents is to instruct mechanics on safety rules. This suggests that lack of knowledge or ignorance of safety rules causes accidents. This suggested answer sounds like a good possibility for being the right answer.)

SUGGESTED ANSWER C
Industrial accidents (C) usually result from inadequate machinery.
(The paragraph does suggest that exposed machines cause accidents, but it doesn't say that it is the usual cause of accidents. The word usually makes this a wrong answer.)

SUGGESTED ANSWER D
Industrial accidents (D) cannot be entirely overcome.
(You may know from your own experience that this is a true statement. But that is not what the paragraph is talking about. Therefore, it is NOT the correct answer.)

SUGGESTED ANSWER E
Industrial accidents (E) result in damage to machinery.
(This is a statement that may or may not be true, but in any case it is NOT covered by the paragraph.)

Looking back, you see that the one suggested answer of the five given that BEST matches what the paragraph says is: Industrial accidents (B) may be due to ignorance.

The CORRECT answer then is B.

Be sure to read ALL the possible answers before you make your choice. You may think that none of the five answers is really good, but choose the BEST one of the five.

---

2. Probably few people realize, as they drive on a concrete road, that steel is used to keep the surface flat in spite of the weight of the busses and trucks. Steel bars, deeply embedded in the concrete, provide sinews to take the stresses so that the stresses cannot crack the slab or make it wavy.
   The paragraph BEST supports the statement that a concrete road
   A. is expensive to build
   B. usually cracks under heavy weights
   C. looks like any other road
   D. is used only for heavy traffic
   E. is reinforced with other material

2.____

ANALYSIS

This paragraph is commenting on the fact that
   1. few people realize, as they drive on a concrete road, that steel is deeply embedded
   2. steel keeps the surface flat
   3. steel bars enable the road to take the stresses without cracking or becoming wavy

SELECTION

Now read and think about the possible answers:
   A. A concrete road is expensive to build. (Maybe so but that is not what the paragraph is about.)
   B. A concrete road usually cracks under heavy weights. (The paragraph talks about using steel bars to prevent heavy weights from cracking concrete roads. It says nothing about how usual it is for the roads to crack. The word usually makes this suggested answer wrong.)
   C. A concrete road looks like any other road. (This may or may not be true. The important thing to note is that it has nothing to do with what the paragraph is about.)
   D. A concrete road is used only for heavy traffic. (This answer at least has something to do with the paragraph—concrete roads are used with heavy traffic—but it does not say "used only.")
   E. A concrete road is reinforced with other material. (This choice seems to be the correct one on two counts: First, the paragraph does suggest that concrete roads are made

stronger by embedding steel bars in them. This is another way of saying "concrete roads are reinforced with steel bars." Second, by the process of elimination, the other four choices are ruled out as correct answers simply because they do not apply.)

You can be sure that not all the reading questions will be so easy as these.

HINTS FOR ANSWERING READING QUESTIONS

1. Read the paragraph carefully. Then read each suggested answer carefully. Read every word, because often one word can make the difference between a right and a wrong answer.

2. Choose that answer which is supported in the paragraph itself. Do not choose an answer which is a correct statement unless it is based on information in the paragraph.

3. Even though a suggested answer has many of the words used in the paragraph, it may still be wrong.

4. Look out for words—such as *always*, *never*, *entirely*, or *only*—which tend to make a suggested answer wrong.

5. Answer first those questions which you can answer most easily. Then work on the other questions.

6. If you can't figure out the answer to the question, guess.

READING COMPREHENSION
UNDERSTANDING WRITTEN MATERIALS
COMMENTARY

The ability to read and understand written materials—texts, publications, newspapers, orders, directions, expositions—is a skill basic to a functioning democracy and to an efficient business or viable government.

That is why almost all examinations—for beginning, middle, and senior levels—test reading comprehension, directly or indirectly.

The reading test measures how well you understand what you read. This is how it is done: You read a passage followed by several statements. From these statements, you choose the one statement, or answer, that is BEST supported by, or BEST matches, what is said in the paragraph. PRINT THE LETTER OF THE CORRECT ANSWER IN THE SPACE AT THE RIGHT.

SAMPLE QUESTIONS

DIRECTIONS: Answer Questions 1 and 2 ONLY according to the information given in the following passage.

1. When a fingerprint technician inks and takes rolled impressions of a subject's fingers, the degree of downward pressure the technician applies is important. The correct pressure may best be determined through experience and observation. It is quite important, however, that the subject be cautioned to relax and not help the fingerprint technician by also applying pressure, as this prevents the fingerprint technician from gaging the amount needed. A method which is helpful in getting the subject to relax his hand is to instruct him to look at some distant object and not to look at his hands.

1. According to this passage, the technician tries to relax the subject's hands by　　　　1.____
   A. instructing him to let his hands hang loosely
   B. telling him that being fingerprinted is painless
   C. asking him to look at this hand instead of some distant object
   D. asking him to look at something other than his hand

2. The subject is asked NOT to press down on his fingers while being fingerprinted　　　　2.____
   because
   A. the impressions taken become rolled
   B. the subject may apply too little downward pressure and spoil the impressions
   C. the technician cannot tell whether he is applying the right degree of pressure
   D. he doesn't have the experience to apply the exact amount of pressure

　　　　　　　　CORRECT ANSWERS
　　　　　　　　　1. D
　　　　　　　　　2. C

EXAMINATION SECTION
TEST 1

DIRECTIONS: Questions 1 through 3 are to be answered on the basis of the following reading passage. *PRINT THE LETTER OF THE CORRECT ANSWER IN THE SPACE AT THE RIGHT.*

Thermostats should be tested in hot water for proper opening. A bucket should be filled with sufficient water to cover the thermostat and fitted with a thermometer suspended in the water so that the sensitive bulb portion does not rest directly on the bucket. The water is then heated on a stove. As the temperature of the water passes the 160-165° range, the thermostat should start to open and should be completely opened when the temperature has risen to 185-190°. Lifting the thermostat into the air should cause a pronounced closing action and the unit should be closed entirely within a short time.

1. The thermostat described above is a device which opens and closes with changes in the
    A. position   B. pressure   C. temperature   D. surroundings

 1.____

2. According to the above passage, the closing action of the thermostat should be tested by
    A. working the thermostat back and forth
    B. permitting the water to cool gradually
    C. adding cold water to the bucket
    D. removing the thermostat from the bucket

 2.____

3. The bulb of the thermometer should not rest directly on the bucket because
    A. the bucket gets hotter than the water
    B. the thermometer might be damaged in that position
    C. it is difficult to read the thermometer in that position
    D. the thermometer might interfere with operation of the thermostat

 3.____

KEY (CORRECT ANSWERS)

1. C
2. D
3. A

TEST 2

DIRECTIONS: Questions 1 through 3 are to be answered on the basis of the following reading passage. *PRINT THE LETTER OF THE CORRECT ANSWER IN THE SPACE AT THE RIGHT.*

    All idle pumps should be turned daily by hand, and should be run under power at least once a week. Whenever repairs are made on a pump, a record should be kept so that it will be possible to judge the success with which the pump is performing its functions. If a pump fails to deliver liquid, there may be an obstruction in the suction line, the pump's parts may be badly worn, or the packing defective.

1. According to the above passage, pumps 1.____
   A. in use should be turned by hand every day
   B. which are not in use should be run under power every day
   C. which are in daily use should be run under power several times a week
   D. which are not in use should be turned by hand every day

2. According to the above passage, the reason for keeping records of repairs made on pumps is to 2.____
   A. make certain that proper maintenance is being performed
   B. discover who is responsible for improper repairs
   C. rate the performance of the pumps
   D. know when to replace worn parts

3. The one of the following causes of pump failure which is NOT mentioned in the above passage is 3.____
   A. excessive suction lift   B. clogged lines
   C. bad packing   D. worn parts

KEY (CORRECT ANSWERS)

1. A
2. C
3. A

TEST 3

DIRECTIONS: Questions 1 through 5 are to be answered on the basis of the following reading passage. *PRINT THE LETTER OF THE CORRECT ANSWER IN THE SPACE AT THE RIGHT.*

Floors in warehouses, storerooms, and shipping rooms must be strong enough to stay level under heavy loads. Unevenness of floors may cause boxes of materials to topple and fall. Safe floor load capacities and maximum heights to which boxes may be stacked should be posted conspicuously so all can notice it. Where material in boxes, containers, or cartons of the same weight is regularly stored, it is good practice to paint a horizontal line on the wall indicating the maximum height to which the material may be piled. A qualified expert should determine floor load capacity from the building plans, the age and condition of the floor supports, the type of floor, and other related information.

Working aisles are those from which material is placed into and removed from storage. Working aisles are of two types: transportation aisles, running the length of the building, and cross aisles, running across the width of the building. Deciding on the number, width, and location of working aisles is important. While aisles are necessary and determine boundaries of storage areas, they reduce the space actually used for storage.

1. According to the above passage, how should safe floor load capacities be made known to employees? They should be
    A. given out to each employee
    B. given to supervisors only
    C. printed in large red letters
    D. posted so that they are easily seen

1.____

2. According to the above passage, floor load capacities should be determined by
    A. warehouse supervisors   B. the fire department
    C. qualified experts   D. machine operators

2.____

3. According to the above passage, transportation aisles
    A. run the length of the building
    B. run across the width of the building
    C. are wider than cross aisles
    D. are shorter than cross aisles

3.____

4. According to the above passage, working aisles tend to
    A. take away space that could be used for storage
    B. add to space that could be used for storage
    C. slow down incoming stock
    D. speed up outgoing stock

4.____

5. According to the above passage, unevenness of floors may cause
    A. overall warehouse deterioration   B. piles of stock to fall
    C. materials to spoil   D. many worker injuries

5.____

KEY (CORRECT ANSWERS)

1. D
2. C
3. A
4. A
5. B

TEST 4

DIRECTIONS: Questions 1 through 3 are to be answered on the basis of the following reading passage. *PRINT THE LETTER OF THE CORRECT ANSWER IN THE SPACE AT THE RIGHT.*

In a retail establishment, any overweight means a distinct loss to the merchant, and even an apparently inconsequential overweight on a single package or sale when multiplied by the total number of transactions, could run into large figures. In addition to the use of reliable scales and weights, and their maintenance in proper condition, there must be proper supervision of the selling force. Such supervision is a difficult matter, particularly on the score of carelessness, as the depositing of extra amounts of material on the scale and failure to remove the same when it overbalances the scale may become a habit. In case of underweight, either in the weighing or by the use of fraudulent scales and weights, the seller soon will hear of it, but there is no reason why the amount weighed out should be in excess of what the customer pays for. Checking sales records against invoices and inventories can supply some indication of the tendency of the sales force to become careless in this field.

1. Of the following, the MOST valid implication of the above passage is that
   A. all overweights which occur in retail stores are in small amounts
   B. even-arm and uneven-arm balances and weights which are unreliable lead more often to underweights than to overweights
   C. overweights due to errors of salesclerks necessarily lead to large losses by a retailer
   D. supervision to prevent overweights is more important to a retailer than remedial measures after their occurrence

2. Of the following, the MOST valid implication of the above passage is that
   A. depositing of insufficient amounts of commodities on scales and failure to add to them may become a habit with salesclerks
   B. salesclerks should be trained in understanding and maintenance of scale mechanisms
   C. supervision of salesclerks to prevent careless habits in weighing must depend upon personal observation

3. According to the above passage, the MOST accurate of the following statements is:
   A. For the most part, the ideas expressed in the passage do not apply to wholesale establishments.
   B. Inventories of commodities prepacked in the store are the only ones which can be used in checking losses due to overweight.
   C. Invoices which give the value and weight of merchandise received are useful in checking losses due to overweights.
   D. The principal value of inventories is to indicate losses due to overweights.

1.____

2.____

3.____

KEY (CORRECT ANSWERS)

1. D
2. C
3. C

TEST 5

DIRECTIONS: Questions 1 through 5 are to be answered on the basis of the following reading passage. *PRINT THE LETTER OF THE CORRECT ANSWER IN THE SPACE AT THE RIGHT.*

TITANIC AIR COMPRESSOR

Valves: The compressors are equipped with Titanic plate valves which are automatic in operation. Valves are so constructed that an entire valve assembly can readily be removed from the head. The valves provide large port areas with short lift and are accurately guided to insure positive seating.

Starting Unloader: Each compressor (or air end) is equipped with a centrifugal governor which is bolted directly to the compressor crank shaft. The governor actuates cylinder relief valves so as to relieve pressure from the cylinders during starting and stopping. The motor is never required to start the compressor tinder load.

Air Strainer: Each cylinder air inlet connection is fitted with a suitable combination air strainer and muffler.

Pistons: Pistons are lightweight castings, ribbed internally to secure strength, and are accurately turned and ground. Each piston is fitted with four (4) rings, two of which are oil control rings. Piston pins are hardened and tempered steel of the full floating type. Bronze bushings are used between piston pin and piston

Connecting Rods: Connecting rods are of solid bronze designed for maximum strength, rigidity, and wear. Crank pins are fitted with renewable steel bushings. Connecting rods are of the one-piece type, there being no bolts, nuts, or cotter pins which can come loose. With this type of construction, wear is reduced to a negligible amount, and adjustment of wrist pin and crank pin bearings is unnecessary.

Main Bearings: Main bearings are of the ball type and are securely held in position by spacers. This type of bearing entirely eliminates the necessity of frequent adjustment or attention. The crank shaft is always in perfect alignment.

Crank Shaft: The crank shaft is a one-piece heat-treated forging of best quality open-hearth steel, of rugged design and of sufficient size to transmit the motor power and any additional stresses which may occur in service. Each crank shaft is counter-balanced (dynamically balanced to reduce vibration to a minimum, and is accurately machined to properly receive the ball-bearing races, crank pin bushing, flexible coupling, and centrifugal governor. Suitable provision is made to insure proper lubrication of all crank shaft bearings and bushings with the minimum amount of attention.

Coupling: Compressor and motor shafts are connected through a Morse Chain Company all-metal enclosed flexible coupling. This coupling consists of two sprockets, one mounted on, and keyed to, each shaft; the sprockets are wrapped by a single Morse Chain, the entire assembly being enclosed in a split aluminum grease-packed cover.

1. The crank pin of the connecting rod is fitted with a renewable bushing made of   1.____
    A. solid bronze   B. steel
    C. a lightweight casting   D. ball bearings

2. When the connecting rod is of the one-piece type,
   A. the wrist pins require frequent adjustment
   B. the crank pins require frequent adjustment
   C. the cotter pins frequently will come loose
   D. wear is reduced to a negligible amount

3. The centrifugal governor is bolted directly to the
   A. compressor crank shaft   B. main bearing
   C. piston pin   D. muffler

4. The number of oil control rings required for each piston is
   A. one   B. two   C. three   D. four

5. The compressor and motor shafts are connected through a flexible coupling. These couplings are _____ to the shafts.
   A. keyed   B. brazed   C. soldered   D. press-fit

KEY (CORRECT ANSWERS)

1. B
2. D
3. A
4. B
5. A

TEST 6

DIRECTIONS: Questions 1 through 6 are to be answered on the basis of the following reading passage. *PRINT THE LETTER OF THE CORRECT ANSWER IN THE SPACE AT THE RIGHT.*

Perhaps the strongest argument the mass transit backer has is the advantage in efficiency that mass transit has over the automobile in the urban traffic picture. It has been estimated that given comparable location and construction conditions, the subway can carry four times as many passengers per hour and cost half as much to build as urban highways. Yet public apathy regarding the mass transportation movement in the 1960's resulted in the building of more roads. Planned to provide 42,000 miles of highways in the period from 1956-72, including 7,500 miles within cities, the Federal Highway System project is now about two-thirds completed. The Highway Trust Fund supplies 90 percent of the cost of the system, with state and local sources putting up the rest of the money. By contrast, a municipality as had to put up the bulk of the cost of a rapid transit system. Although the system and its Trust Fund have come under attack in the past few years from environmentalists and groups opposed to the continued building of urban freeways—considered to be the most expensive, destructive, and inefficient segments of the system—a move by them to get the Trust Fund transformed into a general transportation fund at the expiration of the present program in 1972 seems to be headed nowhere.

1. Given similar building conditions and locations, a city that builds a subway instead of a highway can expect to receive for each dollar spent _____ as much transport value.
   A. half   B. twice   C. four times   D. eight times

1.____

2. The general attitude of the public in the past ten years toward the mass transportation movement has been
   A. favorable   B. indifferent   C. enthusiastic   D. unfriendly

2.____

3. The number of miles of highways still to be completed in the Federal Highway System project is MOST NEARLY
   A. 2,500   B. 5,000   C. 14,000   D. 28,000

3.____

4. What do certain groups who object to some features of the Federal Highway System program want to do with the Highway Trust Fund after 1972?
   A. Extend it in order to complete the project
   B. Change it so that the money can be used for all types of transportation
   C. End it even if the project is not completed
   D. Change it so that the money will be used only for urban freeways

4.____

5. Which one of the following statements is a VALID conclusion based on the facts in the above passage?
   A. The advantage of greater efficiency is the only argument that supporters of the mass transportation movement can offer.
   B. It was easier for cities to build roads rather than mass transit systems in the last 15 years because of the large financial contribution made by the Federal Government.

5.____

15

     C. Mass transit systems cause as much congestion and air pollution in cities as automobiles.
     D. In 1972, the Highway Trust Fund becomes a general transportation fund.

6. The MAIN idea or theme of the above passage is that the 6.____
     A. cost of the Federal Highway System is shared by the federal, state, and local governments
     B. public is against spending money for building mass transportation facilities in the cities
     C. cities would benefit more from expansion and improvement of their mass transit systems than from the building of more highways
     D. building of mass transportation facilities has been slowed by the Highway Trust Fund

KEY (CORRECT ANSWERS)

1. D
2. B
3. C
4. B
5. B
6. C

TEST 7

DIRECTIONS: Questions 1 through 5 are to be answered on the basis of the following reading passage. *PRINT THE LETTER OF THE CORRECT ANSWER IN THE SPACE AT THE RIGHT.*

The use of role-playing as a training technique was developed during the past decade by social scientists, particularly psychologists, who have been active in training experiments. Originally, this technique was applied by clinical psychologists who discovered that a patient appears to gain understanding of an emotionally disturbing situation when encouraged to act out roles in that situation. As applied in government and business organizations, the purpose of role-playing is to aid employees to understand certain work problems involving interpersonal relations and to enable observers to evaluate various reactions to them. Thus, for example, on the problem of handling grievances, two individuals from the group might be selected to act out extemporaneously the parts of subordinate and supervisor. When this situation is enacted by various pairs among the class and the techniques and results are discussed, the members of the group are presumed to reach conclusions about the most effective means of handling similar situations. Often the use or role reversal, where participants take parts different from their actual work roles, assists individuals to gain more insight into other people's problems and viewpoints. Although role-playing can be a rewarding training device, the trainer must be aware of his responsibilities. If this technique is to be successful, thorough briefing of both actors and observers as to the situation in question, the participants' roles, and what to look for, is essential.

1. The role-playing technique was FIRST used for the purpose of 1.____
   A. measuring the effectiveness of training programs
   B. training supervisors in business organizations
   C. treating emotionally disturbed patients
   D. handling employee grievances

2. When role-playing is used in private business as a training device, the CHIEF aim is to 2.____
   A. develop better relations between supervisor and subordinate in the handling of grievances
   B. come up with a solution to a specific problem that has arisen
   C. determine the training needs of the group
   D. increase employee understanding of the human-relation factors in work situations

3. From the above passage, it is MOST reasonable to conclude that when role-playing is used, it is preferable to have the roles acted out by 3.____
   A. only one set of actors
   B. no more than two sets of actors
   C. several different sets of actors
   D. the trainer or trainers of the group

4. It can be inferred from the above passage that a limitation of role-playing as a training method is that
   A. many work situations do not lend themselves to role-play
   B. employees are not experienced enough as actors to play the roles realistically
   C. only trainers who have psychological training can use it successfully
   D. participants who are observing and not acting do not benefit from it

5. To obtain *good* results from the use of role-play in training, a trainer should give participants
   A. a minimum of information about the situation so that they can act spontaneously
   B. scripts which illustrate the best method for handling the situation
   C. a complete explanation of the problem and the roles to be acted out
   D. a summary of work problems which involve interpersonal relations

---

KEY (CORRECT ANSWERS)

1. C
2. D
3. C
4. A
5. C

READING COMPREHENSION
UNDERSTANDING AND INTERPRETING WRITTEN MATERIAL
EXAMINATION SECTION
TEST 1

DIRECTIONS: All questions are to be answered SOLELY on the basis of the information contained in the passage. Each question or incomplete statement is followed by several suggested answers or completions. Select the one that BEST answers the question or completes the statement. *PRINT THE LETTER OF THE CORRECT ANSWER IN THE SPACE AT THE RIGHT.*

Questions 1-3.

The equipment in a mail room may include a mail-metering machine. This machine simultaneously stamps, postmarks, seals, and counts letters as fast as the operator can feed them. It can also print the proper postage directly on a gummed strip to be affixed to bulky items. It is equipped with a meter which is removed from the machine and sent to the postmaster to be set for a given number of stampings of any denomination. The setting of the meter must be paid for in advance. One of the advantages of metered mail is that it bypasses the cancellation operation and, thereby, facilitates handling by the post office. Mail metering also makes the pilfering of stamps impossible, but does not prevent the passage of personal mail in company envelopes through the meters unless there is established a rigid control or censorship over outgoing mail.

1. According to this statement, the postmaster 1.____
   A. is responsible for training new clerks in the use of mail-metering machines
   B. usually recommends that both large and small firms adopt the use of mail metering machines
   C. is responsible for setting the meter to print a fixed number of stampings
   D. examines the mail-metering machines to see that they are properly installed in the mail room

2. According to this statement, the use of mail-metering machines 2.____
   A. requires the employment of more clerks in a mail room than does the use of postage stamps
   B. interferes with the handling of large quantities of outgoing mail
   C. does not prevent employees from sending their personal letters at company expense
   D. usually involves smaller expenditures for mail room equipment than does the use of postage stamps

3. On the basis of this statement, it is MOST accurate to state that 3.____
   A. mail-metering machines are often used for opening envelopes
   B. postage stamps are generally used when bulky packages are to be mailed
   C. the use of metered mail tends to interfere with rapid mail handling by the post office
   D. mail-metering machines can seal and count letters at the same time

Questions 4-8.

It is the Housing Administration's policy that all tenants, whether new or transferring from one housing development to another, shall be required to pay a standard security deposit of one month's rent based on the rent at the time of admission. There are, however, certain exceptions to this policy. Employees of the Administration shall not be required to pay a security deposit if they secure an apartment in an Administration development. Where the payment of a full security deposit may present a hardship to a tenant, the development's manager may allow a tenant to move into an apartment upon payment of only part of the security deposit. In such cases, however, the tenant must agree to gradually pay the balance of the deposit. If a tenant transfers from one apartment to another within the same project, the security deposit originally paid by the tenant for his former apartment will be acceptable for his new apartment, even if the rent in the new apartment is greater than the rent in the former one. Finally, tenants who receive public assistance need not pay a security deposit before moving into an apartment if the appropriate agency states, in writing, that it will pay the deposit. However, it is the responsibility of the development's manager to make certain that payment shall be received within one month of the date the tenant moves into the apartment.

4. According to the above passage, when a tenant transfers from one apartment to another in the same development, the Housing Administration will
   A. accept the tenant's old security deposit as the security deposit for his new apartment
   B. refund the tenant's old security deposit and not require him to pay a new deposit
   C. keep the tenant's old security deposit and require him to pay a new deposit
   D. require the tenant to pay a new security deposit based on the difference between his old rent and his new rent

5. On the basis of the above passage, it is INCORREC to state that a tenant who receives public assistance may move into an Administration development if
   A. he pays the appropriate security deposit
   B. the appropriate agency gives a written indication that it will pay the security deposit before the tenant moves in
   C. the appropriate agency states, by telephone, that it will pay the security deposit
   D. the appropriate agency writes the manager to indicate that the security deposit will be paid within one month but not less than two weeks from the date the tenant moves into the apartment

6. On the basis of the above passage, a tenant who transfers from an apartment in one development to an apartment in a different department will
   A. forfeit his old security deposit and be required to pay another deposit
   B. have his old security deposit refunded and not have to pay a new deposit
   C. pay the difference between his old security deposit and the new one
   D. have to pay a security deposit based on the new apartment's rent

7. The Housing Administration will NOT require payment of a security deposit if a tenant
   A. is an Administration employee
   B. is receiving public assistance
   C. claims that payment will present a hardship
   D. indicates, in writing, that he will be responsible for any damage done to his apartment

8. Of the following, the BEST title for the above passage is:
   A. Security Deposits – Transfers
   B. Security Deposits – Policy
   C. Exemptions and Exceptions – Security Deposits
   D. Amounts – Security Deposits

Questions 9-11.

Terrazzo flooring will last a very long time if it is cared for properly. Lacquers, shellac or varnish preparations should never be used on terrazzo. Soap cleaners are not recommended, since they dull the appearance of the floor. Alkaline solutions are harmful, so neutral cleaner or non-alkaline synthetic detergents will give best results. If the floor is very dirty, it may be necessary to scrub it. The same neutral cleaning solution should be used for scrubbing as for mopping. Scouring powder may be sprinkled at particularly dirty spots. Do not use steel wool for scrubbing. Small pieces of steel filings left on the floor will rust and discolor the terrazzo. Non-woven nylon or open-mesh fabric abrasive pads are suitable for scrubbing terrazzo floors.

9. According to the above passage, the BEST cleaning agent for terrazzo flooring is a(n)
   A. soap cleaner   B. varnish preparation
   C. neutral cleaner   D. alkaline solution

10. According to the above passage, terrazzo floors should NOT be scrubbed with
    A. non-woven nylon abrasive pads   B. steel wool
    C. open-mesh fabric abrasive pads   D. scouring powder

11. As used in the above passage, the word *discolor* means MOST NEARLY
    A. crack   B. scratch   C. dissolve   D. stain

Questions 12-15.

Planning for the unloading of incoming trucks is not easy since generally little or no advance notice of truck arrivals is received. The height of the floor of truck bodies and loading platforms sometimes are different; this makes necessary the use of special unloading methods. When available, hydraulic ramps compensate for the differences in platform and truck floor levels. When hydraulic ramps are not available, forklift equipment can sometimes be used, if the truck sprigs are strong enough to support such equipment. In a situation like this, the unloading operation does not differ much from unloading a railroad box car in the cases where the forklift truck or a hydraulic pallet jack cannot be used inside the truck, a pallet dolly should be placed inside the truck, so that the empty pallet can be loaded close to the truck contents and rolled easily to the truck door and platform.

12. According to the above passage, unloading trucks are
    A. easy to plan since the time of arrival is usually known beforehand
    B. the same as loading a railroad box car
    C. hard to plan since trucks arrive without notice
    D. a very normal thing to do

13. According to the above passage, which materials-handling equipment can make up for the difference in platform and truck floor levels?
    A. Hydraulic jacks   B. Hydraulic ramps
    C. Forklift trucks   D. Conveyors

14. According to the above passage, what materials-handling equipment can be used when a truck cannot support the weight of forklift equipment?
    A. A pallet dolly   B. A hydraulic ramp
    C. Bridge plates   D. A warehouse tractor

15. Which of the following is the BEST title for the above passage?
    A. Unloading Railroad Box Cars   B. Unloading Motor Trucks
    C. Loading Rail Box   D. Loading Motor Trucks

Questions 16-19.

Ventilation, as used in firefighting operations, means opening up a building or structure in which a fire is burning to release the accumulated heat, smoke, and gases. Lack of knowledge of the principle of ventilation on the part of firemen may result in unnecessary punishment due to ventilation being neglected or improperly handled. While ventilation itself extinguishes no fires, when used in an intelligent manner, it allows firemen to get at the fire more quickly, easily, and with less danger and hardship.

16. According to the above passage, the MOST important result of failure to apply the principles of ventilation at a fire may be
    A. loss of public confidence   B. disciplinary action
    C. waste of water   D. excessive use of equipment
    E. injury to fireman

17. It may be inferred from the above passage that the CHIEF advantage of ventilation is that it
    A. eliminates the need for gas masks
    B. reduces smoke damage
    C. permits firemen to work closer to the fire
    D. cools the fire
    E. enables firemen to use shorter hose lines

18. Knowledge of the principles of ventilation, as defined in the above passage, would be LEAST important in a fire in a
    A. tenement house   B. grocery store   C. ship's hold
    D. lumberyard   E. office building

19. We may conclude from the above passage that, for the well-trained and equipped fireman, ventilation is
    A. a simple matter
    B. rarely necessary
    C. relatively unimportant
    D. a basic tool
    E. sometimes a handicap

19.____

Questions 20-22.

Many public service and industrial organizations are becoming increasingly insistent that supervisors at the work level be qualified instructors. The reason for this is that technological improvements and overall organizational growth require the acquisition of new skills and knowledge by workers. These skills and knowledge can be acquired in two ways. They can be gained either by absorption-rubbing shoulders with the job or through planned instruction. Permitting the acquisition of new skills and knowledge is to be haphazard and uncertain is too costly. At higher supervisory levels, the need for instructing subordinate is not so obvious, but it is just as important as at the lowest work level. A high-ranking supervisor accomplishes the requirements of his position only if his subordinate supervisors perform their work efficiently. Regardless of one's supervisory position, the ability to instruct easily and efficiently helps to insure well-qualified and thoroughly-trained subordinates. There exists an unfounded but rather prevalent belief that becoming a competent instructor is a long, arduous, and complicated process. This belief arises partially as a result of the requirement of a long period of college preparation involved in preparing teachers for our school system. This time is necessary because teachers must learn a great deal of subject matter. The worker who advances to a supervisory position generally has superior skill and knowledge; therefore, he has only to learn the techniques by which he can impart his knowledge in order to become a competent instructor.

20. According to the above passage, a prolonged period of preparation for instructing is NOT generally necessary for a worker who is advanced to a supervisory position because
    A. he may already possess some of the requirements of a competent instructor
    B. his previous job knowledge is generally sufficient to enable him to begin instructing immediately
    C. in his present position there is less need for the specific job knowledge of the ordinary worker
    D. the ability to instruct follows naturally from superior skill and knowledge

20.____

21. According to the above passage, it is important for the higher-level supervisor to be a good instructor because
    A. at this level there is a tendency to overlook the need for instruction of both subordinate supervisors and workers
    B. good training practices will then be readily adopted by lower-level supervisors
    C. the need for effective training is more critical at the higher levels of responsibility
    D. training can be used to improve the supervisory performance of his subordinate supervisors

21.____

22. According to the above passage, the acquisition of new skills and knowledge by workers is BEST accomplished when
    A. the method of training allows for the use of absorption
    B. organizational growth and technological improvement indicate a need for further training
    C. such training is the result of careful planning
    D. the cost factor involved in training can be readily justified

Questions 23-25.

The organization of any large agency falls into three broad general zones: top management, middle management, and rank-and-file operations. The normal task of middle management is to supervise, direct, and control the performance of operations within the scope of law, policy, and regulations already established. Where policy is settled and well defined, middle management is basically a set of standard operations, although they may call for high-developed skills. Where, however, policy is not clearly stated, is ambiguous, or is rapidly shifting, middle management is likely to have an important influence upon emergency policy trends. Persons working in the zone of middle management usually become specialists. They need specialist knowledge of law, rules, and regulations, and court decisions governing their organization if they are to discharge their duties effectively. They will also have acquired specialist knowledge of relationships and sequences in the normal flow of business. Further, their attention is brought to bear on a particular administrative task, in a particular jurisdiction, with a particular clientele. The importance of middle management is obviously great. The reasons for such importance are not difficult to find: Here it is that the essential action of government in behalf of citizens is taken; here it is that citizens deal with government when they pass beyond their first contacts; here is a training ground from which a considerable part of top management emerges; and here it is that the spirit and temper of the public service and its reputation are largely made.

23. According to the above passage, the critical importance of middle management is due to the fact that it is at this level that
    A. formal executive training can be most useful
    B. the greatest amount of action is taken on the complaints of the general public
    C. the official actions taken have the greatest impact on general attitudes towards the public service
    D. the public most frequently comes in contact with governmental operations and agencies

24. According to the above passage, the one of the following statements which is NOT offered as an explanation of the tendency for middle management responsibility to produce specialists is that
    A. middle-management personnel frequently feel that their work is the most important in an organization
    B. specialized knowledge is acquired during the course of everyday work
    C. specialized knowledge is necessary for effective job performance
    D. their work assignments are directed to specific problems in specific situations

25. According to the above passage, the GREATEST impact of middle management in policy determination would be likely to be felt in the situation in which
    A. middle management possesses highly developed operational skills
    B. several policy directives from top management are subject to varying interpretations
    C. the authority of middle management to supervise, direct, and control operations has been clearly established
    D. top management has neglected to consider the policy views of middle management

KEY (CORRECT ANSWERS)

1.	C		11.	D
2.	C		12.	C
3.	D		13.	B
4.	A		14.	A
5.	C		15.	B
6.	D		16.	E
7.	A		17.	C
8.	B		18.	D
9.	C		19.	D
10.	B		20.	A

21. D
22. C
23. C
24. A
25. B

TEST 2

DIRECTIONS: All questions are to be answered SOLELY on the basis of the information contained in the passage. Each question or incomplete statement is followed by several suggested answers or completions. Select the one that BEST answers the question or completes the statement. *PRINT THE LETTER OF THE CORRECT ANSWER IN THE SPACE AT THE RIGHT.*

Questions 1-2.

    Metal spraying is used for many purposes. Worn bearings on shafts and spindles can be readily restored to original dimensions with any desired metal or alloy. Low-carbon steel shafts may be supplied with high-carbon steel journal surfaces, which can then be ground to size after spraying. By using babbitt wire, bearings can be lined or babbited while rotating. Pump shafts and impellers can be coated with any desired metal to overcome wear and corrosion. Valve seats may be re-surfaced. Defective castings can be repaired by filling in blowholes and checks. The application of metal spraying to the field of corrosion resistance is growing, although the major application in this field is in the use of sprayed zinc. Tin, lead, and aluminum have been used considerably. The process is used for structural and tank applications in the field as well as in the shop.

1. According to the above passage, worn bearing surface on shafts are metal-sprayed in order to
     A. prevent corrosion of the shaft
     B. fit them into larger-sized impellers
     C. returns them to their original sizes
     D. replaces worn babbitt metal

   1.____

2. According to the above passage, rotating bearings can be metal-sprayed using
     A. babbitt wire   B. high-carbon steel
     C. low-carbon steel   D. any desired metal

   2.____

Questions 3-5.

    The method of cleaning which should generally be used is the space assignment method. Under this method, the buildings to be cleaned are divided into different sections. Within each section, each crew of Custodial Assistants is assigned to do one particular cleaning job. For example, within a section, one crew may be assigned to cleaning offices, another to scrubbing floors, a third to collecting trash, and so on. Other methods which may be used are the post-assignment methods and the gang-cleaning method. Under the post-assignment method, a Custodial Assistant is assigned to one area of a building and performs all cleaning jobs in that area. This method is seldom used except where buildings are so small and distant from each other that it is not economical to use the space-assigned method. Under the gang-cleaning method, a Custodial Foreman takes a number of Custodial Assistants through a section of the building. These Custodial Assistants work as a group and complete the various cleaning jobs as they go. This method is generally used only where the building contains very large open areas.

2 (#2)

3. According to the above passage, under the space-assignment method, each crew generally
    A. works as a group and does a variety of different cleaning jobs
    B. is assigned to one area and performs all cleaning jobs in that area
    C. does one particular cleaning job within a section of a building
    D. follows the Custodial Foreman through a building containing large, open areas

3._____

4. According to the above passage, the post-assignment method is used mostly where the buildings to be cleaned are _____ in size and situated _____.
    A. large; close together   B. small; close together
    C. large; far apart   D. small; far apart

4._____

5. As used in the above passage, the word *economical* means MOST NEARLY
    A. thrifty   B. agreed   C. unusual   D. wasteful

5._____

Questions 6-9.

The desirability of complete refuse collection by municipalities is becoming generally accepted. In many cases, however, such ideal service is economically impractical and certain limits must be imposed. Some municipal authorities find it necessary to regulate the quantity of refuse, by weight or volume, which will be collected from a single residence or place of business at one collection. The purpose of the regulations is twofold: First, to maintain the degree of service rendered on a somewhat uniform basis; and, second, to insure a more or less constant collection from week to week. If left unregulated, careless producers might permit large quantities of refuse to accumulate on their premises over long periods and place abnormal amounts out for collection at irregular intervals, thus upsetting the collection schedule. Regulation is especially applied to large wholesale, industrial, and manufacturing enterprises which, in the great majority of cases, are required to dispose of all or part of their refuse themselves, at their own expense. The maximum quantities permitted by regulation should obviously be sufficient to take care of a normal accumulation at a household over the established interval between regular collections. In commercial districts, the maximum quantity limitations are often fixed on arbitrary bases rather than on normal production.

6. According to the above passage, many municipalities do not have complete refuse collections because
    A. it costs too much   B. it is difficult to regulate
    C. it is not a municipal function D. they don't consider it desirable

6._____

7. According to the above passage, regulation by municipalities of the amount of refuse collected per collection from any one place of business does NOT contribute to
    A. accumulation of refuse by careless producers
    B. maintenance of collection schedules
    C. steady collection from one week to the next
    D. uniform service

7._____

8. According to the above passage, regulations by municipalities of refuse collection from certain enterprises helps to cut down
   A. accumulation of refuse for private collection
   B. the amount of refuse produced
   C. variation in the volume of refuse produced
   D. variation in collection service

8.____

9. According to the above passage, municipalities limit the amount of refuse collected in commercial districts on an arbitrary basis rather than on the basis of a normal accumulation. This is probably done because
   A. arbitrary standards are easy to establish and enforce
   B. normal accumulation is different for each district
   C. normal accumulation would require the collection of too much refuse
   D. there is no such thing as a normal accumulation

9.____

Questions 10-13.

The following passage is adapted from an old office manual:

Modern office methods, geared to ever higher speeds and aimed at ever greater efficiency, are largely the result of the typewriter. The typewriter is a substitute for handwriting and, in the hands of a skilled typist, not only turns out letters and other documents at least three times faster than a penman can do the work, but turns out the greater volume more uniformly and legibly. With the use of carbon paper and onionskin paper, identical copies can be made at the same time.

The typewriter, besides its effect on the conduct of business and government, has had a very important effect on the position of women. The typewriter has done much to bring women into business and government and today there are vastly more women than men typists. Many women have used the keys of the typewriter to climb the ladder to responsible managerial positions.

The typewriter, as its name implies, employs type to make an ink impression on paper. For many years, the manual typewriter was the standard machine used. Today, the electric typewriter is dominant, and completely automatic typewriters are coming into wider use.

The mechanism of the office manual typewriter includes a set of keys arranged systematically in rows; a semicircular frame of type, connected to the keys by levers; the carriage, or paper carrier; a rubber roller, called a platen, against which the type strikes; and an inked ribbon which makes the impression of the type character when the key strikes it.

10. The above passage mentions a number of good features of the combination of a skilled typist and a typewriter. Of the following, the feature which is NOT mentioned in the passage is
    A. speed   B. uniformity   C. reliability   D. legibility

10.____

11. According to the above passage, a skilled typist can
    A. turn out at least five carbon copies of typed matter
    B. type at least three times faster than a penman can write
    C. type more than 80 words a minute
    D. readily move into a managerial position

11.____

12. According to the above passage, which of the following is NOT part of the mechanism of a manual typewriter? 12.____
    A. Carbon paper
    B. Paper carrier
    C. Platen
    D. Inked ribbon

13. According to the above passage, the typewriter has helped 13.____
    A. men more than women in business
    B. women in career advancement into management
    C. men and women equally, but women have taken better advantage of it
    D. more women than men, because men generally dislike routine typing work

Questions 14-18.

Reductions in pipe size of a building heating system are made with eccentric fittings and are pitched downward. The ends of mains with gravity return shall be at least 18" above the water line of the boiler. As condensate flows opposite to the steam, run outs are one size larger than the vertical pipe and are pitched upward. In a one-pipe system, an automatic air vent must be provided at each main to relieve air pressure and to let steam enter the radiator. As steam enters the radiator, a *thermal* device causes the vent to close, thereby holding the steam. Steam mains should not be less than two inches in diameter. The end of the steam main should have a minimum size of one-half of its greatest diameter. Small steam systems should be sized for a 2-oz. pressure drop. Large steam systems should be sized for a 4-oz. pressure drop.

14. The word *thermal*, as used in the above passage, means MOST NEARLY 14.____
    A. convector   B. heat   C. instrument   D. current

15. According to the above passage, the one of the following that is one size larger than the vertical pipe is the 15.____
    A. steam main   B. valve   C. water line   D. run out

16. According to the above paragraph, small steam systems should be sized for a pressure drop of _____ oz. 16.____
    A. 2   B. 3   C. 4   D. 5

17. According to the above passage, ends of mains with gravity return shall be AT LEAST 17.____
    A. 18" above the water line of the boiler
    B. one-quarter of the greatest diameter of the main
    C. twice the size of the vertical pipe in the main
    D. 18" above the steam line of the boiler

18. According to the above passage, the one of the following that is provided at each main to relieve air pressure is a(n) 18.____
    A. gravity return   B. convector   C. eccentric   D. vent

Questions 19-21.

The bearings of all electrical equipment should be subjected to careful inspection at scheduled periodic intervals in order to secure maximum life. The newer type of sleeve bearing requires very little attention since the oil does not become contaminated and oil leakage is negligible. Maintenance of the correct oil level is frequently the only upkeep required for years of service with this type of bearing.

19. According to the above passage, the MAIN reason for making periodic inspections of electrical equipment is to
    A. reduce waste of lubricants
    B. prevent injury to operators
    C. make equipment last longer
    D. keeps operators "on their toes"

19.____

20. According to the above passage, the bearings of electrical equipment should be inspected
    A. whenever the equipment isn't working properly
    B. whenever there is time for inspections
    C. at least once a year
    D. at regular times

20.____

21. According to the above passage, when using the newer type of sleeve bearings,
    A. oil leakage is slight
    B. the oil level should be checked every few years
    C. oil leakage is due to carelessness
    D. oil soon becomes dirty

21.____

Questions 22-25.

There is hardly a city in the country that is not short of fire protection in some areas within its boundaries. These municipalities have spread out and have re-shuffled their residential, business, and industrial districts without readjusting the existing protective fire forces; or creating new protection units. Fire stations are still situated according to the needs of earlier times and have not been altered or improved to house modern firefighting equipment. They are neither efficient for carrying out their tasks nor livable for the men who must occupy them.

22. Of the following, the title which BEST describes the central idea of the above passage is:
    A. The Dynamic Nature of Contemporary Society
    B. The Cost of Fire Protection
    C. The Location and Design of Fire Stations
    D. The Design and Use of Firefighting Equipment
    E. The Growth of American Cities

22.____

23. According to the above passage, fire protection is inadequate in the United Sates in
    A. most areas of some cities
    B. some areas of most cities
    C. some areas in all cities
    D. all areas in some cities
    E. most areas in most cities

23.____

24. The one of the following criteria for planning of fire stations which is NOT mentioned in the above passage is:
    A. Comfort of Firemen
    B. Proper Location
    C. Design for Modern Equipment
    D. Efficiency of Operation
    E. Cost of Construction

    24.____

25. Of the following suggestions for improving the fire service, the one which would BEST deal with the problem discussed in the above passage would involve
    A. specialized training in the use of modern fire apparatus
    B. replacement of obsolete fire apparatus
    C. revision of zoning laws
    D. longer basic training for probationary firemen
    E. reassignment of fire districts

    25.____

Questions 26-30.

Stopping, standing, and parking of motor vehicles is regulated by law to keep the public highways open for a smooth flow of traffic, and to keep stopped vehicles from blocking intersections, driveways, signs, fire hydrants, and other areas that must be kept clear. These established regulations apply in all situations, unless otherwise indicated by signs. Other local restrictions are posted in the areas to which they apply. Three examples of these other types of restrictions, which may apply singly or in combination with one another are:
NO STOPPING: This means that a driver may not stop a vehicle for any purpose except when necessary to avoid interference with other vehicles, or in compliance with directions of a police officer or signal.
NO STANDING: This means that a driver may stop a vehicle only temporarily to actually receive or discharge passengers.
NO PARKING: This means that a driver may stop a vehicle only temporarily to actually load or unload merchandise or passengers. When stopped, it is advisable to turn on warning flashers, if equipped with them. However, one should never use a directional signal for this purpose, because it may confuse other drivers. Some NO PARKING signs prohibit parking between certain hours on certain days. For example, the sign may read NO PARKING 8 A.M. to 11 A.M., MONDAY, WEDNESDAY, FRIDAY. These signs are usually utilized on streets where cleaning operations take place on alternate days.

26. The parking regulation that applies to fire hydrants is an example of _____ regulations.
    A. local   B. established   C. posted   D. temporary

    26.____

27. When stopped in a NO PARKING zone, it is advisable to
    A. turn on the right directional signal to indicate to other drivers that you will remain stopped
    B. turn on the left directional signal to indicate to other drivers that you may be leaving the curb after a period of time
    C. turn on the warning flashers if your car is equipped with them
    D. put the vehicle in reverse so that the backup lights will be on to warn approaching cars that you have temporarily stopped

    27.____

28. You may stop a vehicle temporarily to discharge passengers in an area under the restriction of a _____ zone.
    A. NO STOPPING – NO STANDING
    B. NO STANDING – NO PARKING
    C. NO PARKING – NO STOPPING
    D. NO STOPPING – NO STANDING – NO PARKING

28._____

29. A sign reads "NO PARKING 8 A.M. to 11 A.M., MONDAY, WEDNESDAY, FRIDAY."
    Based on this sign, an enforcement officer would issue a summons to a car that is parked on a
    A. Tuesday at 9:30 A.M.   B. Wednesday at 12:00 A.M.
    C. Friday at 10:30 A.M.   D. Saturday at 8:00 A.M.

29._____

30. NO PARKING signs prohibiting parking between certain hours, on certain days, are usually utilized on streets where
    A. vehicles frequently take on and discharge passengers
    B. cleaning operations take place on alternate days
    C. NO STOPPING signs have been ignored
    D. commercial vehicles take on and unload merchandise

30._____

KEY (CORRECT ANSWERS)

1.	C	11.	B	21.	A
2.	A	12.	A	22.	C
3.	C	13.	B	23.	B
4.	D	14.	B	24.	E
5.	A	15.	D	25.	E
6.	A	16.	A	26.	B
7.	A	17.	A	27.	C
8.	D	18.	D	28.	B
9.	C	19.	C	29.	C
10.	C	20.	D	30.	B

ARITHMETICAL REASONING
EXAMINATION SECTION
TEST 1

DIRECTIONS: Each question or incomplete statement is followed by several suggested answers or completions. Select the one that BEST answers the question or completes the statement. *PRINT THE LETTER OF THE CORRECT ANSWER IN THE SPACE AT THE RIGHT.*

1. A supplier quotes a list price of $172.00 less 15 and 10 percent for twelve tools. The actual cost for these twelve tools is MOST NEARLY   1.____

    A. $146   B. $132   C. $129   D. $112

2. If the diameter of a circular piece of sheet metal is 1 1/2 feet, the area, in square inches, is MOST NEARLY   2.____

    A. 1.77   B. 2.36   C. 254   D. 324

3. The sum of 5'6", 7'3", 9'3 1/2", and 3'7 1/4" is   3.____

    A. 19'8 1/2"   B. 22' 1/2"   C. 25'7 3/4"   D. 28'8 3/4"

4. If the floor area of one shop is 15' by 21'3" and the size of an adjacent shop is 18' by 30'6", then the TOTAL floor area of these two shops is _____ square feet.   4.____

    A. 1127.75   B. 867.75   C. 549.0   D. 318.75

5. The fraction which is equal to 0.875 is   5.____

    A. 7/16   B. 5/8   C. 3/4   D. 7/8

6. The sum of 1/2, 2 1/32, 4 3/16, and 1 7/8 is MOST NEARLY   6.____

    A. 9.593   B. 9.625   C. 9.687   D. 10.593

7. If the base of a right triangle is 9" and the altitude is 12", the length of the third side will be   7.____

    A. 13"   B. 14"   C. 15"   D. 16"

8. If a steel bar 1" in diameter and 12' long weighs 32 lbs., then the weight of a piece of this bar 5'9" long is MOST NEARLY _____ lbs.   8.____

    A. 15.33   B. 15.26   C. 16.33   D. 15.06

9. The diameter of a circle whose circumference is 12" is MOST NEARLY   9.____

    A. 3.82"   B. 3.72"   C. 3.62"   D. 3.52"

10. A dimension of 39/64 inches converted to decimals is MOST NEARLY   10.____

    A. .600"   B. .609"   C. .607"   D. .611"

11. A farm worker was paid a weekly wage of $415.20 for a 44-hour work week. As a result of a new labor contract, he is paid $431.40 a week for a 40-hour work week with time and one-half pay for time worked in excess of 40 hours in any work week.
If he continues to work 44 hours weekly under the new contract, the amount by which his average hourly rate for a 44-hour work week under the new contract exceeds the hourly rate previously paid him lies between _____ and _____, inclusive.

    A. 80¢; $1.00   B. $1.00; $1.20
    C. $1.25; $1.45   D. $1.50; $1.70

12. The sum of 4 feet 3 1/4 inches, 7 feet 2 1/2 inches, and 11 feet 1/4 inch is _____ feet _____ inches.

    A. 21; 6 1/4   B. 22; 6   C. 23; 5   D. 24; 5 3/4

13. The number 0.038 is read as

    A. 38 tenths   B. 38 hundredths
    C. 38 thousandths   D. 38 ten-thousandths

14. Assume that an employee is paid at the rate of $10.86 per hour with time and a half for overtime past 40 hours in a week.
If he works 43 hours in a week, his gross weekly pay is

    A. $434.40   B. $438.40   C. $459.18   D. $483.27

15. The sum of the following dimensions: 3'2 1/4", 8 7/8", 2'6 3/8", 2'9 3/4", and 1'0" is

    A. 16'7 1/4"   B. 10'7 1/4"   C. 10'3 1/4"   D. 9'3 1/4"

16. Two gears are meshed together and have a gear ratio of 6 to 1.
If the small gear rotates 120 revolutions per minute, the large gear rotates at

    A. 20   B. 40   C. 60   D. 720

17. The vacuum side of a compound gage reads 14 inches of vacuum. The barometer reading is 29.76 inches of mercury. The equivalent absolute pressure of the compound gage reading, in inches of mercury, is MOST likely

    A. 15.06   B. 15.76   C. 43.06   D. 43.76

18. The fraction 5/8 expressed as a decimal is

    A. 0.125   B. 0.412   C. 0.625   D. 0.875

19. If 300 feet of a certain size pipe weighs 450 pounds, the number of pounds that 100 feet will weigh is

    A. 1,350   B. 150   C. 300   D. 250

20. As an oiler, you work for a facility that has automobiles that use, on the average, 600 quarts of one grade of lubricating oil every month.
The number of one-gallon cans of the above oil that should be ordered each month to meet this requirement is

    A. 100   B. 125   C. 140   D. 150

21. The inside dimensions of a rectangular oil gravity tank are: height 15", width 9", length 10".
    The amount of oil in the tank, in gallons, (231 cu.in. = 1 gallon), when the oil level is 9" high, is MOST NEARLY

    A. 2.3   B. 3.5   C. 5.2   D. 5.8

22. If 30 gallons of oil cost $76.80, 45 gallons of oil at the same rate will cost

    A. $91.20   B. $115.20   C. $123.20   D. $131.20

23. If an oiler earns $18,000 in the first six months of a year and receives a 10% raise in salary for the next six months of the same year, his TOTAL earnings for the year will be

    A. $36,000   B. $37,500   C. $37,800   D. $39,600

24. If the cost of lubricating oil increases 15%, then a gallon of oil which used to cost $10.00 will now cost MOST NEARLY

    A. $10.50   B. $11.00   C. $11.50   D. $12.00

25. The sum of 7/8", 3/4", 1/2", and 3/8" is

    A. 2 1/8"   B. 2 1/4"   C. 2 3/8"   D. 2 1/2"

KEY (CORRECT ANSWERS)

1. B
2. C
3. C
4. B
5. D

6. A
7. C
8. A
9. A
10. B

11. A
12. B
13. C
14. D
15. C

16. A
17. B
18. C
19. B
20. D

21. B
22. B
23. C
24. C
25. D

SOLUTIONS TO PROBLEMS

1. Actual cost = ($172)(.85)(.90) = $131.58 ≈ $132

2. Radius = .75', then area = (3.14)(.75)^2 ≈ 1.77 sq.ft.
   Since 1 sq.ft. = 144 sq.in., the area ≈ 254 sq.in.

3. 5'6" + 7'3" + 9'3 1/2" + 3'7 1/4" = 24'19 3/4" = 25'7 3/4"

4. Total area = (15)(21.25) + (18)(30.5) = 867.75 sq.ft.

5. .875 = 875/1000 = 7/8

6. 1 1/2 + 2 1/32 + 4 3/16 + 1 7/8 = 8 51/32 = 9 19/32 = 9.593

7. Third side = $\sqrt{9^2+12^2} = \sqrt{225} = 15"$

8. Let x = weight. Then, 12/32 = 5.75/x. Solving, x ≈ 15.33 lbs.

9. 12" = (3.14)(diameter), so diameter ≈ 3.82"

10. $\frac{39}{64}$" = .609375" ≈ .609"

11. Under his new contract, the weekly wage for 44 hours can be found by first determining his hourly rate for the first 40 hours = $431.40 ÷ 40 ≈ $10.80. Now, his time and one-half pay will = ($10.80)(1.5) = $16.20. His weekly wage for the new contract = $431.40 + (4)($16.20) = $496.20. His new hourly rate for 44 hours = $496.20 ÷ 44 ≈ $10.34. Under the old contract, his hourly rate for 44 hours was $415.20 ÷ 44 = $9.44. His hourly rate increase = $10.34 - $9.44 = $0.90. (Answer key: between $0.80 and $1.00)

12. 4'3 1/4" + 7'2 1/2" + 11' 1/4" = 22'6"

13. .038 = 38 thousandths

14. ($10.86)(40) + ($16.29)(3) = $483.27

15. 3'2 1/4" + 8 7/8" + 2'6 3/8" + 2'9 3/4" + 1'0" = 8'25 18/8" = 10'3 1/4"

16. The gear ratio is inversely proportional to the gear size. Let x = large gear's rpm. Then, 6/1 = 120/x. Solving, x = 20

17. Subtract 14 from 29.76

18. 5/8 = .625

19. Let x = number of pounds. Then, 300/450 = 100/x. Solving, x = 150

20. 600 quarts = 150 gallons, since 4 quarts = 1 gallon

21. (9")(9")(10") = 810 cu.in. Then, 810 ÷ 231 ≈ 3.5

22. Let x = unknown cost. Then, 30/$76.80 = 45/x. Solving, x = $115.20

23. $18,000 + ($18,000)(1.10) = $37,800

24. ($10.00)(1.15) = $11.50

25. 7/8" + 3/4" + 1/2" + 3/8" = 20/8" = 2 1/2"

TEST 2

DIRECTIONS: Each question or incomplete statement is followed by several suggested answers or completions. Select the one that BEST answers the question or completes the statement. *PRINT THE LETTER OF THE CORRECT ANSWER IN THE SPACE AT THE RIGHT.*

1. A sheet metal plate has been cut in the form of a right triangle with sides of 5, 12, and 13 inches.
   The area of this plate, in square inches, is

   A. 30   B. 32 1/2   C. 60   D. 78

   1.____

2. If steel weighs 480 lbs. per cubic foot, the weight of an 18" x 18" x 2" steel base plate is _____ lbs.

   A. 180   B. 216   C. 427   D. 648

   2.____

3. By trial, it is found that by using 2 cubic feet of sand, a 5 cubic foot batch of concrete is produced.
   Using the same proportions, the amount of sand, in cubic feet, required to produce 2 cubic yards of concrete is MOST NEARLY

   A. 7   B. 22   C. 27   D. 45

   3.____

4. The total number of cubic yards of earth to be removed to make a trench 3'9" wide, 25'0" long, and 4'3" deep is MOST NEARLY

   A. 53.1   B. 35.4   C. 26.6   D. 14.8

   4.____

5. A large number of 2 x 4 studs, some 10'5" long and some 6'5 1/2" long, are required for a job.
   To minimize waste, it would be PREFERABLE to order lengths of _____ feet.

   A. 16   B. 17   C. 18   D. 19

   5.____

6. A 6" pipe is connected to a 4" pipe through a reducer. If 100 cubic feet of water is flowing through the 6" pipe per minute, the flow, in cubic feet, per minute through the 4" pipe is

   A. 225   B. 100   C. 66.6   D. 44.4

   6.____

7. If steel weighs 0.28 pounds per cubic inch, then the weight, in pounds, of a 2" square steel bar 120" long is MOST NEARLY

   A. 115   B. 125   C. 135   D. 155

   7.____

8. A three-inch diameter steel bar two feet long weighs MOST NEARLY (assume steel weighs 480 lbs./cu.ft.) _____ lbs.

   A. 48   B. 58   C. 68   D. 78

   8.____

9. The area of a circular plate will be reduced by 5% if a sector removed from it has an angle of _____ degrees.

   A. 18   B. 24   C. 32   D. 60

   9.____

10. If a 4 1/16 inch shaft wears six thousandths of an inch, the NEW diameter will be _____ inches.

    A. 4.0031   B. 4.0565   C. 4.0578   D. 4.0605

11. A set of mechanical plan drawings is drawn to a scale of 1/8" = 1 foot.
    If a length of pipe measures 15 7/16" on the drawing, the ACTUAL length of the pipe is _____ feet.

    A. 121.5   B. 122.5   C. 123.5   D. 124.5

12. An electrical drawing is drawn to a scale of 1/4" = 1'. If a length of conduit on the drawing measures 7 3/8", the actual length of the conduit, in feet, is

    A. 7.5   B. 15.5   C. 22.5   D. 29.5

13. Assume that you have assigned 6 mechanics to do a job that must be finished in 4 days. At the end of 3 days, your men have completed only two-thirds of the job. In order to complete the job on time and because the job is such that it cannot be speeded up, you should assign a MINIMUM of _____ extra men.

    A. 3   B. 4   C. 5   D. 6

14. Assume that a trench is 42" wide, 5' deep, and 100' long. If the unit price of excavating the trench is $105 per cubic yard, the cost of excavating the trench is MOST NEARLY

    A. $6,805   B. $15,330   C. $21,000   D. $63,000

15. If the scale on a shop drawing is 1/4 inch to the foot, then the length of a part which measures 2 3/8 inches long on the drawing is ACTUALLY _____ feet.

    A. 9 1/2   B. 8 1/2   C. 7 1/4   D. 4 1/4

16. It is necessary to pour a new concrete floor for a shop. If the dimensions of the concrete slab for the floor are to be 27' x 18' x 6", then the number of cubic yards of concrete that must be poured is

    A. 9   B. 16   C. 54   D. 243

17. The jaws of a vise move 1/4" for each complete turn of the handle.
    The number of complete turns necessary to open the jaws 2 3/4" is

    A. 9   B. 10   C. 11   D. 12

18. Assume that a jobbing shop is to submit a price for a contract involving 300 pieces of work. Assume that material costs 50 cents per piece, labor costs $7.50 an hour, and a lathe operator can complete 5 pieces in an hour.
    If overhead is 40% of material and labor costs and the profit is 10% of all costs, the submitted price for the entire job will be

    A. $630.24   B. $872.80   C. $900.00   D. $924.00

19. The following formula is used in connection with the three-wire method of measuring pitch diameters of screw threads: $G=\frac{0.57735}{N}$, where G = wire size and N = number of threads per inch.
   According to this formula, the proper size of wire for a 1"-8NC thread is MOST NEARLY

   A. .0722"   B. .7217"   C. .0072"   D. .0074"

20. A millimeter is 1/25.4 of an inch and there are 10 millimeters to a centimeter.
   If a piece of stock measures 127 centimeters long, the length of the stock, in feet and inches, would be MOST NEARLY

   A. 2'1"   B. 4'2"   C. 8'4"   D. 41'8"

21. For a certain job, you will need 25 steel bars 1 inch in diameter and 4"6" long.
   If these bars weigh 3 pounds per foot of length, then the TOTAL weight for all 25 bars is _____ pounds.

   A. 13.5   B. 75.0   C. 112.5   D. 337.5

22. If steel weighs 0.30 pounds per cubic inch, then the weight of a 2 inch square steel bar 90 inches long is _____ pounds.

   A. 27   B. 54   C. 108   D. 360

23. A concrete wall is 36' long, 9' high, and 1 1/2' thick. The number of cubic yards of concrete that were needed to make this wall is

   A. 14   B. 18   C. 27   D. 36

24. If the scale on a shop drawing is 1/2 inch to the foot, then the length of a part which measures 41/4 inches long on the drawing has a length of APPROXIMATELY _____ feet.

   A. 2 1/8   B. 4 1/4   C. 8 1/2   D. 10 3/4

25. If the allowable load on a wooden scaffold is 60 pounds per square foot and the scaffold surface area is 3 feet by 12 feet, then the MAXIMUM total distributed load that is permitted on the scaffold is _____ pounds.

   A. 720   B. 1,800   C. 2,160   D. 2,400

KEY (CORRECT ANSWERS)

1. A
2. A
3. B
4. D
5. B

6. B
7. C
8. A
9. A
10. B

11. C
12. D
13. A
14. A
15. A

16. A
17. C
18. D
19. A
20. B

21. D
22. C
23. B
24. C
25. C

SOLUTIONS TO PROBLEMS

1. Area = (1/2)(base)(height) = (1/2)(5")(12") = 30 sq.in.

2. Volume = (18") (18") (2") = 648 cu.in. = 648/1720 cu.ft.
   Then, (480)(648/1720) = ≈ 180 lbs.

3. 2 cu.yds. = 54 cu.ft. Let x = required cubic feet of sand. Then, 2/5 = x/54. Solving, x = 21.6 (or about 22)

4. (3.75')(25')(4.25') = 398.4375 cu.ft. ≈ 14.8 cu.yds.

5. 10'5" + 6'5 1/2" = 16'10 1/2", so lengths of 17 feet are needed

6. The amount of water flowing through each pipe must be equal.

7. (2")(2")(120") = 480 cu. in. Then, (480)(.28) ≈ 135 lbs.

8. Volume = (π) (.125 ')^2 (2) ≈ .1 cu.ft. Then, (.1)(480) = 48 lbs.

9. (360°)(.05) - 18°

10. 4 1/16 - .006 = 4.0625 - .006 = 4.0565

11. 15 7/16" ÷ 1/8" = 247/16 . 8/1 = 123.5. Then, (123.5)(1 ft.) = 123.5 ft.

12. 7 3/8" ÷ 1/4" = 59/8 . 4/1 = 29.5 Then, (29.5)(1 ft.) = 29.5 ft.

13. (6)(4) = 24 man-days normally required. Since after 3 days only the equivalent of (2/3)(24) = 16 man-days of work has been 1 done, 8 man-days of work is still left. 16 ÷ 3 = 5 1/3, which means the crew is equivalent to only 5 1/3 men. To do the 8 man-days of work, it will require at least 8 - 5 1/3 = 2 2/3 = 3 additional men.

14. (3.5')(5')(100') = 1750 cu.ft. ≈ 64.8 cu.yds. Then, (64.8)($105) ≈ $6805

15. 2 3/8" ÷ 1/4" = 19/8 . 4/1 = 9 1/2 Then, (9 1/2)(1 ft.) = 9 1/2 feet

16. (27')(18')(1/2') = 243 cu.ft. = 9 cu.yds. (1 cu.yd. = 27 cu.ft.)

17. 2 3/4" ÷ 1/4" = 11/4 . 4/1 = 11

18. Material cost = (300)($.50) = $150. Labor cost = ($7.50)(300/5) = $450. Overhead = (.40)($150+$450) = $240. Profit = .10($150+$450+$240) = $84. Submitted price = $150 + $450 + $240 + $84 = $924

19. 6 = .57735" ÷ 8 = .0722"

20. 127 cm = 1270 mm = 1270/25.4" ≈ 50" = 4.2"

21. (25)(4.5') = 112.5' Then, (112.5X3) = 337.5 lbs.

22. (2")(2")(90") = 360 cu.in. Then, (360)(30) = 108 lbs.

23. (36')(9')(1 1/2') = 486 cu.ft. = 18 cu.yds. (1 cu.yd. = 27 cu.ft.)

24. 4 1/4" ÷ 1/2" = 17/4 . 2/1 = 8 1/2. Then, (8 1/2)(1 ft.) = 8 1/2 ft.

25. (12')(3') = 36 sq.ft. Then, (36)(60) = 2160 lbs.

TEST 3

DIRECTIONS: Each question or incomplete statement is followed by several suggested answers or completions. Select the one that BEST answers the question or completes the statement. *PRINT THE LETTER OF THE CORRECT ANSWER IN THE SPACE AT THE RIGHT.*

1. A right triangular metal sheet for a roofing job has sides of 36 inches and 4 feet. The length of the remaining side is

   A. 7 feet
   B. 6 feet
   C. 60 inches
   D. 90 inches

2. A U.S. Standard Gauge thickness is given as 0.15625. This thickness, in fractions of an inch, is MOST NEARLY _____ inches.

   A. 1/8   B. 4/32   C. 5/32   D. 3/64

3. The weight per 100 of sheet metal fasteners is given as 2/3 pound. The APPROXIMATE number of fasteners in a 2-pound package is

   A. 166   B. 200   C. 300   D. 266

4. The decimal equivalent of 27/32 is MOST NEARLY

   A. 0.813   B. 0.828   C. 0.844   D. 0.859

5. If a scaled measurement of 1'3" on the drawing of a sheet metal layout represents an actual length of 10"0", then the drawing has been made to a scale of _____ inch to the foot.

   A. 3/4   B. 1 1/4   C. 1 1/2   D. 1 3/4

6. Two and two-thirds tees can be made from one sheet of steel. If 24 tees must be made, then the number of sheets required is

   A. 6   B. 7   C. 8   D. 9

7. A main duct 20 inches in diameter discharges into two branch ducts. The sum of the areas of the branches is to be equal to the area of the main duct. One branch is 12 inches in diameter.
   The diameter of the other branch is _____ inches.

   A. 16   B. 12   C. 10   D. 8

8. If steel weighs 480 lbs. per cubic foot, the weight of 10 sheets, each 6 feet by 3 feet by 1/32 inch, is _____ lbs.

   A. 2,700   B. 1,237   C. 270   D. 225

9. The area, in square inches, of a right triangle that has sides of 12 1/2, 10, and 7 1/2 inches is

   A. 18 1/4   B. 37 1/2   C. 75   D. 60

10. In making a container to hold 1 gallon (231 cu.in.) and to be 6 inches in diameter at the top and 8 inches in diameter at the bottom, the height must be, in inches,

    A. 10.0   B. 8.2   C. 4.6   D. 6

11. A sheet metal worker is given a job to make a transition piece from a 8 1/2" diameter duct to an 11 1/4" diameter duct. If the length of the transition piece is 5 1/2" for each inch change in diameter, then the length of the transition piece is

    A. 14 7/8"   B. 15"   C. 15 1/8"   D. 15 1/4"

12. A duct layout is drawn to a scale of 3/8" to a foot. If the length of a run shown on the drawing scales 7 1/2", then the ACTUAL length of the run is

    A. 19'6"   B. 19'9"   C. 20'0"   D. 20'3"

13. An 18" x 24" duct is to be connected to a 24" x 24" duct by means of an eccentric transition piece (3 sides flush). If the taper is to be 1" in 4", then the length of the transition piece is

    A. 6"   B. 12"   C. 18"   D. 24"

14. Twenty-seven pairs of 3/8" diameter rods each 3'3 1/2" long are needed to support a duct.
    If the available rods are ten feet long, then the MINIMUM number of rods that will be needed to make the twenty-seven sets is

    A. 9   B. 12   C. 15   D. 18

15. A rectangular sheet metal air duct with open ends is 12 feet long and 15" x 20" in cross-section. If one square foot of the sheet metal weighs 1/2 pound, then the TOTAL weight of the duct is _____ lbs.

    A. 10   B. 17 1/2   C. 35   D. 150

16. The sum of 1/12 and 1/4 is

    A. 1/3   B. 5/12   C. 7/12   D. 3/8

17. The product of 12 and 2 1/3 is

    A. 27   B. 28   C. 29   D. 30

18. If 4 1/2 is subtracted from 7 1/5, the remainder is

    A. 3 7/10   B. 2 7/10   C. 3 3/10   D. 2 3/10

19. The number of cubic yards in 47 cubic feet is MOST NEARLY

    A. 1.70   B. 1.74   C. 1.78   D. 1.82

20. A wall 8'0" high by 12'6" long has a window opening 4'0" high by 3'6" wide. The net area of the wall (allowing for the window opening) is, in square feet,

    A. 86   B. 87   C. 88   D. 89

21. A worker's hourly rate is $11.36.
    If he works 11 1/2 hours, he should receive

    A. $129.84   B. $130.64   C. $131.48   D. $132.24

22. The number of cubic feet in 3 cubic yards is

    A. 81   B. 82   C. 83   D. 84

23. At an annual rate of $.40 per $100, what is the fire insurance premium for one year on a house that is insured for $80,000?

    A. $120   B. $160   C. $240   D. $320

24. A meter equals approximately 1.09 yards.
    How much longer, in yards, is a 100-meter dash than a 100-yard dash?

    A. 6   B. 8   C. 9   D. 12

25. A train leaves New York City at 8:10 A.M. and arrives in Buffalo at 4:45 P.M. on the same day. How long, in hours and minutes, does it take the train to make the trip?
    _____ hours, _____ minutes.

    A. 6; 22   B. 7; 16   C. 7; 28   D. 8; 35

KEY (CORRECT ANSWERS)

1. C		11. C	
2. C		12. C	
3. C		13. D	
4. C		14. D	
5. C		15. C	
6. D		16. A	
7. A		17. B	
8. D		18. B	
9. B		19. B	
10. D		20. A	

21. B
22. A
23. D
24. C
25. D

SOLUTIONS TO PROBLEMS

1. Let x = remaining side. Converting to inches, $x^2 = 36^2 + 48^2$ So, $x^2 = 3600$. Solving, x = 60 inches.

2. $.15625 = \dfrac{15,625}{100,000} = \dfrac{5}{32}$

3. 2 ÷ 2/3 = 3. Then, (3)(100) = 300 fasteners

4. 27/32 = .84375 ≈ .844

5. 1'3" ÷ 10 = 15" ÷ 10 = 1 1/2"

6. 24 ÷ 2 2/3 = 24/1.3/8 = 9

7. Area of main duct = $(\pi)(10^2) = 100\pi$. One of the branches has an area of $(\pi)(6^2) = 36\pi$. Thus, the area of the 2nd branch = $100\pi - 36\pi = 64\pi$. The 2nd branch's radius must be 8" and its diameter must be 16".

8. Volume = (1/384')(6')(3') = .046875 cu.ft. Then, 10 sheets have a volume of .46875 cu.ft. Now, (.46875)(480) = 225 lbs.

9. Note that $(7\ 1/2)^2 + (10)^2 = (12\ 1/2)^2$, so that this is a right triangle. Area = (1/2)(10")(7 1/2") = 37 1/2 sq.in.

10. $231 = \dfrac{h}{3}[(\pi)(3)^2 + (\pi)(4)^2 + \sqrt{(9\pi)(16\pi)}]$, where h = required height. Then,

    $231 = \dfrac{h}{3}(9\pi + 16\pi + 12\pi)$. Simplifying, $231 = 37\pi h/3$.
    Solving, h ~ 5.96" or 6"

11. 11 1/4 - 8 1/2 = 2 3/4. Then, (2 3/4)(5 1/2) = 11/4 .11/2 = 15 1/8

12. 7 1/2 " ÷ 3/8" = 15/2 .8/3 = 20 Then, (20)(1 ft.) = 20 feet

13. 24" - 18" = 6" Then, (6")(4) = 24"

14. 3'3 1/2" = 39.5". Now, (27)(2)(39.5") = 2133". 10 ft. = 120". Finally, 2133 ÷ 120 = 17.775, so 18 rods are needed.

15. Surface area = (2)(12')(1 1/4') + (2)(12')(1 2/3') = 70 sq.ft. Then, (70)(1/2 lb.) - 35 lbs.

16. 1/12 + 1/4 = 4/12 = 1/3

17. (12)(2 1/3) = 12/1 . 7/3 = 28

18. 7 1/5 - 4 1/2 = 7 2/10 - 4 5/10 = 6 12/10 - 4 5/10 = 2 7/10

19. 47 cu.ft. = 47/27 cu.yds. = 1.74 cu.yds.

20. (8')(12.5') - (4')(3.5') = 86 sq.ft.

21. ($11.36)(11.5) = $130.64

22. 1 cu.yd. = 27 cu.ft., so 3 cu.yds. = 81 cu.ft.

23. $80,000 ÷ $100 = 800. Then, (800)($.40) = $320

24. 100 meters = 109 yds. Then, 109 - 100 = 9 yds.

25. 4:45 P.M. - 8:10 AM. = 8 hrs. 35 min.

ABSTRACT REASONING

EXAMINATION SECTION
COMMENTARY

Since intelligence exists in many forms or phases and the theory of differential aptitudes is now firmly established in testing, other manifestations and measurements of intelligence than verbal or purely arithmetical must be identified and measured.

Classification inventory, or figure classification, involves the aptitude of form perception, i.e., the ability to perceive pertinent detail in objects or in pictorial or graphic material. It involves making visual comparisons and discriminations and discerning slight differences in shapes and shading figures and widths and lengths of lines.

Leading examples of presentation are the figure analogy and the figure classification. The Section that follows presents progressive and varied samplings of this type of question.

SAMPLE QUESTIONS

DIRECTIONS: In each of these sample questions, look at the symbols in the first two boxes. Something about the three symbols in the first box makes them alike; something about the two symbols in the other box with the question mark makes them alike. Look for some characteristic that is common to all symbols in the same box, yet makes them different from the symbols in the other box. Among the five answer choices, find the symbol that can BEST be substituted for the question mark, because it is *like* the symbols in the second box, and, *for the same reason,* different from those in the first box.

1.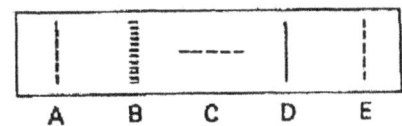

1.____

In sample question 1, all the symbols in the first box are vertical lines. The second box has two lines, one broken and one solid. Their *likeness* to each other consists in their being horizontal; and their being horizontal makes them *different* from the vertical lines in the other box. The answer must be the only one of the five lettered choices that is a horizontal line, either broken or solid. Therefore, the CORRECT answer is C.

2.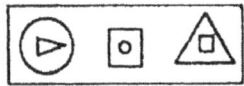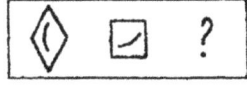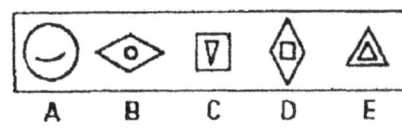

2.____

The CORRECT answer is A.

EXAMINATION SECTION
TEST 1

DIRECTIONS: In each of these question, look at the symbols in the first two boxes. Something about the three symbols in the first box makes them alike; something about the two symbols in the other box with the question mark makes them alike. Look for some characteristic that is common to all symbols in the same box, yet makes them different from the symbols in the other box. Among the five answer choices, find the symbol that can BEST be substituted for the question mark, because it is *like* the symbols in the second box, and, *for the same reason,* different from those in the first box.

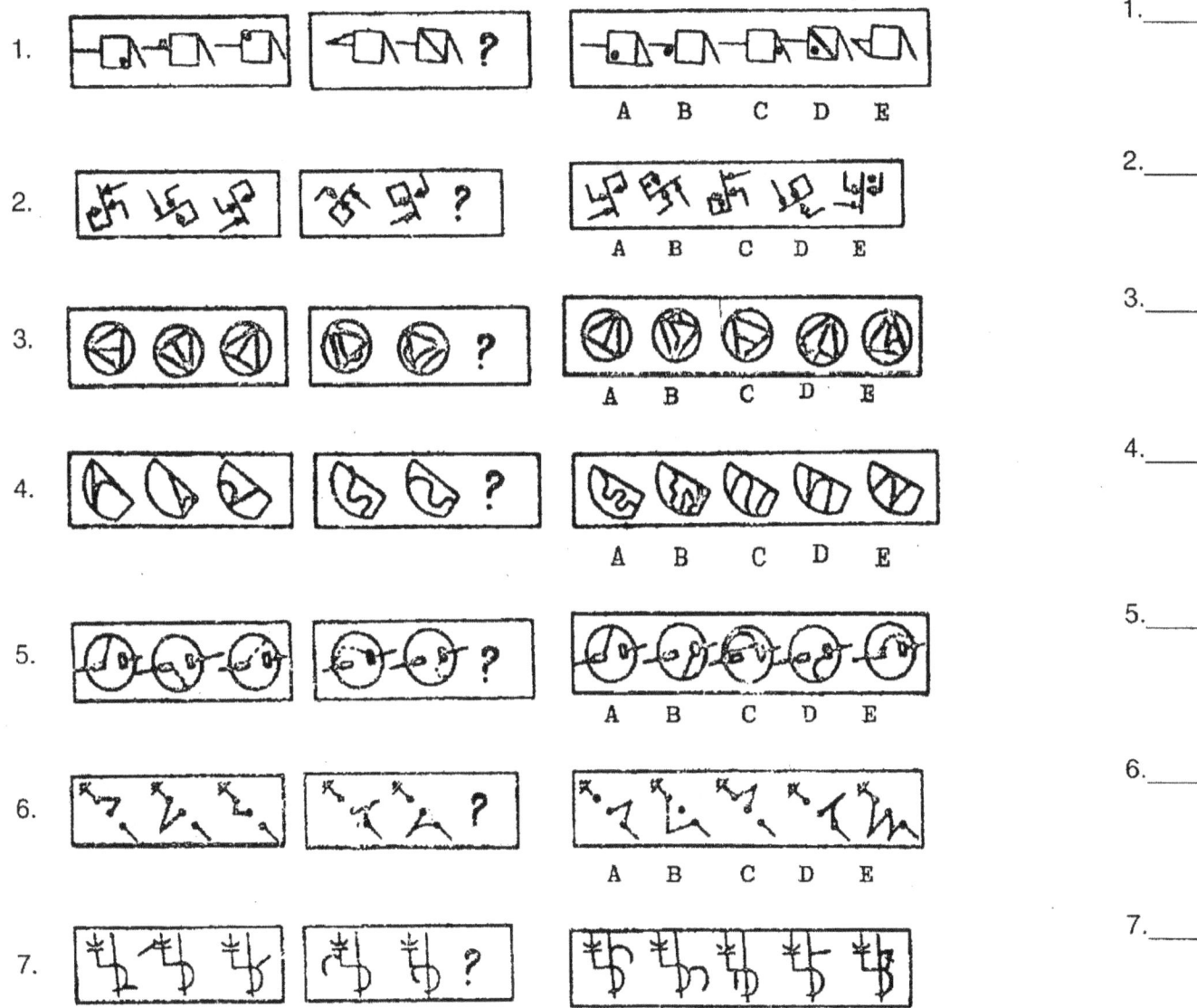

2 (#1)

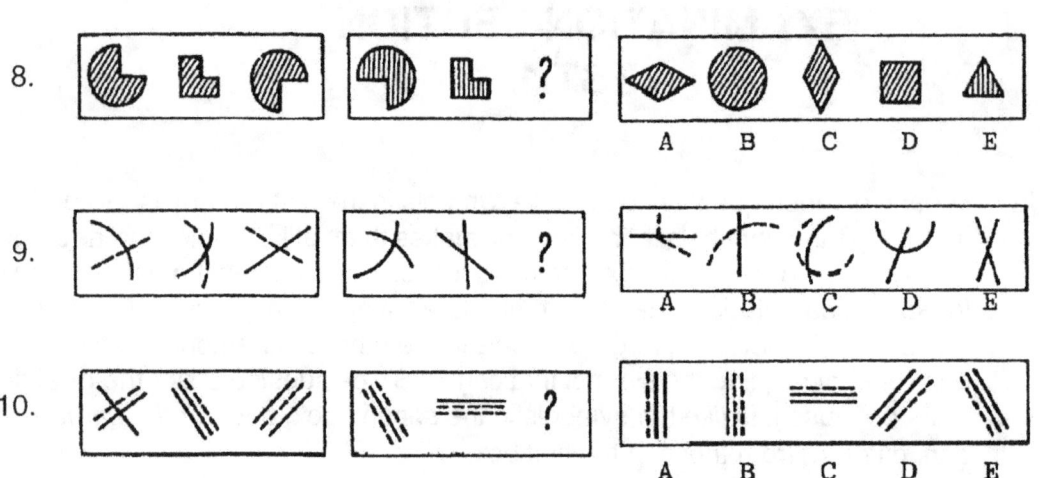

KEY (CORRECT ANSWERS)

1. E
2. D
3. B
4. A
5. D

6. D
7. A
8. E
9. D
10. B

TEST 2

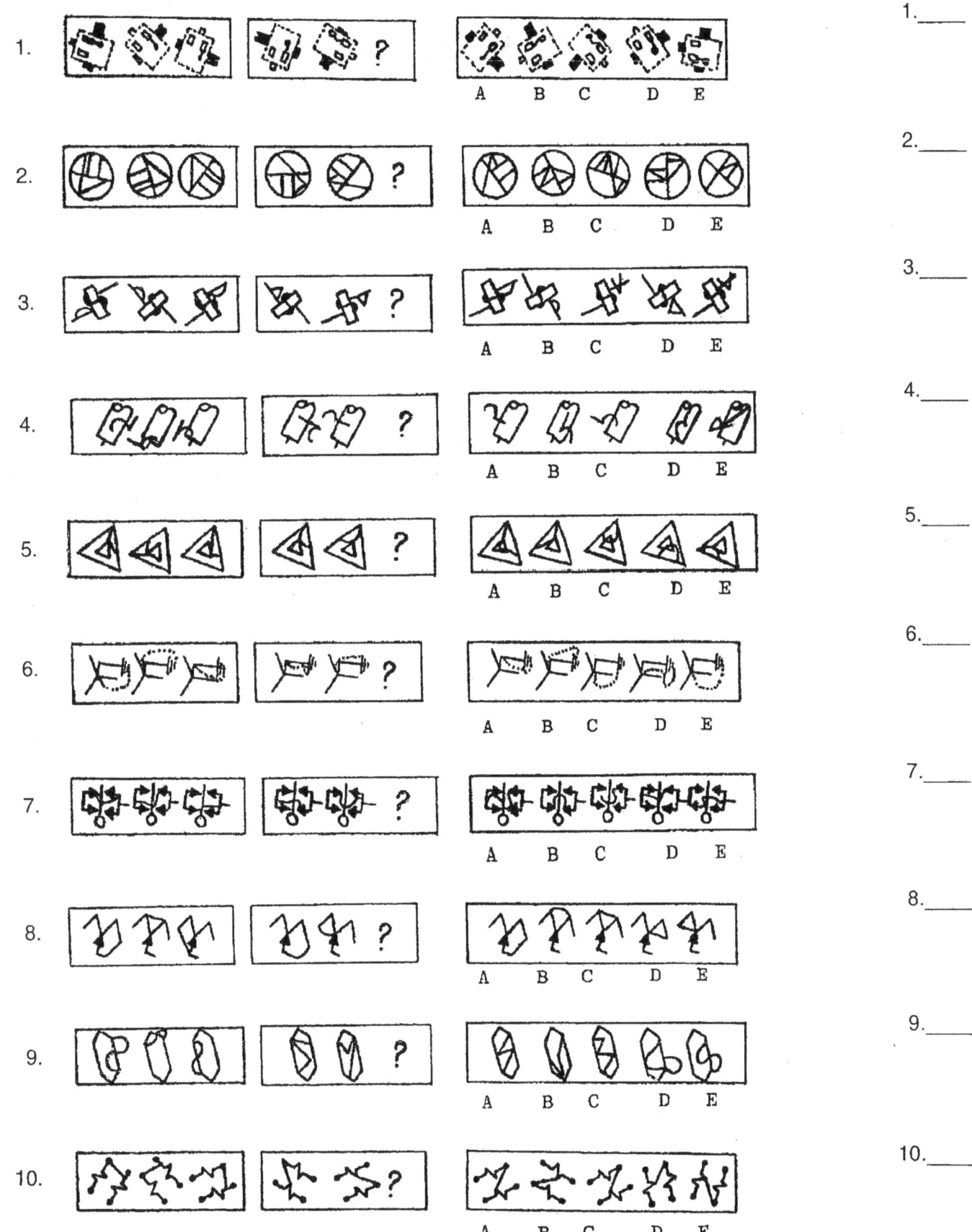

KEY (CORRECT ANSWERS)

1. C
2. A
3. D
4. A
5. E

6. C
7. E
8. B
9. B
10. D

TEST 3

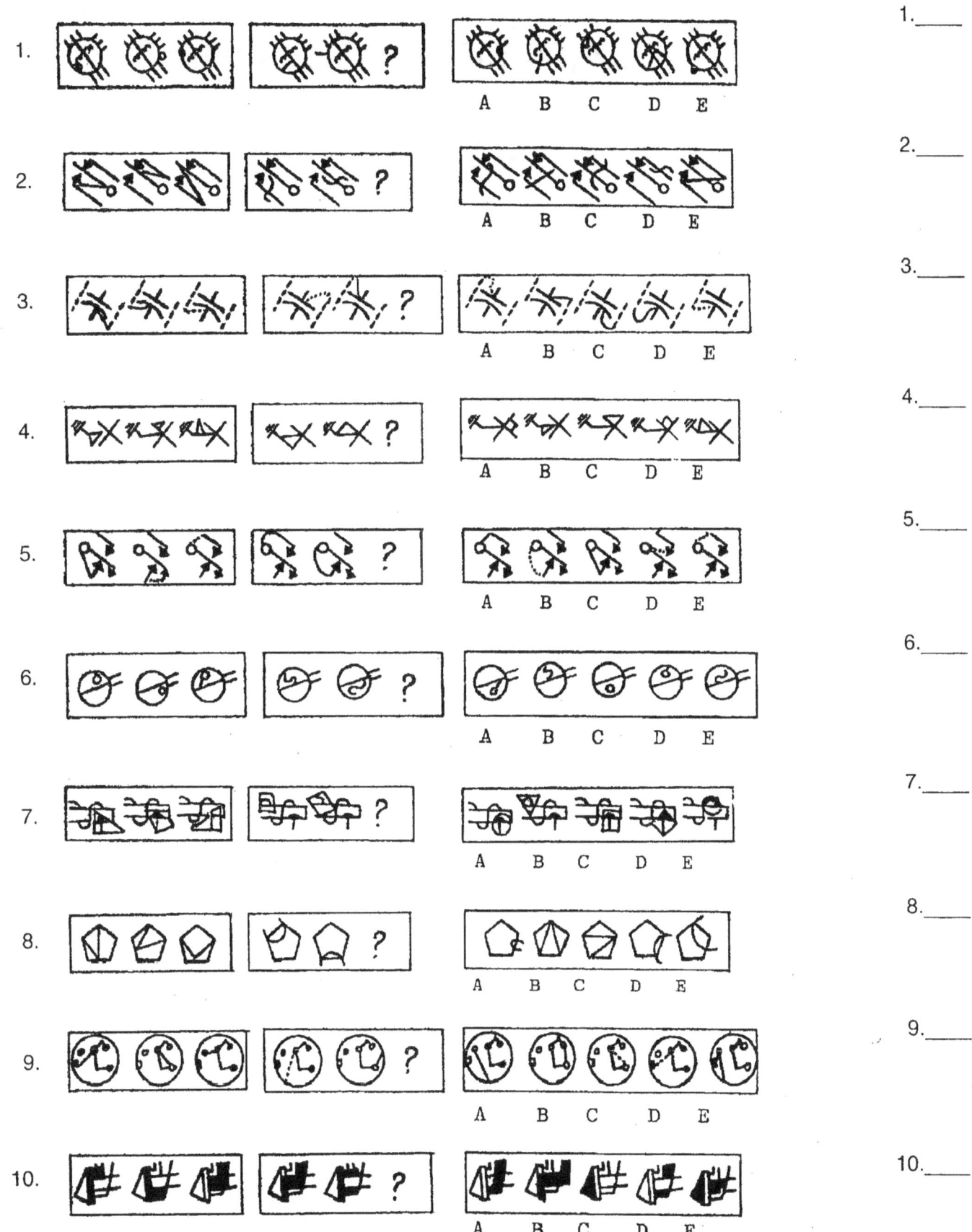

KEY (CORRECT ANSWERS)

1. B
2. D
3. A
4. C
5. B

6. E
7. B
8. D
9. A
10. B

ABSTRACT REASONING

SPATIAL RELATIONS

COMMENTARY

Since intelligence exists in many forms or phases and the theory of differential aptitudes is now firmly established in testing, other manifestations and measurements of intelligence than verbal or purely arithmetical must be identified and measured.

The spatial relations test, including that phase designated as spatial perception, involves and measures the ability to solve problems, drawn up in the form of outlines or pictures, which are concerned with the shapes of objects or the interrelationship of their parts. While, concededly, little is known about the nature and scope of this aptitude, it appears that this ability is required in science, mathematics, engineering, and drawing courses and curricula. Accordingly, tests of spatial perception involving the reconstruction of three-dimensional patterns, are presented in this section.

It is to be noted that the relationships expressed in spatial tests are geometric, definitive, and exact. Keeping these basic characteristics in mind, the applicant is to proceed to solve the spatial perception problems in his own way. There is no set method of solving these problems. The examinee may find that there are different methods for different types of spatial problems. Therefore, the BEST way to prepare for this type of test is to *TAKE* and study the work-practice problems in three-dimensional patterns provided in this section.

EXAMINATION SECTION

PART/1

For questions 1 through 15 you are to examine the four INTERIOR angles and rank each in terms of degrees from SMALL TO LARGE. Choose the alternative that has the correct ranking.

EXAMPLE: (Do not mark these on the answer sheet)

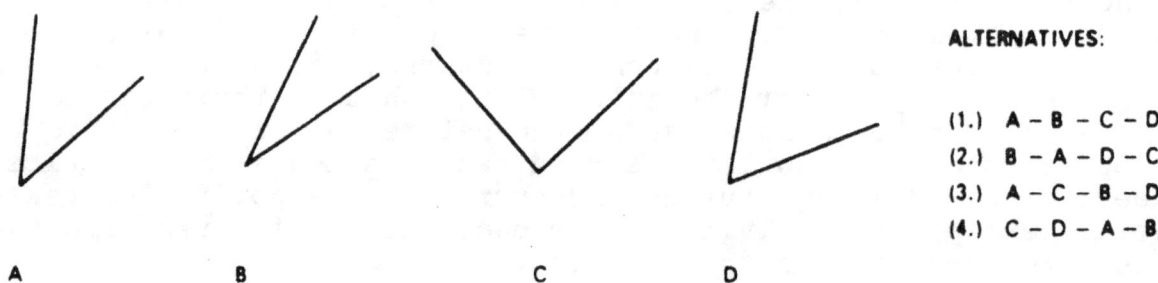

ALTERNATIVES:

(1.) A – B – C – D
(2.) B – A – D – C
(3.) A – C – B – D
(4.) C – D – A – B

The correct ranking of the angles from small to large is B – A – D – C; therefore, alternative (2) is correct. Now, proceed to the questions marking the correct alternative on your answer sheet.

PROCEED TO QUESTIONS

1.

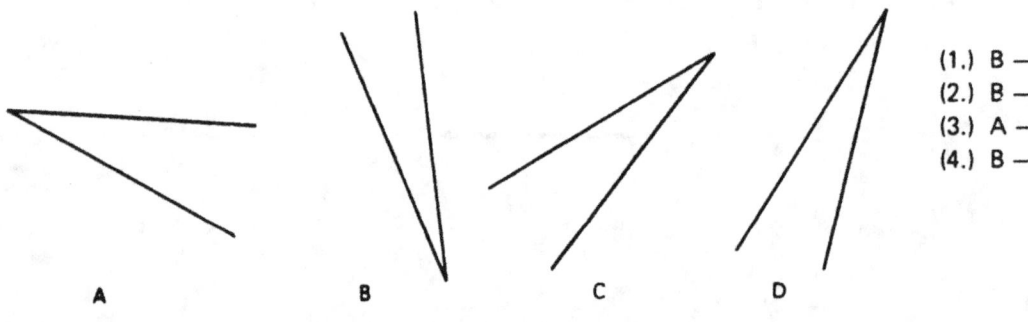

(1.) B – A – C – D
(2.) B – A – D – C
(3.) A – B – C – D
(4.) B – D – C – A

2.

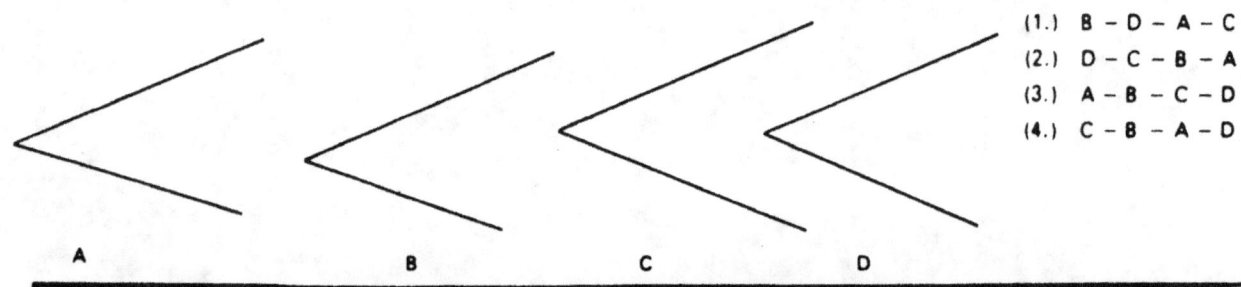

(1.) B – D – A – C
(2.) D – C – B – A
(3.) A – B – C – D
(4.) C – B – A – D

3.

  A   B   C   D

(1.) C - A - D - B
(2.) A - C - D - B
(3.) A - C - B - D
(4.) C - B - A - D

4.

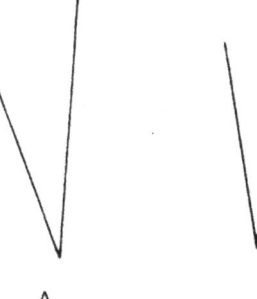 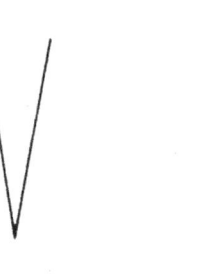 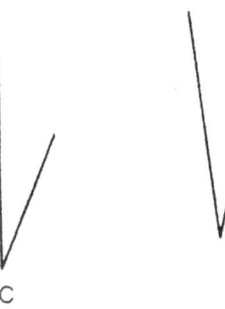

  A   B   C   D

(1.) D - C - B - A
(2.) B - D - A - C
(3.) B - D - C - A
(4.) D - B - C - A

5.

  A   B   C   D

(1.) C - A - D - B
(2.) A - D - C - B
(3.) C - D - B - A
(4.) C - A - B - D

6.

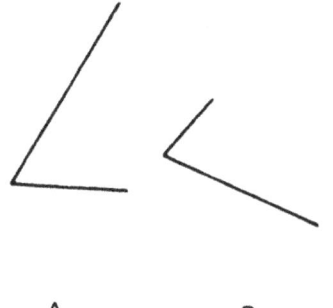 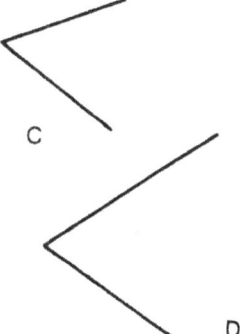

  A   B   C   D

(1.) C - A - B - D
(2.) A - C - B - D
(3.) C - A - D - B
(4.) A - C - D - B

7.

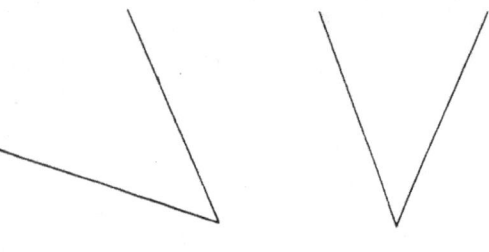

(1.) B – A – C – D
(2.) B – A – D – C
(3.) A – B – C – D
(4.) B – D – C – A

8.

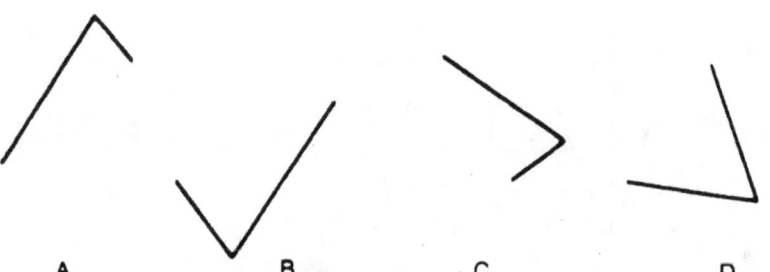

(1.) C · B · D · A
(2.) D · C · B · A
(3.) C · D · A · B
(4.) D · A · C · B

9.

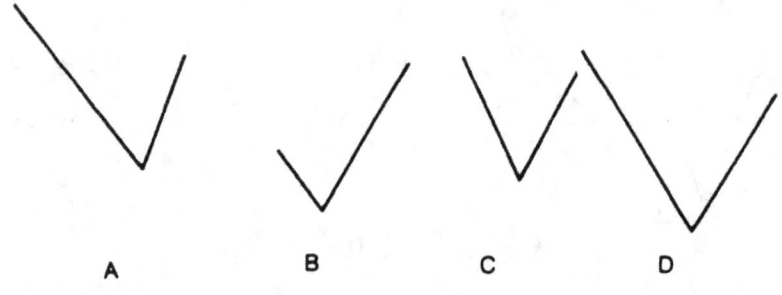

(1.) C · A · B · D
(2.) A · C · B · D
(3.) C · A · D · B
(4.) A · C · D · B

10.

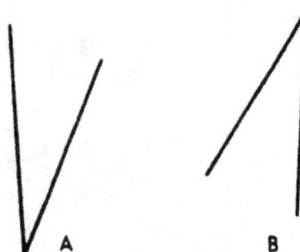 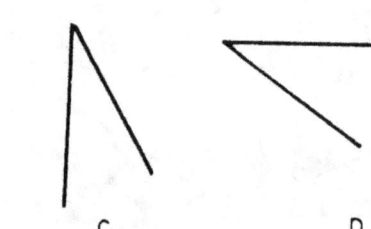

(1.) C · A · D · B
(2.) A · C · D · B
(3.) A · B · C · D
(4.) C · A · B · D

11.

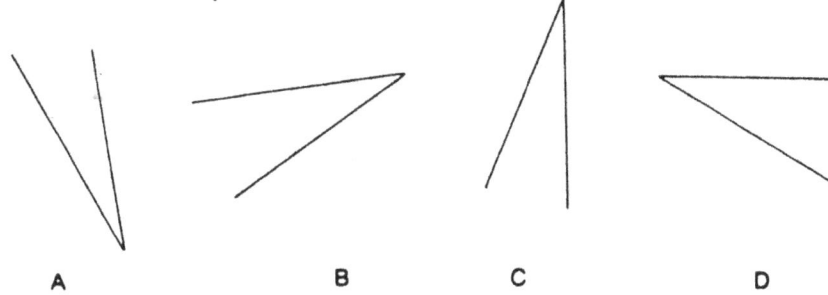

(1.) C · A · D · B
(2.) A · C · D · B
(3.) A · C · B · D
(4.) C · B · A · D

A   B   C   D

12.

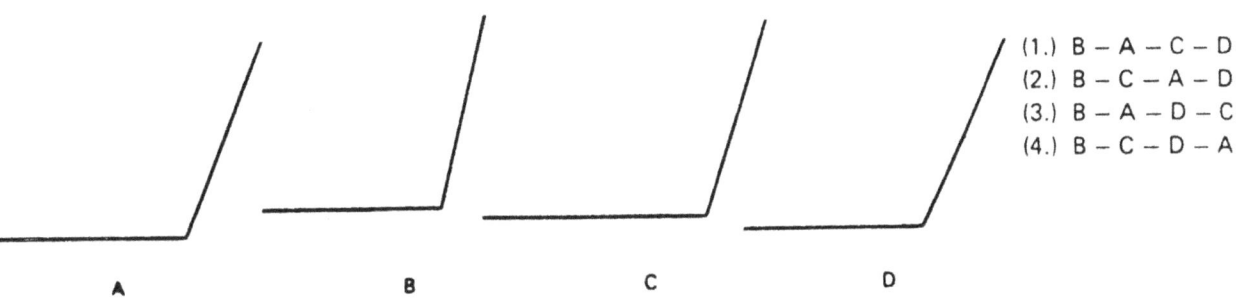

(1.) B — A — C — D
(2.) B — C — A — D
(3.) B — A — D — C
(4.) B — C — D — A

A   B   C   D

13.

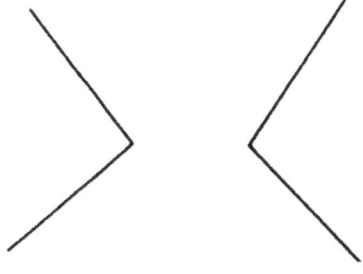 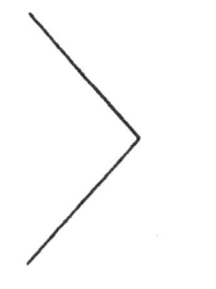

(1.) D — A — B — C
(2.) A — D — C — B
(3.) D — A — C — B
(4.) A — D — B — C

A   B   C   D

14.

(1.) C · A · B · D
(2.) A · B · C · D
(3.) B · D · A · C
(4.) A · C · B · D

A   B   C   D

15.

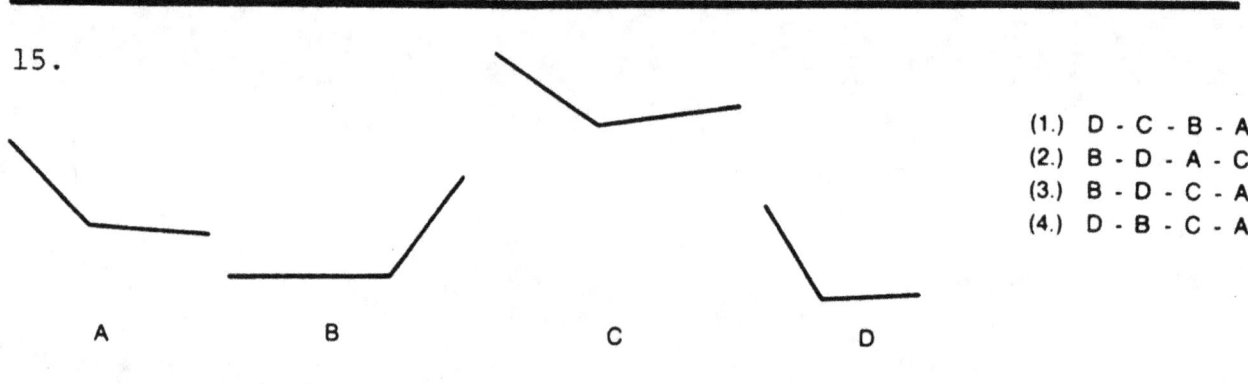

(1.) D - C - B - A
(2.) B - D - A - C
(3.) B - D - C - A
(4.) D - B - C - A

DO NOT STOP – READ DIRECTIONS FOR PART 2 AND CONTINUE

PART/2

For questions **16** through **30**

The pictures that follow are top, front, and end views of various solid objects. The views are without perspective. That is, the points in the viewed surface are viewed along parallel lines of vision. The projection of the object looking DOWN on it is shown in the upper left-hand corner (TOP VIEW). The projection looking at the object from the FRONT is shown in the lower left-hand corner (FRONT VIEW). The projection looking at the object from the END is shown in the lower right-hand corner (END VIEW). These views are ALWAYS in the same positions and are labeled accordingly.

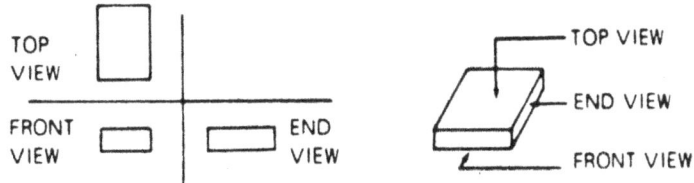

If there were a hole in the block, the views would look like this:

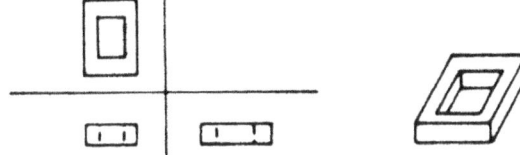

Note that lines that cannot be seen on the surface in some particular view are DOTTED in that view.

In the problems that follow, two views will be shown, with four alternatives to complete the set. You are to select the correct one and mark its number on the answer sheet.

EXAMPLE: Choose the correct END VIEW.

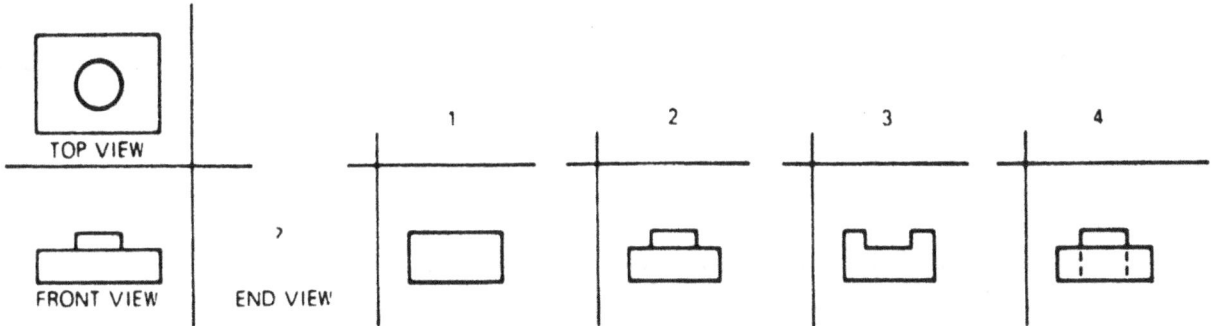

The front view shows that there is a smaller block on the base and that there is no hole. The top view shows that the block is round and in the center of the base. The answer, therefore, must be number 2.

In the problems that follow, it is not always the end view that must be selected, sometimes it is the top view or front view that is missing. Now, proceed to the questions marking the number of the correct view on your answer sheet.

PROCEED TO QUESTIONS

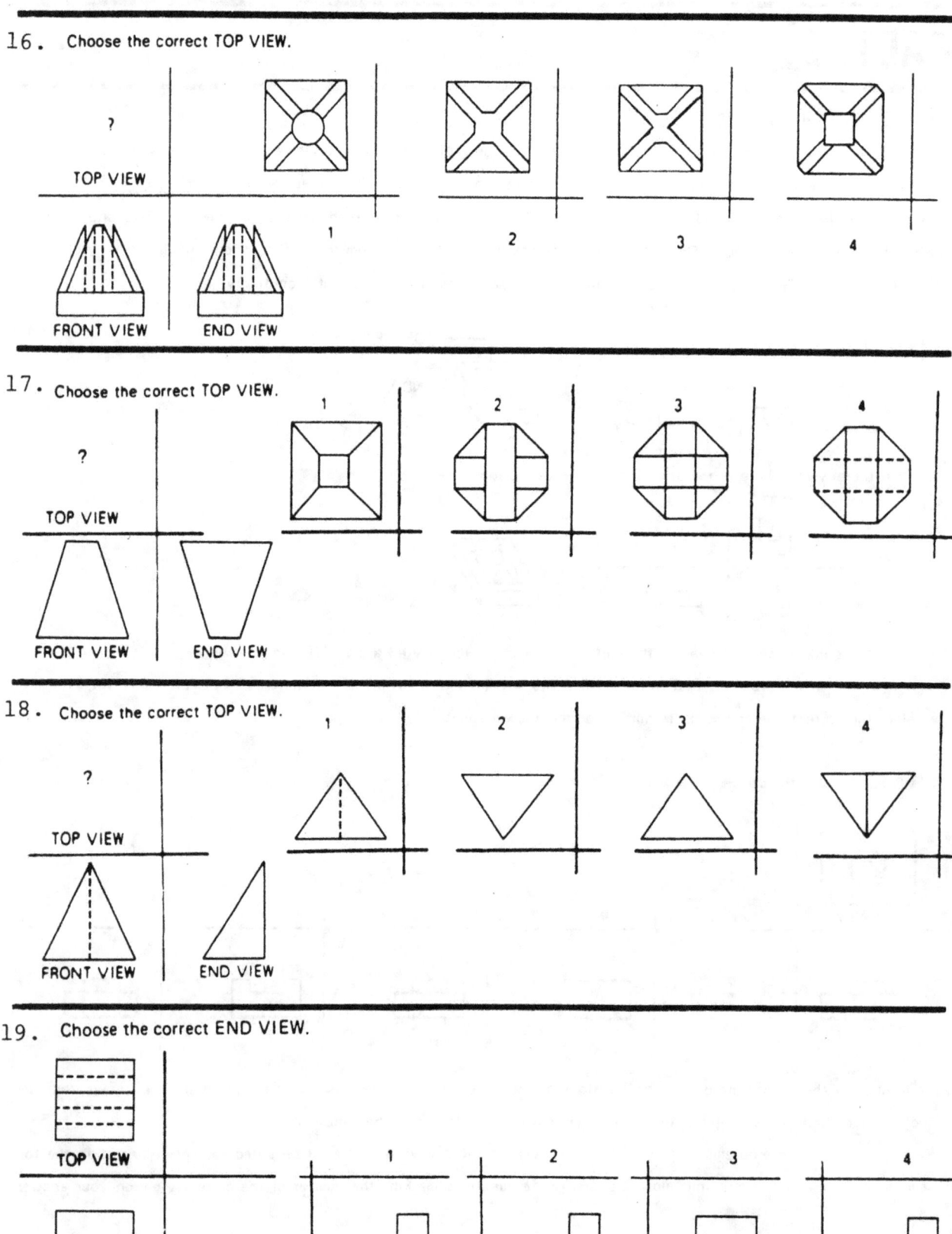

20. Choose the correct FRONT VIEW

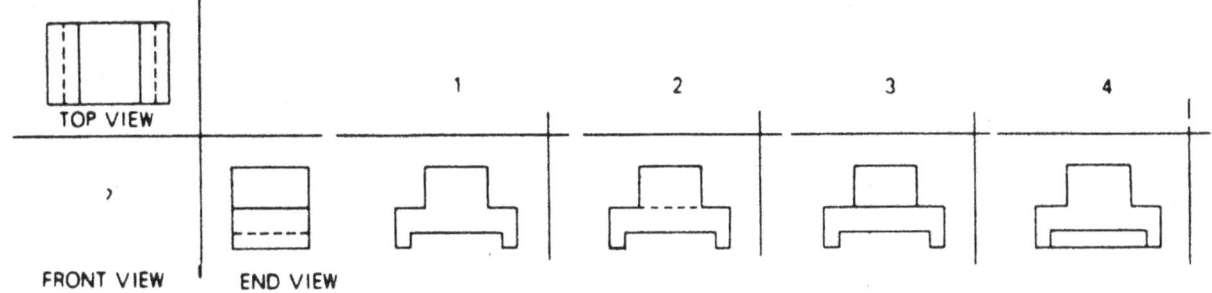

21. Choose the correct END VIEW.

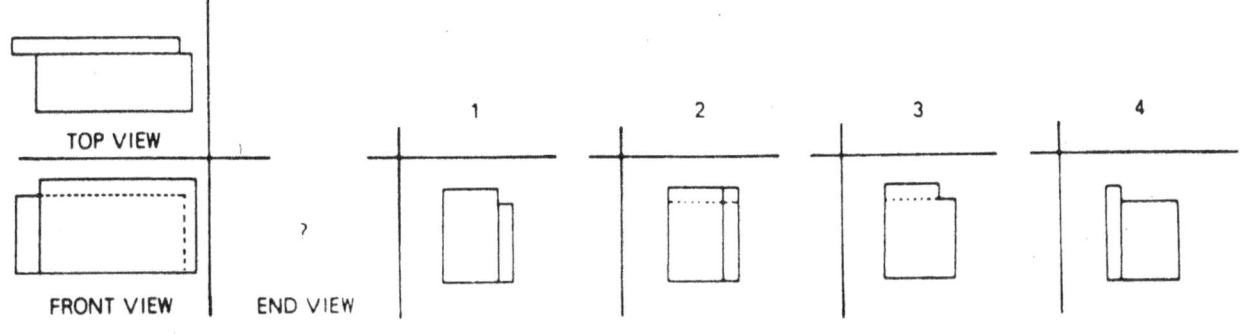

22. Choose the correct END VIEW.

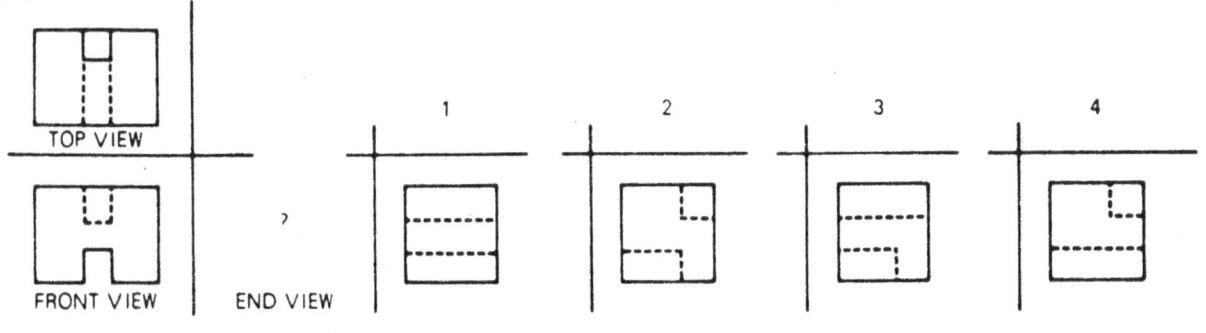

23. Choose the correct END VIEW.

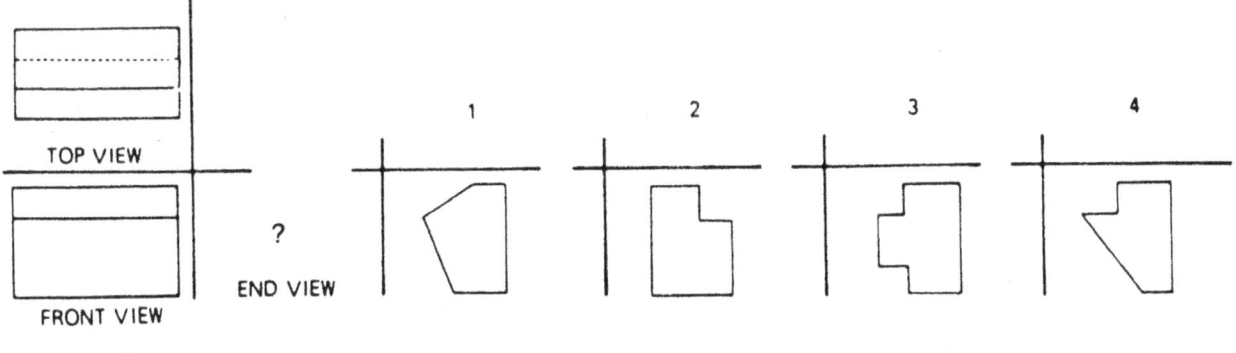

24. Choose the correct TOP VIEW.

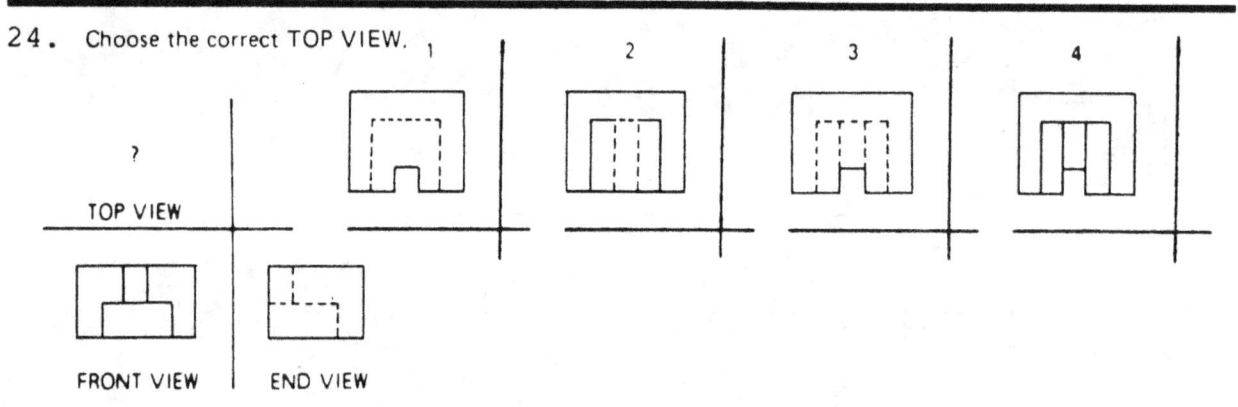

25. Choose the correct END VIEW.

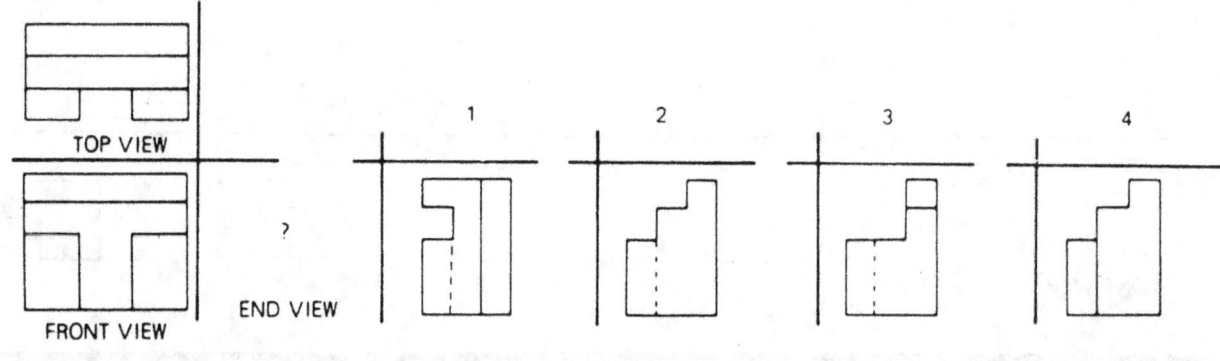

26. Choose the correct END VIEW.

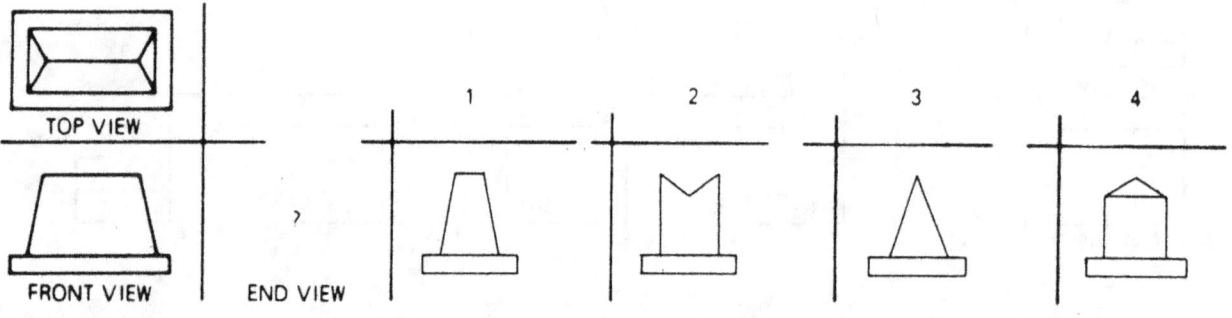

27. Choose the correct END VIEW.

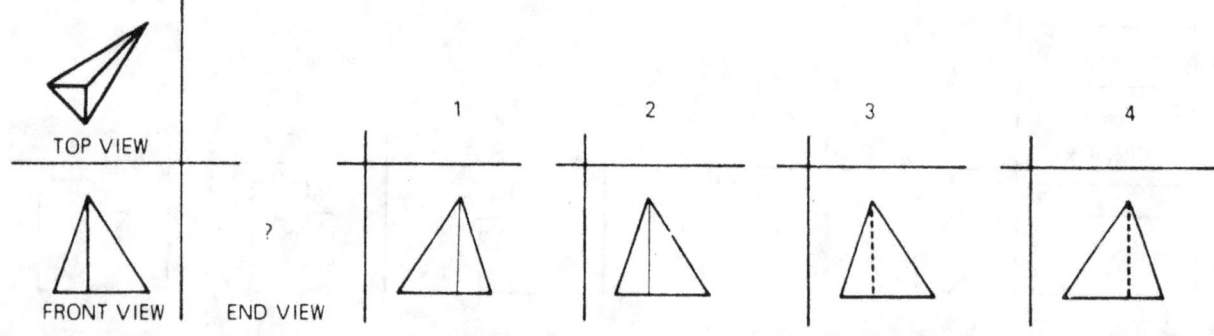

28. Choose the correct TOP VIEW.

29. Choose the correct FRONT VIEW

30. Choose the correct TOP VIEW.

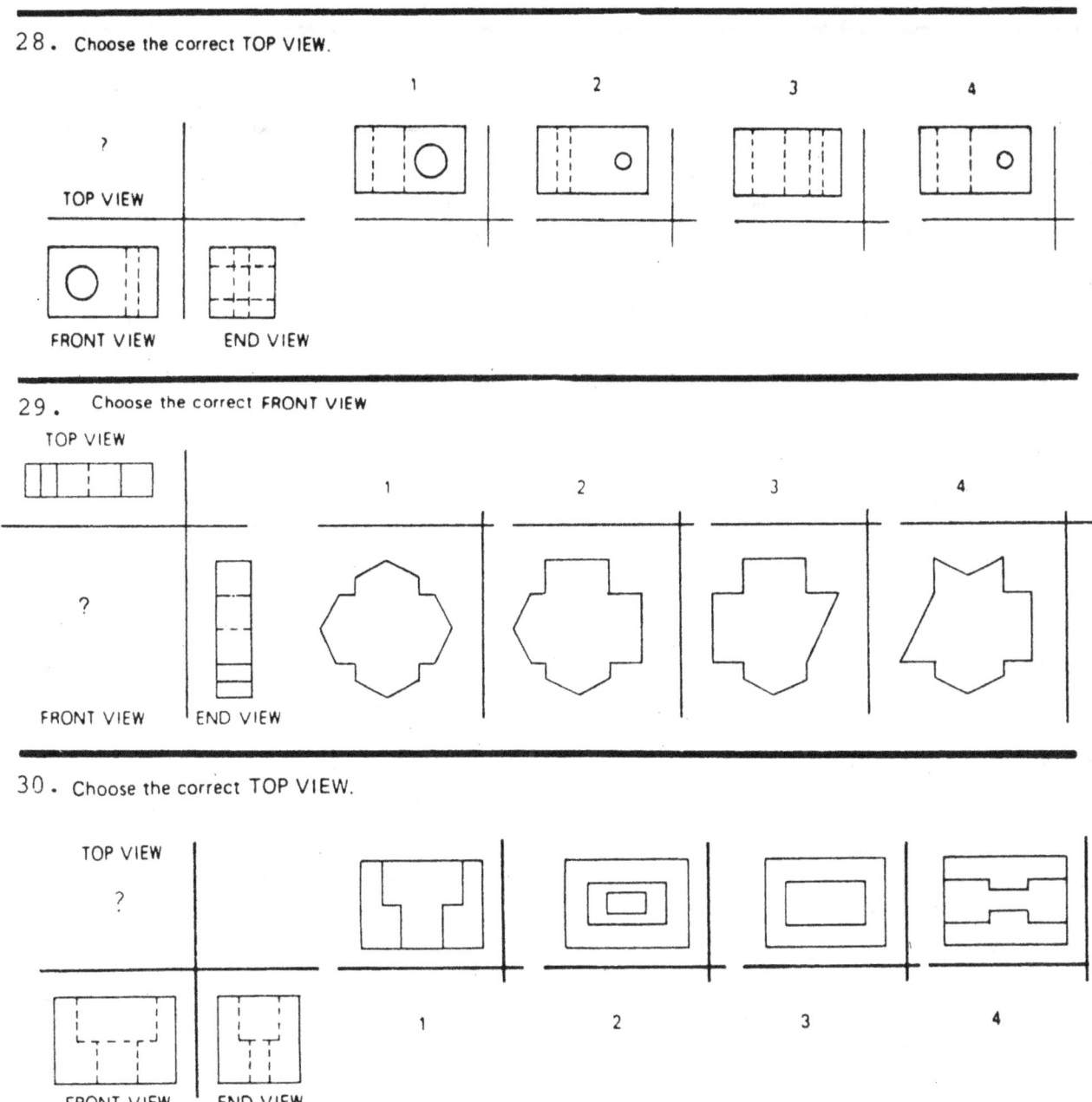

DO NOT STOP — READ DIRECTIONS FOR PART 3 AND CONTINUE

PART/3

Each group of cubes has been made by cementing together cubes of the same size. After being cemented together, each group was PAINTED ON ALL EXPOSED SIDES EXCEPT THE BOTTOM ON WHICH IT IS RESTING.

For questions 31 through 42 you are to examine each figure closely and then determine HOW MANY CUBES have:

one of their exposed sides painted.
two of their exposed sides painted.
three of their exposed sides painted.
four of their exposed sides painted.
five of their exposed sides painted.

Note: There are no problems for which the answer zero (0) is a correct answer.

Example: (Do not mark these on the answer sheet)

PROBLEM Z

In Figure Z how many cubes have

702. two of their exposed sides painted?
703. four of their exposed sides painted?
704. five of their exposed sides painted?

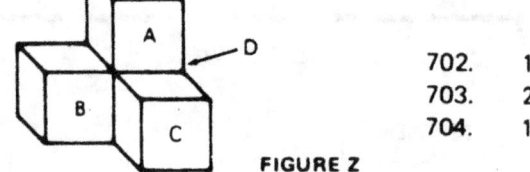

FIGURE Z

ANSWERS:

702. 1
703. 2
704. 1

Now, proceed to the questions. Mark on your answer sheet the number of cubes that have the different number of exposed sides painted. Remember, after being cemented together, each group was PAINTED ON ALL EXPOSED SIDES EXCEPT THE BOTTOM.

PROCEED TO QUESTIONS

PROBLEM A

In Figure A how many cubes have

31. two of their exposed sides painted?
32. four of their exposed sides painted?

FIGURE A

PROBLEM B

In Figure B how many cubes have

33. two of their exposed sides painted?
34. three of their exposed sides painted?

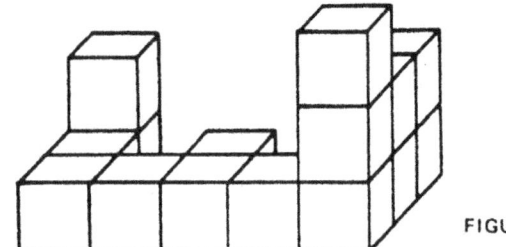

FIGURE B

PROBLEM C

In Figure C how many cubes have

35. two of their exposed sides painted?
36. three of their exposed sides painted?
37. four of their exposed sides painted?

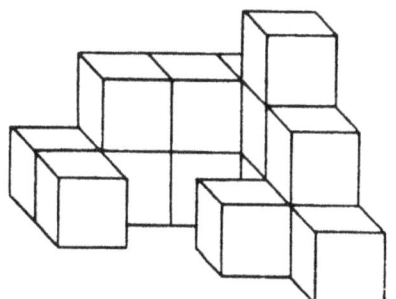

FIGURE C

PROBLEM D

In Figure D how many cubes have

38. two of their exposed sides painted?
39. three of their exposed sides painted?

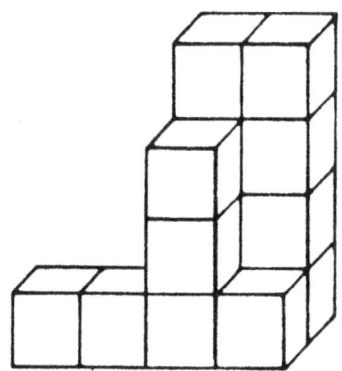

FIGURE D

PROBLEM E

In Figure E how many cubes have

40. one of their exposed sides painted?
41. two of their exposed sides painted?
42. three of their exposed sides painted?

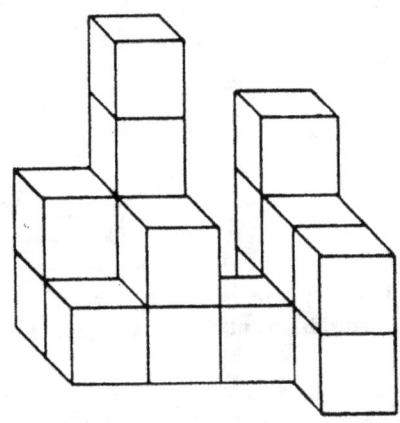

FIGURE E

DO NOT STOP – READ DIRECTIONS FOR PART 4 AND CONTINUE

PART/4

For questions 43 through 60

This visualization test consists of a number of items similar to the sample below. A three-dimensional object is shown at the left. This is followed by outlines of five apertures or openings.

In each item the task is exactly the same. *First*, you are to imagine how the object looks from *all* directions (rather than from a single direction as shown). *Then*, pick from the five apertures outlined, the opening through which the object could pass directly if the proper side were inserted first. *Finally*, mark on your answer sheet (after the number of the item) the letter corresponding to the answer you have chosen.

Here are the rules:

1. Prior to passing through the aperture, the irregular solid object may be turned in any direction. It may be started through the aperture on a side not shown.

2. Once the object is started through the aperture, it may not be twisted or turned. It must pass completely through the opening. The opening is always the exact shape of the appropriate external outline of the object.

3. Both objects and apertures are drawn to the same scale. Thus it is possible for an opening to be the correct shape but too small for the object. In all cases, however, differences are large enough to judge by eye.

4. There are no irregularities in any hidden portion of the object. However, if the figure has symmetric indentations, the hidden portion is symmetric with the part shown.

5. For each object there is only one correct aperture.

EXAMPLE: (Do not mark these on the answer sheet)

The correct answer is 3 since the object would pass through this aperture if the side at the left were introduced first.

PROCEED TO QUESTIONS

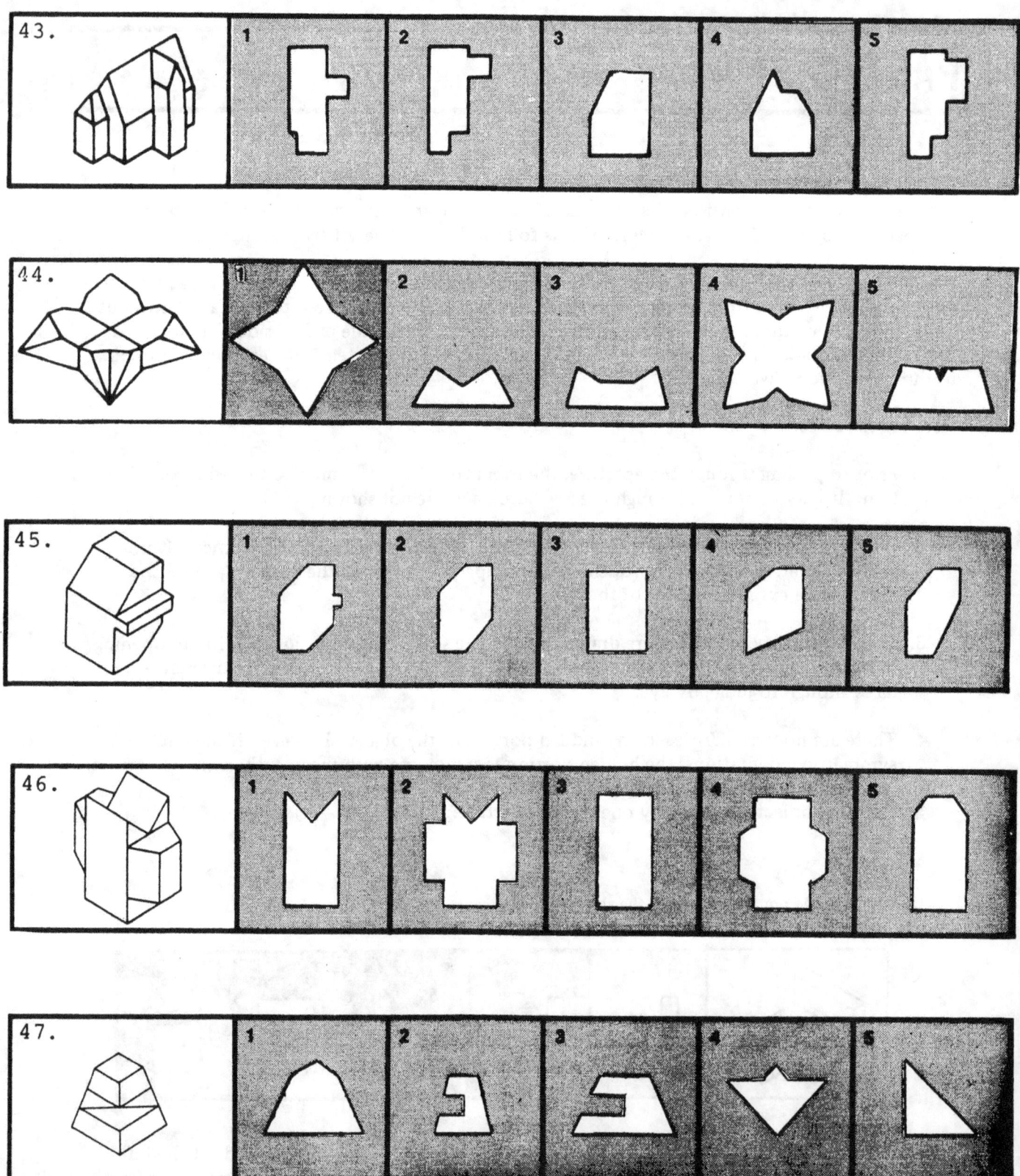

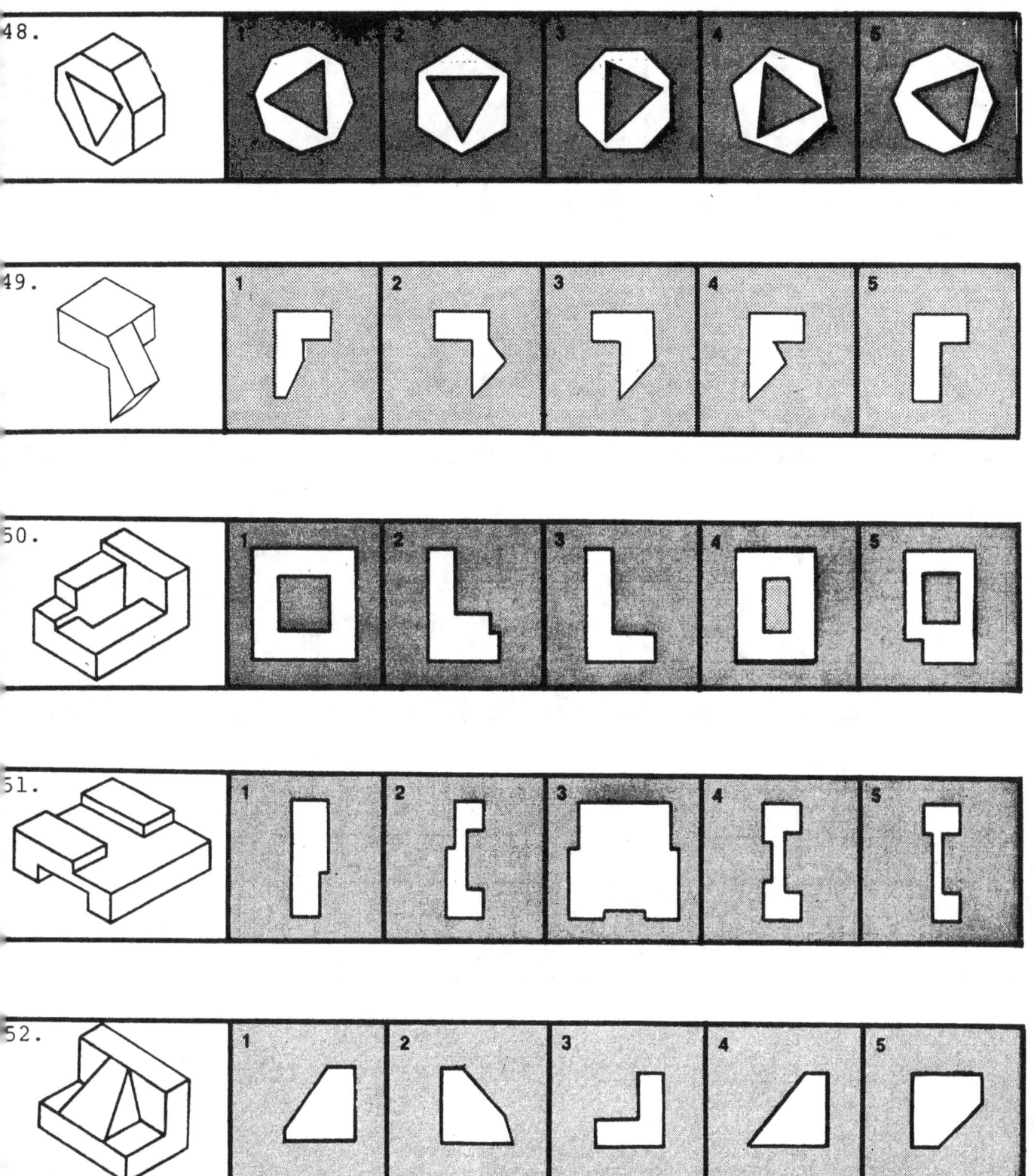

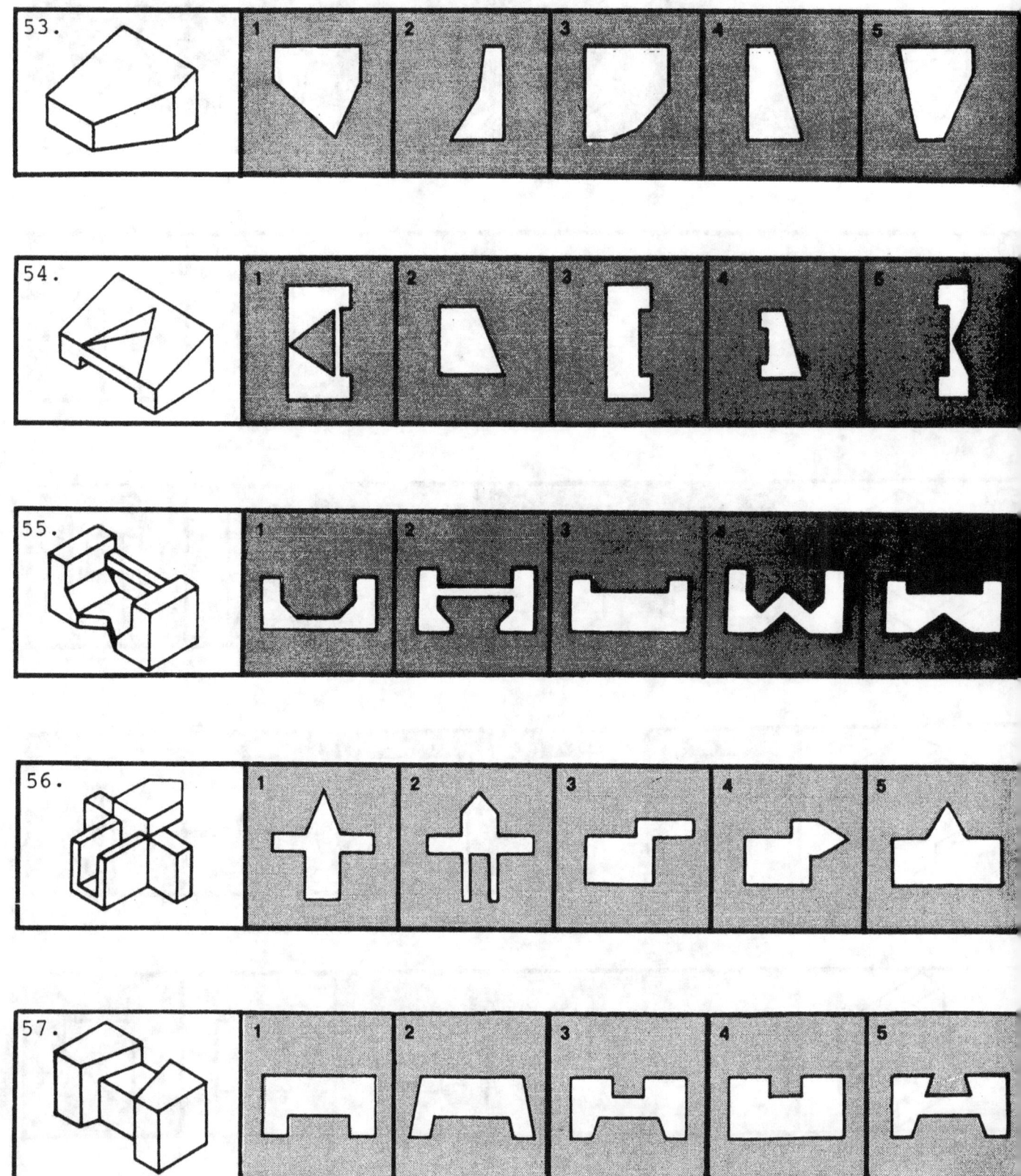

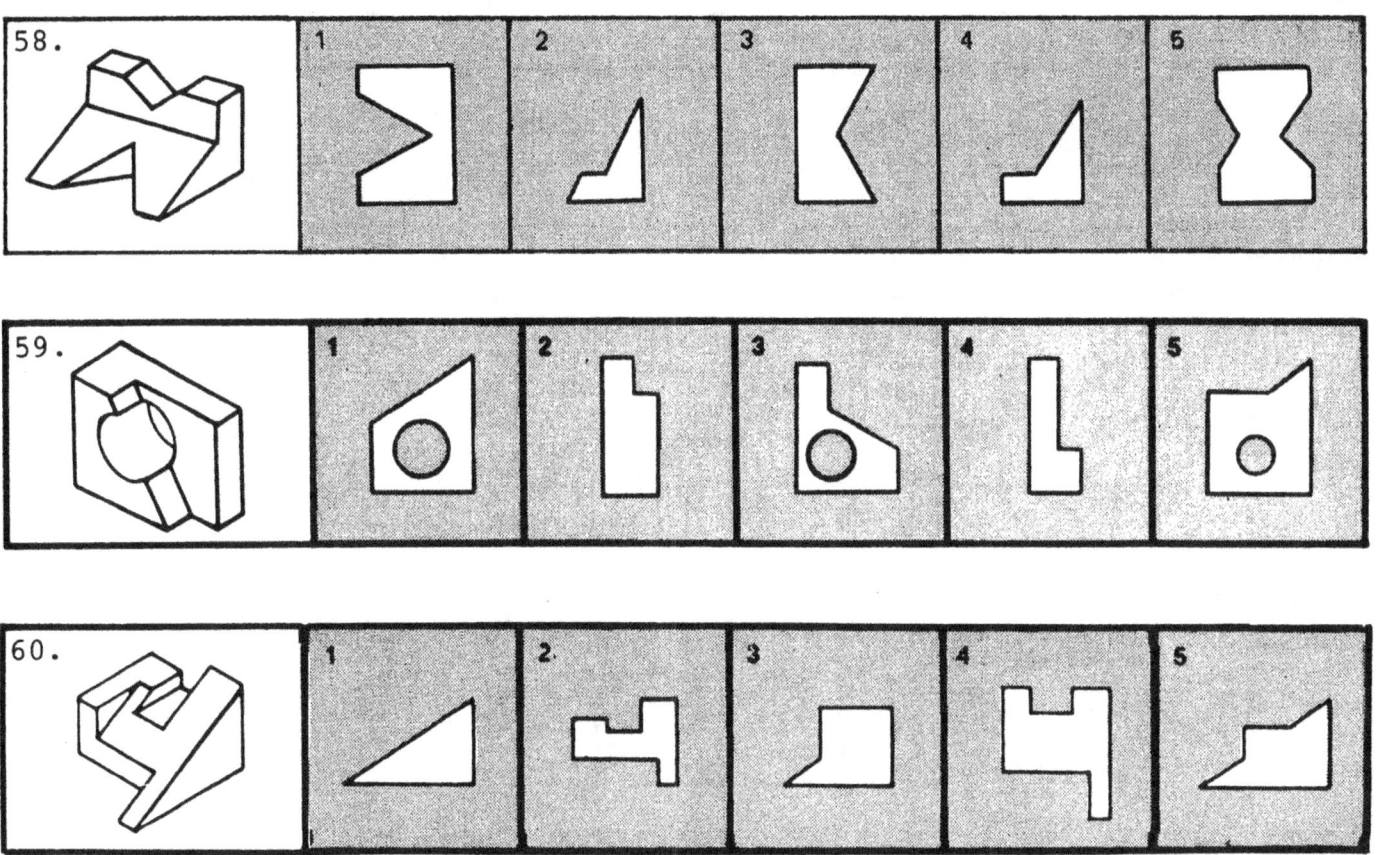

KEY (CORRECT ANSWERS)

1. 4	16. 2	31. 3	46. 1
2. 3	17. 4	32. 4	47. 1
3. 3	18. 3	33. 3	48. 1
4. 3	19. 1	34. 8	49. 5
5. 1	20. 1	35. 5	50. 4
6. 3	21. 1	36. 3	51. 2
7. 2	22. 4	37. 5	52. 5
8. 2	23. 4	38. 4	53. 4
9. 3	24. 1	39. 5	54. 3
10. 3	25. 2	40. 2	55. 3
11. 3	26. 3	41. 3	56. 3
12. 2	27. 3	42. 6	57. 4
13. 3	28. 4	43. 3	58. 4
14. 3	29. 2	44. 1	59. 2
15. 4	30. 2	34. 2	60. 5

MECHANICAL APTITUDE EXAMINATION SECTION
TEST 1

MECHANICAL COMPREHENSION

DIRECTIONS: Questions 1 through 4 test your ability to understand general mechanical devices. Pictures are shown and questions asked about the mechanical devices shown in the picture. Read each question and study the picture. Each question is followed by four choices. For each question, choose the one BEST answer (A, B, C, or D). Then, *PRINT THE LETTER OF THE CORRECT ANSWER IN THE SPACE AT THE RIGHT.*

1.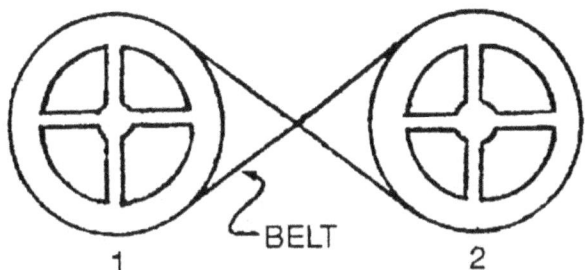

   The reason for crossing the belt connecting these wheels is to
   A. make the wheels turn in opposite directions
   B. make wheel 2 turn faster than wheel 1
   C. save wear on the belt
   D. take up slack in the belt

2.

   The purpose of the small gear between the two large gears is to
   A. increase the speed of the larger gears
   B. allow the larger gears to turn in different directions
   C. decrease the speed of the larger gears
   D. make the larger gears turn in the same direction

2 (#1)

3.

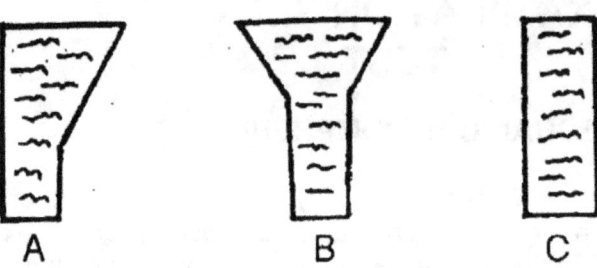

Each of these three-foot-high water cans have a bottom with an area of one square foot.
The pressure on the bottom of the cans is
   A. least in A   B. least in B   C. least in C   D. the same in all

4.

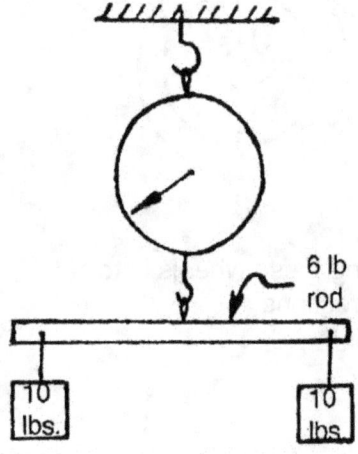

The reading on the scale should be
   A. zero   B. 10 pounds   C. 13 pounds   D. 26 pounds

KEY (CORRECT ANSWERS)

1. A
2. D
3. D
4. D

TEST 2

DIRECTIONS: Questions 1 through 6 test knowledge of tools and how to use them. For each question, decide which one of the four things shown in the boxes labeled A, B, C, or D normally is used with or goes best with the thing in the picture on the left. *PRINT THE LETTER OF THE CORRECT ANSWER IN THE SPACE AT THE RIGHT.*

NOTE: All tools are NOT drawn to the same scale.

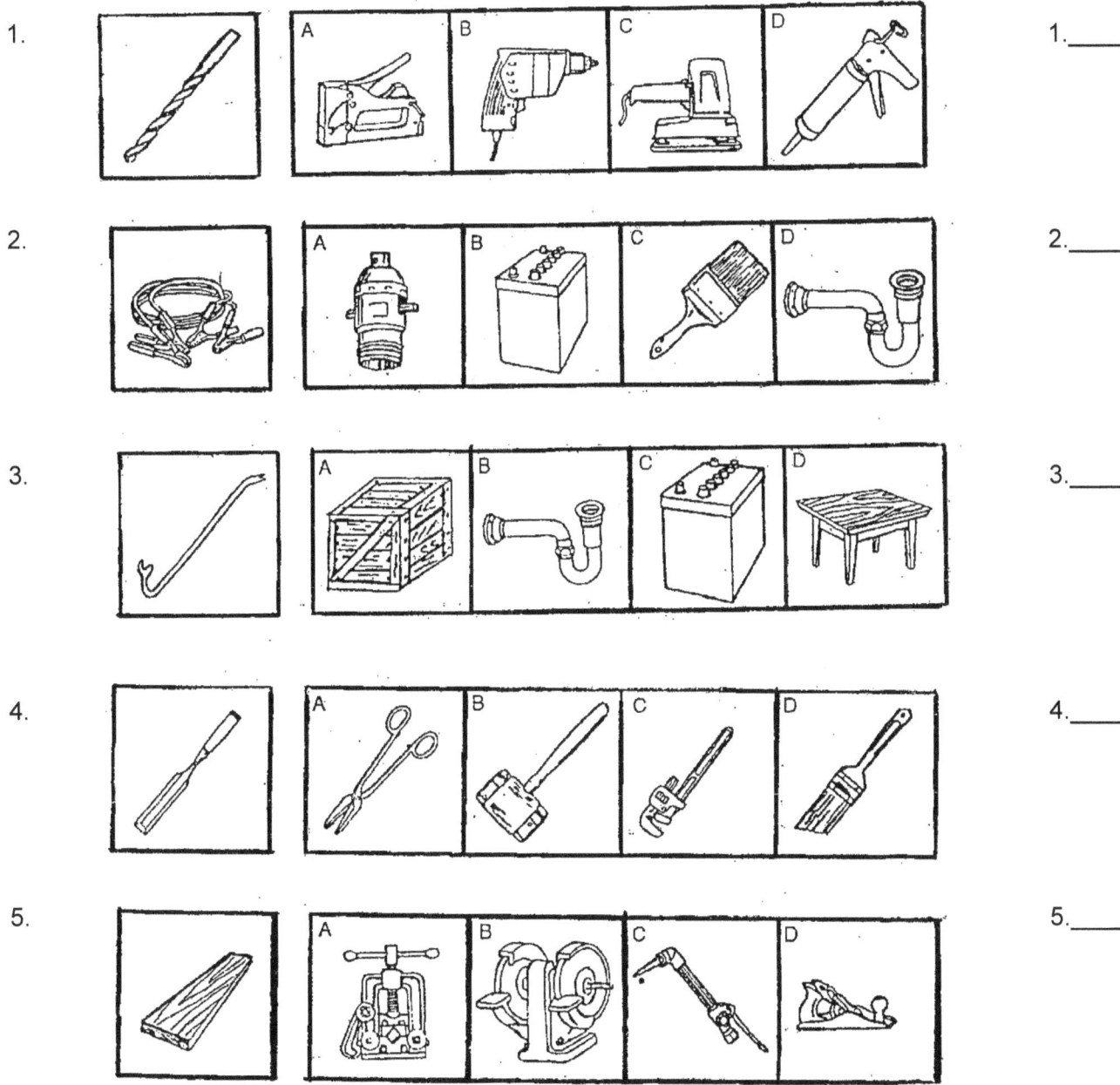

2 (#2)

6. 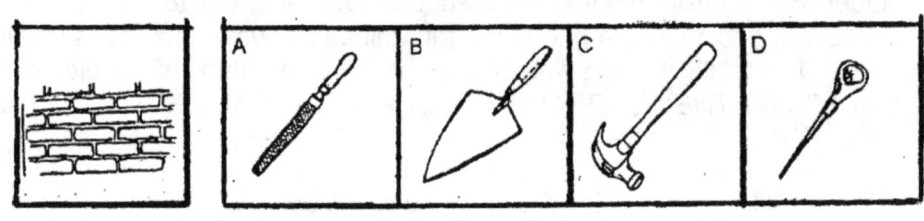 6._____

KEY (CORRECT ANSWERS)

1. B 4. B
2. B 5. D
3. A 6. B

TOOLS

EXAMINATION SECTION
TEST 1

DIRECTIONS: Each question or incomplete statement is followed by several suggested answers or completions. Select the one that BEST answers the question or completes the statement. *PRINT THE LETTER OF THE CORRECT ANSWER IN THE SPACE AT THE RIGHT.*

1. It is NOT good practice to cut thin-walled copper tubing with an ordinary three-wheel pipe cutter because

    A. the cutters will be dulled
    B. too much time is required
    C. the tubing end must be reamed after cutting
    D. the tubing is likely to collapse

2. Wedges are used under vertical shoring timbers to

    A. utilize scrap wood
    B. permit the use of very short timbers
    C. obtain rigid shoring
    D. absorb construction noise

3. The LONGEST nail of the following is a _____-penny nail.
    A. 12 B. 10 C. 6 D. 4

4. A commonly used priming coat for structural steel is
    A. enamel B. varnish C. red lead D. lacquer

5. A nail set is a tool used for

    A. straightening bent nails
    B. cutting nails to specified size
    C. sinking a nail head in wood
    D. measuring nail size

6. The sketch at the right shows a gauge used to
    A. measure the depth of a hole
    B. determine if a board has been smoothly planed
    C. check the width of a brick
    D. scribe a line on a board parallel to its edge

7. The gauge box shown at the right is used for measuring the dry volume of a concrete mix. If the gauge box is to have a volume of 1 cubic yard, dimension H must be APPROXIMATELY _____ feet.
  A. 2.39
  B. 1.69
  C. 1.45
  D. .63

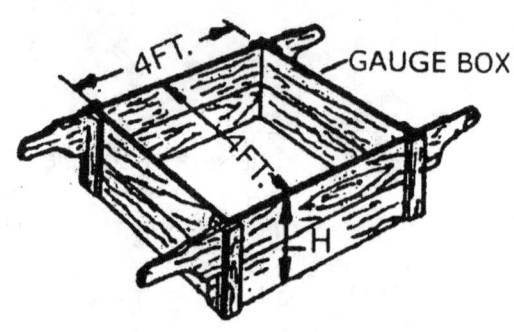

Questions 8-27.

DIRECTIONS: Questions 8 through 27 refer to the use of tools shown below. Refer to these tools when answering these questions.

3 (#1)

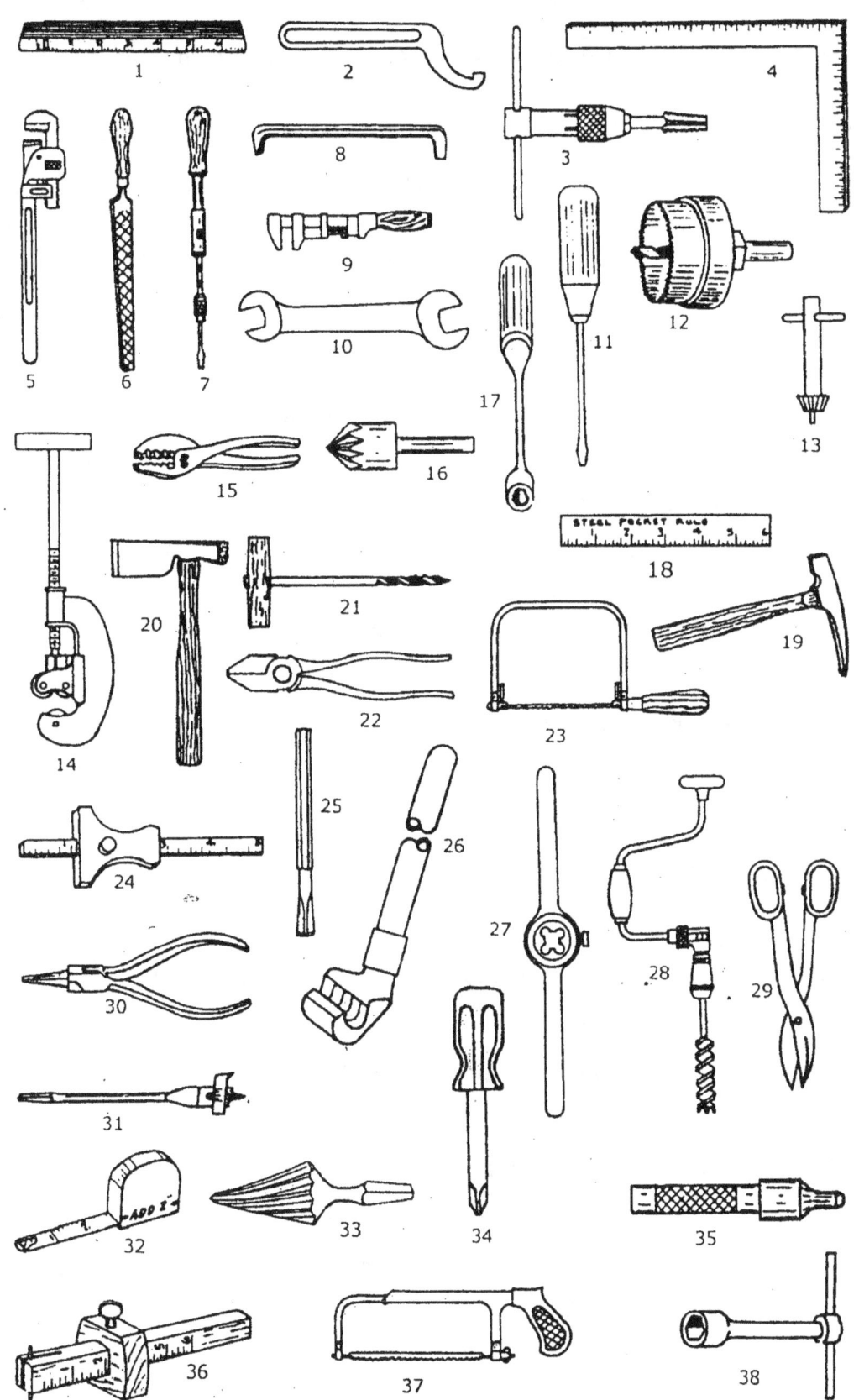

8. Tool number 38 is properly called a(n) _____ wrench.
   A. box   B. open-end   C. socket   D. tool

9. Two tools which are used for cutting large circular holes in thin sheets are numbers _____ and _____.
   A. 12; 31   B. 28; 33   C. 12; 28   D. 31; 33

10. If there is a possible danger of electric shock when you are taking measurements, it would be BEST to use number
    A. 1   B. 4   C. 18   D. 32

11. A 1/2-inch steel pipe is preferably cut with number
    A. 14   B. 23   C. 27   D. 29

12. A nut for a #8 machine screw should be tightened using number
    A. 9   B. 15   C. 17   D. 38

13. The hexagon nut for a 1/2-inch diameter machine bolt should be tightened using number
    A. 5   B. 10   C. 22   D. 26

14. If a small piece must be chipped off a brick in order to clear an obstruction when a brick wall is being built, the MOST suitable tool to use is number
    A. 16   B. 19   C. 20   D. 33

15. A large number of wood screws can be screwed into a board MOST quickly by using number
    A. 7   B. 8   C. 11   D. 17

16. A number of different diameter holes can be MOST easily bored through a heavy wood plank by using number
    A. 3   B. 13   C. 21   D. 31

17. The tool to use in order to form threads in a hole in a steel block is number
    A. 2   B. 3   C. 27   D. 31

18. Curved designs in thin wood are preferably cut with number
    A. 12   B. 23   C. 29   D. 37

19. The driving of Phillips-head screws requires the use of number
    A. 7   B. 8   C. 11   D. 34

20. In order to properly flare one end of a piece of copper tubing, the tool to use is number
    A. 13   B. 25   C. 33   D. 35

21. Tool number 16 is used for
    A. counterboring   B. cutting concrete
    C. countersinking   D. reaming

22. A tool that can be used to drill a hole in a concrete wall to install a lead anchor is number   22.____

    A. 3   B. 16   C. 21   D. 25

23. After cutting a piece of steel pipe, the burrs are BEST removed from the inside edge with   23.____
    number

    A. 6   B. 13   C. 16   D. 33

24. The MOST convenient tool for measuring the depth of a 1/2-inch diameter hole is number   24.____

    A. 24   B. 31   C. 32   D. 36

25. A 1" x 1" x 1/8" angle iron would usually be cut using number   25.____

    A. 12   B. 26   C. 29   D. 37

26. Wood screws located in positions NOT accessible to an ordinary screwdriver would be   26.____
    removed using number

    A. 2   B. 8   C. 13   D. 30

27. A small hole can be quickly bored through an 1/8-inch thick plywood board with number   27.____

    A. 3   B. 7   C. 21   D. 31

28. The hammer shown to the right would be used by a   28.____
    A. carpenter
    B. bricklayer
    C. tinsmith
    D. plumber

29. Which of the following pairs of tools would be used to tighten a nut on a screw?   29.____

    A. Two open-end wrenches
    B. One open-end wrench and one adjustable wrench
    C. A screwdriver and a wrench
    D. A vise wrench and an adjustable screwdriver

30. In order to determine if a surface is truly horizontal, it should be checked with a   30.____

    A. carpenter's square   B. plumb bob
    C. steel rule   D. spirit level

KEY (CORRECT ANSWERS)

1.	D	16.	D
2.	C	17.	B
3.	A	18.	B
4.	C	19.	D
5.	C	20.	D
6.	D	21.	C
7.	B	22.	D
8.	C	23.	D
9.	A	24.	A
10.	A	25.	D
11.	A	26.	B
12.	C	27.	C
13.	B	28.	B
14.	B	29.	C
15.	A	30.	D

TEST 2

DIRECTIONS: Each question or incomplete statement is followed by several suggested answers or completions. Select the one that BEST answers the question or completes the statement. *PRINT THE LETTER OF THE CORRECT ANSWER IN THE SPACE AT THE RIGHT.*

1. After a wedge-shaped hole has been cut into the large stone, the three-legged lifting device is inserted to lift the stone. The CORRECT order for inserting the three legs is
   A. 1, 2, 3
   B. 3, 2, 1
   C. 2, 3, 1
   D. 1, 3, 2

   1.____

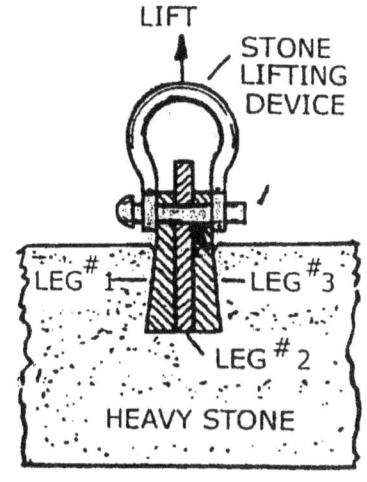

2. Brushes which have been used to apply shellac are BEST cleaned with

   A. alcohol
   B. water
   C. carbon tetrachloride
   D. acetic acid

   2.____

3. When timbers are bolted together, a flat washer is GENERALLY used under the head of the bolt to

   A. prevent the bolt from turning
   B. increase the strength of the bolt
   C. reduce crushing of the wood when the bolt is tightened
   D. make it easier to turn the bolt

   3.____

4. A claw hammer is PROPERLY used for

   A. driving a cold chisel
   B. driving brads
   C. setting rivets
   D. flattening a 1/4" metal bar

   4.____

5. Open-end wrenches are made with the sides of the jaws at about a 15° angle to the line of the handle. This angle

   A. is useful when working the wrench in close quarters
   B. increases the strength of the jaws
   C. prevents extending the handle with a piece of pipe
   D. serves only to improve the appearance of the wrench

   5.____

6. It is BEST to cut a piece of sheet metal with a pair of snips by starting each cut with the metal sheet

   A. out near the points of the snips
   B. as far back in the jaws as possible
   C. midway between the snip points and the pivot
   D. one-quarter the way between the snip points and the pivot

7. Cement-lined drain pipe should be cut with a

   A. chisel
   B. file
   C. star drill
   D. hacksaw

8. A riser is GENERALLY a pipe run which is

   A. horizontal
   B. curved
   C. vertical
   D. at a 45 angle

Questions 9-18.

DIRECTIONS: Questions 9 through 18 refer to the use of the tools shown below. Read the item, and for the operation given, select the PROPER tool to be used from those shown.

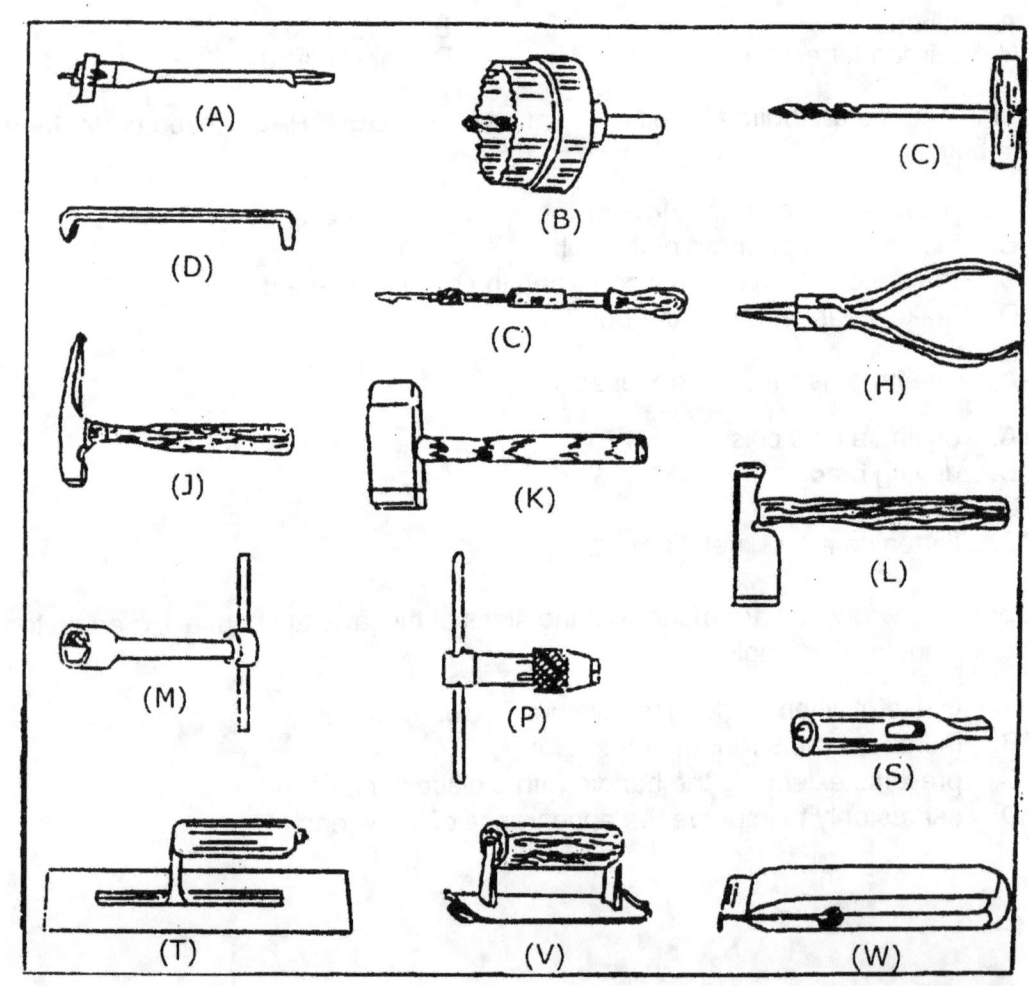

3 (#2)

9. Turning a screw tap when threading a hole in a steel block. 9._____

10. Boring a number of different diameter holes through a heavy wood plank. 10._____

11. Quickly screwing a number of wood screws into a board. 11._____

12. Setting a groove in a cement floor before hardening of the cement. 12._____

13. Plastering a wall. 13._____

14. Chipping a small piece out of a brick to clear a projecting steel rod when building a brick wall. 14._____

15. Tightening a large nut. 15._____

16. Quickly boring a small hole through a 1/8" board. 16._____

17. Unfastening wood screws located in a position inaccessible to an ordinary screwdriver. 17._____

18. Making a 1 1/2" hole in a steel plate. 18._____

19. A pneumatic bucker is used in 19._____

    A. riveting   B. brazing
    C. soldering   D. reinforcing concrete

20. To make certain two points separated by a vertical distance of 8 feet are in perfect vertical alignment, it would be BEST to use a 20._____

    A. surface gage   B. height gage
    C. protractor   D. plumb bob

21. When repair work is being done on the elevated structure, canvas spreads are suspended under the working area MAINLY to 21._____

    A. reduce noise   B. discourage crowds
    C. protect the structure   D. protect pedestrians

22. When grinding a weld smooth, it is MOST important to avoid 22._____

    A. overheating the surrounding metal
    B. grinding too much of the weld away
    C. grinding too slowly
    D. grinding after the weld has cooled off

23. A gouge is a tool used for 23._____

    A. planing wood smooth   B. grinding metal
    C. drilling steel   D. chiseling wood

24. The tool that should be used to cut a 1" x 4" plank down to a 3" width is a 24._____

    A. hacksaw   B. crosscut saw
    C. rip saw   D. backsaw

4 (#2)

25. Threads are cut on the ends of a length of steel pipe by the use of a   25.___
    A. brace and bit   B. counterbore
    C. stock and die   D. doweling jig

26. A bit brace can be locked so that the bit will turn in only one direction by means of a   26.___
    A. feed screw   B. rachet device
    C. universal chuck   D. ball-bearing device

27. A reamer is used to   27.___
    A. enlarge drilled holes to an exact size
    B. punch holes to desired size
    C. line up adjacent holes
    D. lay out holes before drilling

28. The tool shown at the right is a   28.___
    A. countersink
    B. counterbore
    C. star drill
    D. burring reamer

29. The saw shown at the right would be used to cut   29.___
    A. curved designs in thin wood
    B. strap iron
    C. asphalt tiles to fit against walls
    D. soft lead pipe

30. The tool shown at the right is a   30.___
    A. float
    B. finishing trowel
    C. hawk
    D. roofing seamer

KEY (CORRECT ANSWERS)

1. D
2. A
3. C
4. B
5. A

6. B
7. D
8. C
9. P
10. A

11. E
12. V
13. T
14. J
15. M

16. C
17. D
18. B
19. B
20. D

21. C
22. B
23. D
24. C
25. C

26. B
27. A
28. D
29. A
30. A

TEST 3

DIRECTIONS: Each question or incomplete statement is followed by several suggested answers or completions. Select the one that BEST answers the question or completes the Statement. *PRINT THE LETTER OF THE CORRECT ANSWER IN THE SPACE AT THE RIGHT.*

Questions 1-8.

DIRECTIONS: Questions 1 through 8 are to be answered on the basis of the following items. The sizes of the items shown are NOT their actual sizes. Each item is identified by a number, For each question, select the answer which gives the identifying number of the item that BEST answers the question.

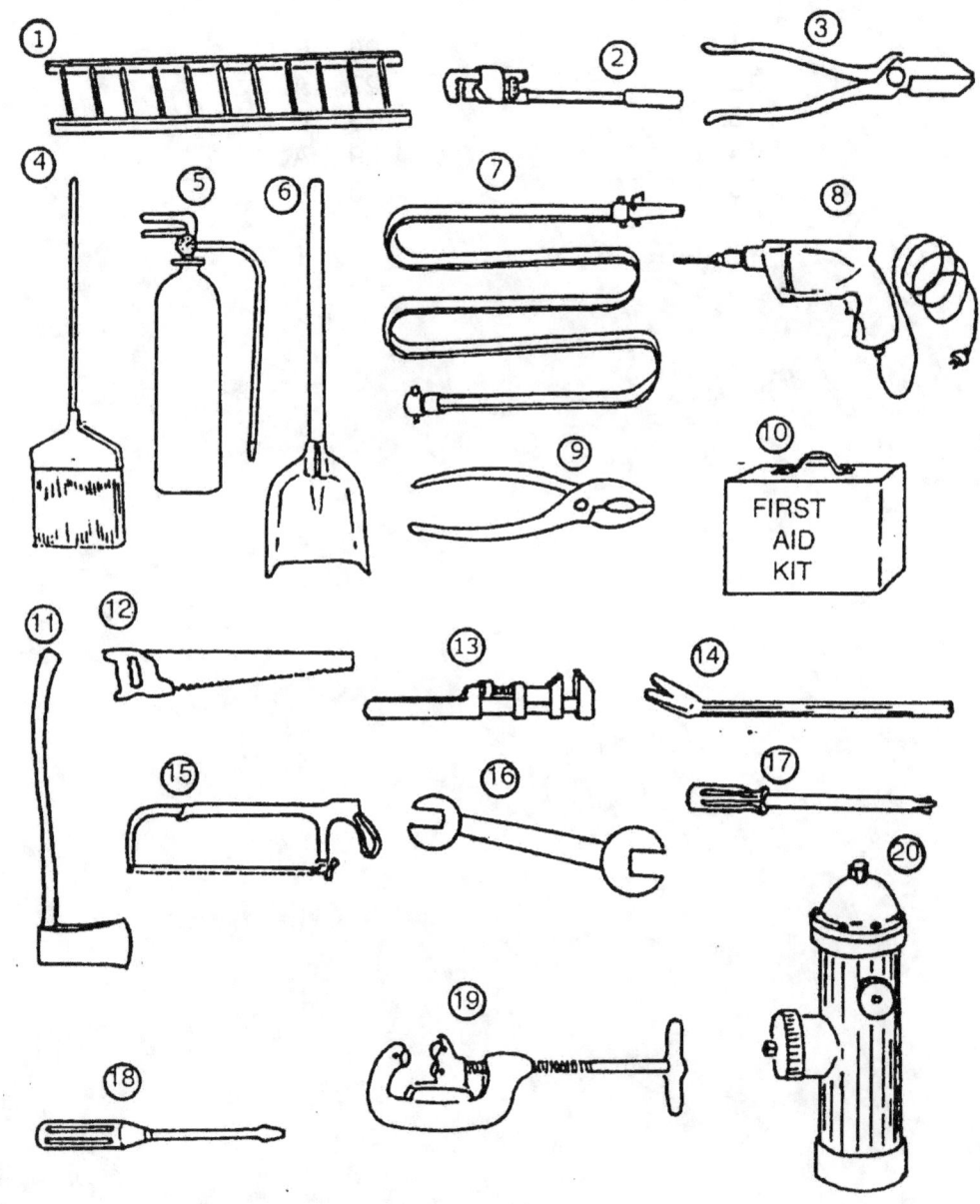

1. Which one of the following items should be connected to a hydrant and used to put out a fire?
   A. 5   B. 7   C. 8   D. 17

2. Which one of the following pairs of items should be used after a fire to clean a floor covered with small pieces of burned material?
   A. 1 and 14   B. 4 and 6   C. 10 and 12   D. 11 and 13

3. Which one of the following pairs of items should be used for cutting a branch from a tree?
   A. 2 and 3   B. 8 and 9   C. 11 and 12   D. 14 and 15

4. Which one of the following items should be used to rescue a victim from a second floor window?
   A. 1   B. 10   C. 15   D. 20

5. Which one of the following pairs of items should be used to tighten a nut on a screw?
   A. 2 and 3   B. 8 and 19   C. 9 and 14   D. 16 and 18

6. Which one of the following items should be used to repair a leaky faucet?
   A. 4   B. 5   C. 12   D. 13

7. Which one of the following items should be used as a source of water at a fire?
   A. 2   B. 6   C. 9   D. 20

8. Which item should be used for cutting metal?
   A. 6   B. 13   C. 15   D. 18

Questions 9-18.

DIRECTIONS: Questions 9 through 18, inclusive, in Column I are articles or terms used in structure maintenance and repair work, each of which is associated primarily (though not exclusively) with one of the trade specialties listed in Column II. For each article or term in Column I, select the trade specialty from Column II in which it is in greatest use. Indicate in the space at the right, the letter preceding your selected trade specialty.

COLUMN I
(Articles or Terms)

9. Drift pin
10. Studding
11. Elbow
12. Header course
13. Dowel
14. Screeding
15. Cleanout
16. Air jam
17. Curing
18. Mortise and tenon

COLUMN II
(Trade Specialties)

A. Carpentry
B. Masonry
C. Ironwork
D. Plumbing

19. Practically all valves used in plumbing work are made so that the handwheel is turned clockwise instead of counterclockwise to close the valve.
    The PROBABLE reason is that

    A. it is easier to remember since screws and nuts move inward when turned clockwise
    B. the handwheel is less likely to loosen
    C. greater force can be exerted
    D. most people are righthanded

20. Sharpening a hand saw consists of

    A. jointing, shaping, setting, and filing
    B. adzing, clinching, forging, and machining
    C. brazing, chiseling, grinding, and mitering
    D. bushing, dressing, lapping, and machining

21. A hacksaw blade having 32 teeth to the inch is the BEST blade to use when cutting

    A. cold rolled steel shafting
    B. wrought iron pipe
    C. stainless steel plate
    D. copper tubing

22. Good practice dictates that an adjustable open-end wrench should be used PRIMARILY when the

    A. nut to be turned is soft and must not be scored
    B. extra leverage is needed
    C. proper size of fixed wrench is not available
    D. location is cramped permitting only a small turning angle

23. When a hacksaw blade is designated as an 18-32, the numbers 18 and 32 refer to, respectively, the blade's

    A. stroke and thickness
    B. thickness and length
    C. length and teeth per inch
    D. teeth per inch and stroke

24. When a machine screw is designated as a 10-32, the numbers 10 and 32 refer to, respectively, the screw's

    A. length and head type
    B. threads per inch and length
    C. diameter and threads per inch
    D. head type and diameter

25. An offset screwdriver is MOST useful for turning a wood screw when

    A. a strong force needs to be applied
    B. the screw head is marred
    C. space is limited
    D. speed is desired

26. Of the following orders for tools or materials used in the building trades, the one which is INCOMPLETE is 26.____

    A. 1 paintbrush, flat, 2 in. wide
    B. 1 drill, twist, straight shank, high speed, 3/8 in.
    C. 1 snake, steel, 3/4 in. wide by 1/8 in. thick
    D. 1 keg of nails, 10 penny, common wire, galvanized

27. The tool that is GENERALLY used to slightly elongate a round hole in strap-iron is a 27.____

    A. rat-tail file   B. reamer
    C. drill   D. rasp

28. The BEST way to locate a point on the floor directly below a given point on the ceiling is by using a 28.____

    A. plumber's snake   B. plumb bob
    C. flashlight   D. chalk line

29. The wrench that would prove LEAST useful in uncoupling several pieces of pipe is a _____ wrench. 29.____

    A. socket   B. chain   C. strap   D. stillson

30. Of the following, the tool that is LEAST easily broken is a 30.____

    A. file   B. pry bar
    C. folding rule   D. hacksaw blade

KEY (CORRECT ANSWERS)

1. B
2. B
3. C
4. A
5. D

6. D
7. D
8. C
9. C
10. A

11. B
12. D
13. A
14. B
15. D

16. C
17. B
18. A
19. A
20. A

21. D
22. C
23. C
24. C
25. C

26. C
27. A
28. B
29. A
30. B

EXAMINATION SECTION
TEST 1

DIRECTIONS: Each question or incomplete statement is followed by several suggested answers or completions. Select the one that BEST answers the question or completes the statement. *PRINT THE LETTER OF THE CORRECT ANSWER IN THE SPACE AT THE RIGHT.*

1. A bit is held in a hand drill by means of a(n)

    A. arbor B. chuck C. collet D. clamp

2. The type of screw that MOST often requires a countersunk hole is a _____ head.

    A. flat B. round C. fillister D. hexagon

3. Instead of using the ordinary 1 piece screwdriver, a screwdriver bit is MOST often used with a brace because of the

    A. increased length of the brace
    B. different types of bits available
    C. increased leverage of the brace
    D. ability to work in tight corners

4. A thread gage is usually used to measure the

    A. thickness of a thread
    B. diameter of a thread
    C. number of threads per inch
    D. height of a thread

5. The wheel of a glass cutter is BEST lubricated with

    A. kerosene
    B. linseed oil
    C. varnolene
    D. diesel oil

6. A nail set is a

    A. group of nails of the same size and type
    B. group of nails of different sizes but the same type
    C. tool used to extract nails
    D. tool used to drive nails below the surface of wood

7. To test for leaks in a gas line, it is BEST to use

    A. a match
    B. soapy water
    C. a colored dye
    D. ammonia

8. Routing is the process of cutting a

    A. strip out of sheet metal
    B. groove in wood
    C. chamfer on a shaft
    D. core out of concrete

9. A hacksaw frame has a wing nut mainly to

    A. make it easier to replace blades
    B. increase the strength of the frame
    C. prevent vibration of the blade
    D. adjust the length of the frame

10. A mitre box is usually used with a _____ saw.

    A. hack   B. crosscut   C. rip   D. back

11. A continuous flexible saw blade is MOST often used on a _____ saw.

    A. radial   B. band   C. swing   D. table

12. A pipe reamer is used to

    A. clean out a length of pipe
    B. thread pipe
    C. remove burrs from the ends of pipe
    D. seal pipe joints

13. To lay out a straight cut on a piece of wood at the same angle as the cut on a second piece of wood, the PROPER tool to use is a

    A. bevel   B. cope   C. butt gauge   D. clevis

14. Before drilling a hole in a piece of metal, an indentation should be made with a _____ punch.

    A. pin   B. taper   C. center   D. drift

15. Curved cuts in wood are BEST made with a _____ saw.

    A. jig   B. veneer   C. radial   D. swing

16. A face plate is generally used to

    A. hold material while working with it on a lathe
    B. smooth out irregularities in a metal plate
    C. protect the finish on a metal plate
    D. locate centers of holes to be drilled on a drill press

17. A die would be used to

    A. gage the groove in a splined shaft
    B. cut a thread on a metal rod
    C. hold a piece to be machined on a milling machine
    D. control the depth of a hole to be drilled in a piece of metal

18. Before using a ladle to scoop up molten solder, you should make sure that the ladle is dry.
    This is done to prevent

    A. the solder from sticking to the ladle
    B. impurities from getting into the solder
    C. injuries due to splashing solder
    D. cooling of the solder

19. To PROPERLY adjust the gap on a spark plug, you should use a(n)   19.____
    A. inside caliper   B. center gauge
    C. wire type feeler gauge D. micrometer

20. The length of the MOST common type of folding wood rule is _____ feet.   20.____
    A. 4   B. 5   C. 6   D. 7

21. A four-foot mason's level is usually used to determine whether the top of a wall is level and whether it is   21.____
    A. square   B. plumb   C. rigid   D. in line

22. To match a tongue in a board, the matching board MUST have a   22.____
    A. rabbet   B. chamfer   C. bead   D. groove

23. When driving screws in close quarters, the BEST type of screwdriver to use is a(n)   23.____
    A. Phillips   B. offset   C. butt   D. angled

24. The term 12-24 refers to a _____ screw.   24.____
    A. wood   B. lag
    C. sheet metal D. machine

25. To measure the length of a curved line on a drawing or plan, the PROPER tool to use in addition to a ruler is(are)   25.____
    A. dividers   B. calipers
    C. surface gage D. radius gage

26. For the standard machine screw, the diameter of a tap drill is generally   26.____
    A. *equal* to the diameter of the shaft of the screw at the base of the threads (the root diameter)
    B. *larger* than the root diameter, but smaller than the diameter of the screw
    C. *equal* to the diameter of the screw
    D. *larger* than the diameter of the screw

27. In order to drill a 1" hole accurately with a drill press, you should   27.____
    A. drill at high speeds
    B. use very little pressure on the drill
    C. drill partway down, release pressure on the drill, and then continue drilling
    D. drill a pilot hole first

28. Before taking apart an electric motor to repair, punch marks are sometimes placed on the casing near each other.   28.____
    The MOST probable reason for doing this is to

    A. make sure the parts lock together on reassembly
    B. properly line up the parts that are next to each other
    C. keep track of the number of parts in the assembly
    D. identify all the parts as coming from the one motor

29. To locate a point on a floor directly under a point on the ceiling, the PROPER tool to use is a

   A. square
   B. line level
   C. height gage
   D. plumb bob

Question 30.

DIRECTIONS: Question 30 is based on the diagram appearing below.

30. In the above diagram, the full P required to lift the weight a distance of four feet is MOST NEARLY _____ lbs.

   A. 50 B. 67 C. 75 D. 100

31. The EASIEST tool to use to determine whether the edge of a board is at right angles to the face of the board is a

   A. rafter square
   B. try square
   C. protractor
   D. marking gage

32. *Whetting* refers to

   A. tempering of tools by dipping them in water
   B. annealing of tools by heating and slow cooling
   C. brazing of carbide tips on tools
   D. sharpening of tools

33. The MOST difficult part of a plank to plane is the

   A. face B. side C. end D. back

34. To prevent wood from splitting when drilling with an auger, it is BEST to

   A. use even pressure on the bit
   B. drill at a slow speed
   C. hold the wood tightly in a vise
   D. back up the wood with a piece of scrap wood

35. The term *dressing a grinding wheel* refers to

    A. setting up the wheel on the arbor
    B. restoring the sharpness of a wheel face that has become clogged
    C. placing flanges against the sides of the wheel
    D. bringing the wheel up to speed before using it

    35.____

36. Heads of rivets are BEST cut off with a

    A. hacksaw
    B. cold chisel
    C. fly cutter
    D. reamer

    36.____

37. A *V-block* is especially useful to

    A. prevent damage to work held in a vise
    B. hold round stock while a hole is being drilled into it
    C. prevent rolling of round stock stored on the ground
    D. shim up the end of a machine so that it is level

    37.____

38. A full set of taps for a given size usually consists of a _____ tap.

    A. taper and bottoming
    B. taper and plug
    C. plug and bottoming
    D. taper, plug, and bottoming

    38.____

39. Round thread cutting dies are usually held in stock by means of

    A. wing nuts   B. clamps   C. set screws   D. bolts

    39.____

40. The one of the following diagrams that shows the plan view and the elevation of a counterbored hole is

    40.____

A.

B.

C.

D.

41. With regard to pipe, *I.D.* usually means

    A. inside diameter
    B. inside dressed
    C. invert diameter
    D. installation date

    41.____

42. A compression fitting is MOST often used to

    A. lubricate a wheel
    B. join two pieces of tubing
    C. reduce the diameter of a hole
    D. press fit a gear to a shaft

43. The shape of a mill file is basically

    A. flat   B. half round   C. triangular   D. square

44. Of the following, the ratio of tin to lead that will produce the solder with the LOWEST melting point is

    A. 30-70   B. 40-60   C. 50-50   D. 60-40

45. A safe edge on a file is one that

    A. is smooth and can not cut
    B. has a finer cut than the face of the file
    C. is rounded to prevent scratches
    D. has a coarser cut than the face of the file

46. The MOST frequent use of a file card is to _____ files.

    A. sort out   B. clean
    C. prevent damage to   D. prevent clogging of

47. The BEST way of determining whether a grinding wheel has an internal crack is to

    A. run the wheel at high speed, stop it, and examine the wheel
    B. spray lubricating oil on the sides of the wheel and check the amount of absorption of the oil
    C. hit the wheel with a rubber hammer and listen to the sound
    D. drop the wheel sharply on a table and then check the wheel

48. If a grinding wheel has worn to a smaller diameter, the BEST practice to follow is to

    A. discard the wheel
    B. continue using the wheel as before
    C. use the wheel, but at a faster speed
    D. use the wheel, but at a slower speed

49. With respect to the ordinary awl,

    A. only the tip is hardened
    B. the entire blade is hardened
    C. the tip is tempered, and the rest of the blade is hardened
    D. the entire blade is tempered

50. To prevent overheating of drills, it is BEST to use _____ oil.

    A. cutting   B. lubricating
    C. penetrating   D. heating

KEY (CORRECT ANSWERS)

1. B	11. B	21. B	31. B	41. A
2. A	12. C	22. D	32. D	42. B
3. C	13. A	23. B	33. C	43. A
4. C	14. C	24. D	34. D	44. D
5. A	15. A	25. A	35. B	45. A
6. D	16. A	26. B	36. B	46. B
7. B	17. B	27. D	37. B	47. C
8. B	18. C	28. B	38. D	48. C
9. A	19. C	29. D	39. C	49. A
10. D	20. C	30. D	40. A	50. A

TEST 2

DIRECTIONS: Each question or incomplete statement is followed by several suggested answers or completions. Select the one that BEST answers the question or completes the statement. *PRINT THE LETTER OF THE CORRECT ANSWER IN THE SPACE AT THE RIGHT.*

1. Crocus cloth is commonly used to   1.____

   A. protect finely machined surfaces from damage while the machines are being repaired
   B. remove rust from steel
   C. protect floors and furniture while painting walls
   D. wipe up oil and grease that has spilled

2. Before using a new paint brush, the FIRST operation should be to   2.____

   A. remove loose bristles
   B. soak the brush in linseed oil
   C. hang the brush up overnight
   D. clean the brush with turpentine

3. When sharpening a hand saw, the FIRST operation is to   3.____

   A. file the teeth down to the same height
   B. shape the teeth to the proper profile
   C. bend the teeth over to provide clearance when sawing
   D. clean the gullies with a file

4. To prevent solder from dripping when soldering a vertical seam, it is BEST to   4.____

   A. hold a waxed rag under the soldering iron
   B. use the soldering iron in a horizontal position
   C. tin the soldering iron on one side only
   D. solder the seam in the order from bottom to top

5. If a round nut has two holes in the face, the PROPER type wrench to use to tighten this nut is a(n)   5.____

   A. Stillson   B. monkey   C. spanner   D. open end

6. A box wrench is BEST used on   6.____

   A. pipe fittings   B. flare nuts
   C. hexagonal nuts   D. Allen screws

7. To prevent damage to fine finishes on metal work that is to be held in a vise, you should   7.____

   A. clamp the work lightly
   B. use brass inserts on the vise
   C. wrap the work with cloth before inserting it in the vise
   D. substitute a smooth face plate for the serrated plate on the vise

8. The MOST frequent use for a turnbuckle is to

   A. tighten a guy wire
   B. adjust shims on a machine
   C. bolt a bracket to a wall
   D. support electric cable from a ceiling

9. To form the head of a tinner's rivet, the PROPER tool to use is a rivet

   A. anvil   B. plate   C. set   D. brake

10. A socket speed handle MOST closely resembles a

    A. screwdriver   B. brace   C. spanner   D. spin grip

11. Tips of masonry drills are usually made of

    A. steel   B. carbide   C. corundum   D. monel

12. The BEST flux to use for soldering galvanized iron is

    A. resin
    B. sal ammoniac
    C. borax
    D. muriatic acid

13. The one of the following that is NOT a common type of oilstone is

    A. silicon carbide
    B. aluminum oxide
    C. hard Arkansas
    D. pumice

14. A method of joining metals using temperatures intermediate between soldering and welding is

    A. corbelling   B. brazing   C. annealing   D. lapping

15. When an unusually high degree of accuracy is required with woodwork, lines should be marked with a

    A. pencil ground to a chisel point
    B. pencil line over a crayon line
    C. sharp knife point
    D. scriber

16. The MOST important difference between pipe threads and V threads on bolts is that pipe threads are usually

    A. longer
    B. sharper
    C. tapered
    D. more evenly spaced

17. A street elbow differs from the ordinary elbow in that the street elbow has

    A. different diameter threads at each end
    B. male threads at one end and female threads at the other
    C. female threads at both ends
    D. male threads at both ends

18. Water hammer in a pipe line can MOST often be stopped by the installation of a(n)

    A. pressure reducing valve
    B. expansion joint
    C. flexible coupling
    D. air chamber

19. If water is leaking from the top part of a bibcock, the part that should be replaced is MOST likely the

    A. bibb washer
    B. packing
    C. seat
    D. bibb screw

20. When joining electric wires together in a fixture box, the BEST thing to use are wire

    A. connectors   B. couplings   C. clamps   D. bolts

21. If the name plate of a motor indicates that it is a split phase motor, it is LIKELY that this motor

    A. is a universal motor
    B. operates on DC only
    C. operates on AC only
    D. operates either on DC at full power or on AC at reduced power

22. To make driving of a screw into hard wood easier, it is BEST to lubricate the threads of the screw with

    A. varnoline
    B. penetrating oil
    C. beeswax
    D. cutting oil

23. Assume that a thermostatically controlled oil heater fails to operate. To determine whether it is the thermostat that is at fault, you should

    A. check the circuit breaker
    B. connect a wire across the terminals of the thermostat
    C. replace the contacts on the thermostat
    D. put an ammeter on the line

24. The function of the carburetor on a gasoline engine is to

    A. mix the air and gasoline properly
    B. filter the fuel
    C. filter the air to engine
    D. pump the gasoline into the cylinder

25. If a car owner complains that the battery in his car is constantly running dry, the item that should be checked FIRST is the

    A. fan belt
    B. generator
    C. voltage regulator
    D. relay

26. On MOST modern automobiles, foot brake pressure is transmitted to the brake drums by

    A. air pressure
    B. mechanical linkage
    C. hydraulic fluid
    D. electro-magnetic force

27. Assume that the engine of a car remains cold even though it is run for a period of time. The part that is MOST likely at fault is the

    A. heat by-pass valve
    B. thermostat
    C. heater control
    D. choke

28. To permit easy stripping of concrete forms, they should be

    A. dried B. oiled C. wet down D. cleaned

29. To prevent honey combing in concrete, the concrete should be

    A. vibrated
    C. heated in cold weather
    B. cured
    D. protected from the rain

30. The MAIN reason for using wire mesh in connection with concrete work is to

    A. strain the impurities from the sand
    B. increase the strength of the concrete
    C. hold the forms together
    D. protect the concrete till it hardens

31. Segregation of concrete is MOST often caused by pouring concrete

    A. in cold weather
    B. from too great a height
    C. too rapidly
    D. into a form in which the concrete has already begun to harden

32. Headers in carpentry are MOST closely associated with

    A. trimmers
    C. posts
    B. cantilevers
    D. newels

33. Joists are very often supported by

    A. suspenders
    C. anchor bolts
    B. base plates
    D. bridal irons

34. At outside corners, the type of joint MOST frequently used on a baseboard is the

    A. plowed
    C. mortise and tenon
    B. mitered
    D. butt

35. The vehicle used with latex paints is usually

    A. linseed oil
    C. varnish
    B. shellac
    D. water

36. *Boxing* of paint refers to the _____ of paints.

    A. mixing B. storage C. use D. canning

37. When painting wood, nail holes should be puttied

    A. *before* applying the prime coat
    B. *after* applying the prime coat but before the second coat
    C. *after* applying the second coat but before the third coat
    D. *after* applying the third coat

38. In laying up a brick wall, you find that at the end of the wall there is not enough space for a full brick.
    You should use a

    A. stretcher B. bat C. corbel D. bull nose

39. Pointing a brick wall is the same as

    A. truing up the wall
    B. topping the wall with a waterproof surface
    C. repairing the mortar joints in the wall
    D. providing a foundation for the wall

39._____

40. The pigment MOST often used in a prime coat of paint on steel to prevent rusting is

    A. lampblack   B. calcimine
    C. zinc oxide   D. red lead

40._____

41. If you find a co-worker lying unconscious across an electric wire, the FIRST thing you should do is

    A. get him off the wire   B. call the foreman
    C. get a doctor   D. shut off the power

41._____

42.

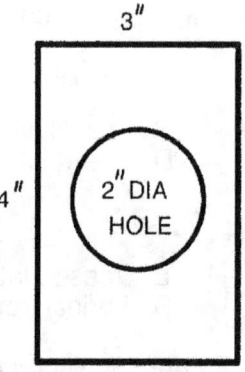

The area of the metal plate shown above, minus the hole area, is MOST NEARLY _____ square inches.

    A. 8.5   B. 8.9   C. 9.4   D. 10.1

42._____

43.

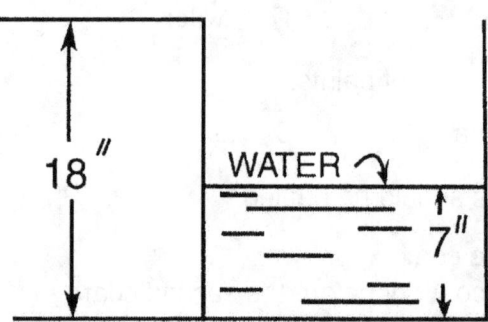

The percentage of the above tank that is filled with water is MOST NEARLY

    A. 33   B. 35   C. 37   D. 39

43._____

44.

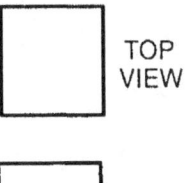

The top and front view of an object are shown above. The right side view will MOST likely look like

A.    B.    C.    D.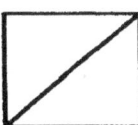

45.

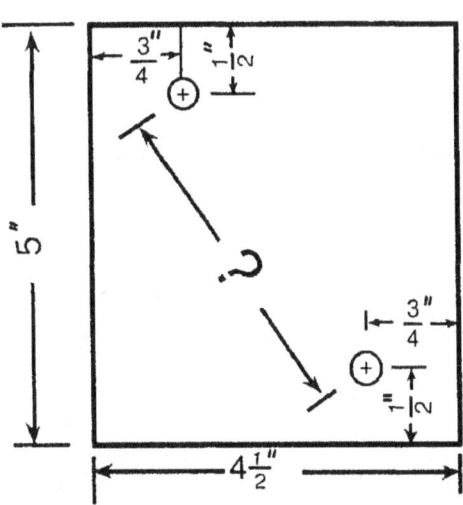

The distance between centers of the holes in the above diagram is MOST NEARLY

A. $4\frac{1}{2}"$ B. 4 3/4"   C. 5"   D. $5\frac{1}{4}"$

Questions 46-48.

DIRECTIONS: Questions 46 through 48, inclusive, are to be answered in accordance with the paragraph below.

A steam heating system with steam having a pressure of less than 10 pounds is called a low-pressure system. The majority of steam-heating systems are of this type. The steam may be provided by low-pressure boilers installed <u>expressly</u> for the purpose, or it may be gener-

ated in boilers at a higher pressure and reduced in pressure before admitted to the heating mains. In other instances, it may be possible to use exhaust steam which has been made to run engines and other machines and which still contains enough heat to be utilized in the heating system. The first case represents the system of heating used in the ordinary residence or other small building; the other two represent the systems of heating employed in industrial buildings where a power plant is installed for general power purposes.

46. According to the above paragraph, whether or not a steam heating system is considered a low pressure system is determined by the pressure

    A. generated by the boiler
    B. in the heating main
    C. at the inlet side of the reducing valve
    D. of the exhaust

47. According to the above paragraph, steam used for heating is sometimes obtained from steam

    A. generated principally to operate machinery
    B. exhausted from larger boilers
    C. generated at low pressure and brought up to high pressure before being used
    D. generated by engines other than boilers

48. As used in the above paragraph, the word *expressly* means

    A. rapidly   B. specifically
    C. usually   D. mainly

49. Of the following words, the one that is CORRECTLY spelled is

    A. suficient   B. sufficant
    C. sufficient   D. suficiant

50. Of the following words, the one that is CORRECTLY spelled is

    A. fairly   B. fairley   C. farely   D. fairlie

KEY (CORRECT ANSWERS)

1. B	11. B	21. C	31. B	41. D
2. A	12. D	22. C	32. A	42. B
3. A	13. D	23. B	33. D	43. D
4. C	14. B	24. A	34. B	44. A
5. C	15. C	25. C	35. D	45. C
6. C	16. C	26. C	36. A	46. B
7. B	17. B	27. B	37. B	47. A
8. A	18. D	28. B	38. B	48. B
9. C	19. B	29. A	39. C	49. C
10. B	20. A	30. B	40. D	50. A

EXAMINATION SECTION
TEST 1

DIRECTIONS: Each question or incomplete statement is followed by several suggested answers or completions. Select the one that BEST answers the question or completes the statement. *PRINT THE LETTER OF THE CORRECT ANSWER IN THE SPACE AT THE RIGHT.*

Questions 1-8.

DIRECTIONS: Questions 1 through 8 involve tests on the fuse box arrangement shown below. All tests are to be performed with a neon tester or a lamp test bank consisting of two 6-watt, 120-volt lamps connected in series. Do not make any assumptions about the conditions of the circuits. Draw your conclusions only from the information obtained with the neon tester or the two-lamp test bank, applied to the circuits as called for.

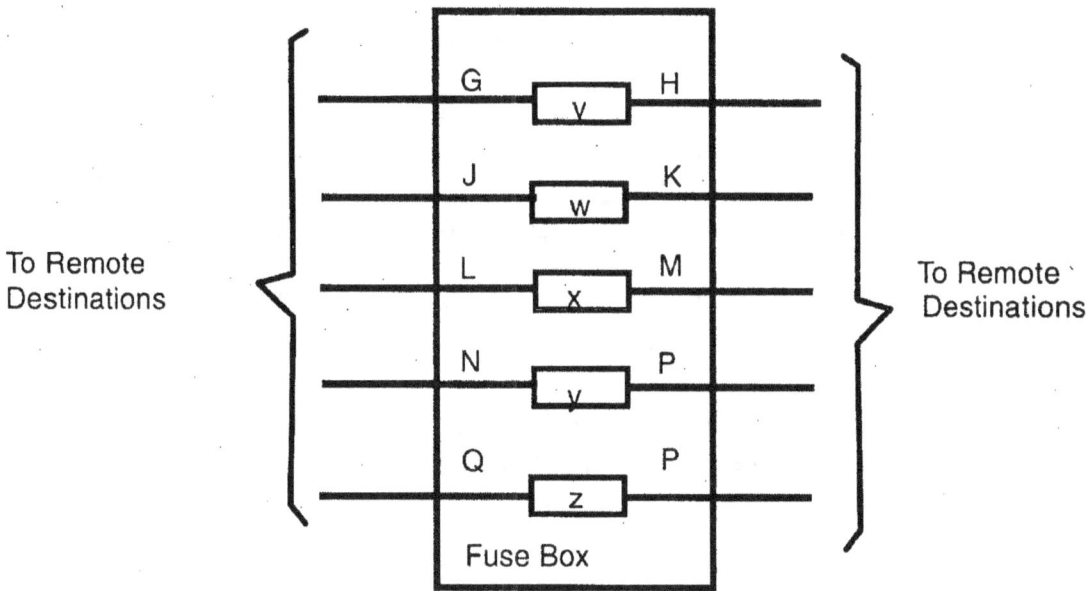

1. The two lamp test bank is placed from point G to joint J, and both lamps light. One of the lamps is momentarily removed from its socket; during that instant, the other lamp in the series-connected test bank should

   A. go dark
   B. get dimmer
   C. remain at same brightness
   D. get brighter

2. The test bank with two 60-watt, 120-volt lamps in series should be used on circuits with

   A. wattages only from 60 to 120 watts
   B. wattages only from 0 to 120 watts
   C. voltages only from 120 to 240 volts
   D. voltages only from 0 to 240 volts

3. The neon tester is placed from point G to point J and only one-half of the neon tester lights.
   It should be concluded that

   A. half of the tester has gone bad
   B. a wire has become disconnected in the circuit
   C. the voltage is AC
   D. the voltage is DC

4. If both lamps in the test bank light when placed directly across one of the above fuses, it should be concluded that

   A. the fuse is good
   B. the fuse is blown
   C. the fuse is overrated
   D. further tests have to be made to determine the condition of the fuse

5. If the lamp test bank does not light when placed directly across one of the above fuses, it should be concluded that

   A. the fuse is good
   B. the fuse is blown
   C. the fuse is overrated
   D. further tests have to be made to determine the condition of the fuse

6. The lamp test bank lights when placed from point G to point J but does not light when placed from point H to point J.
   It should be concluded that

   A. the wire to point H has become disconnected
   B. the wire to point J has become disconnected
   C. fuse v is bad
   D. fuse w is bad

7. The lamp test bank lights when placed from point L to point N but does not light when placed from point M to point P.
   It should be concluded that

   A. both fuses x and y are bad
   B. either fuse x or fuse y is bad or both are bad
   C. both fuses x and y are good
   D. these tests do not indicate the condition of any fuse

8. The lamp test bank is placed from point L to point N, then from N to point Q, and finally from point L to point Q. In each case, both lamps light to full brightness.
   It should be concluded that points L, N, and Q have

   A. three-phase, 120 volts, AC, line-to-line
   B. plus and minus 120 volts, DC
   C. three-phase, 208 volts, AC
   D. plus and minus 240 volts, DC

9. An automatic device used for regulating air temperature is a(n)

   A. rheostat   B. aquastat   C. thermostat   D. duostat

10. Assume that you have just completed a certain maintenance job which you feel is satisfactory, but your foreman asks you to make certain changes.
    The BEST procedure for you to follow is to

    A. request the foreman to assign this work to someone else
    B. have another maintainer verify that the job was done properly
    C. ask the foreman the reasons for the changes
    D. complain to the foreman's superior of this waste of time

11. The PROPER set of tools and equipment to be used to clean and adjust the ignition points of an automobile consists of a

    A. screwdriver, feeler gauge, and point file
    B. wrench, micrometer, and sandpaper
    C. scraper, micrometer, and emery cloth
    D. V-block, pliers, and sandpaper

12. The voltage developed in each cell of an automobile battery is _____ volts.

    A. 2   B. 4   C. 6   D. 12

13. The one of the following tools that is NOT used to clear plumbing stoppages is a

    A. force-cup   B. drain auger
    C. snake   D. pick-out iron

14. Eyebolts are generally fastened to the shells of machinery in order to

    A. act as a leveling device
    B. facilitate lifting
    C. permit easy tagging of the equipment
    D. reinforce the machine shells

15. When grinding a weld smooth, it is MOST important to avoid

    A. grinding too slowly
    B. overheating the surrounding metal
    C. grinding away too much of the weld
    D. grinding after the weld has cooled off

16. A cold chisel whose head has become *mushroomed* should NOT be used because

    A. it is impossible to hit the head squarely
    B. the chisel will not cut accurately
    C. chips might fly from the head
    D. the chisel has lost its *temper*

17. The type of screwdriver specially made to be used in tight spots is the

    A. Phillips   B. offset
    C. square shank   D. truss

18. An indication that a fluorescent lamp in a fixture should be replaced is

    A. humming in the fixture
    B. the ends of the lamp remain black when the lamp is lit
    C. poor or slow starting
    D. the lamp does not shut off each time the OFF button is pressed

19. Asbestos is used as a covering on electrical wires to provide protection from

    A. high voltage
    B. high temperatures
    C. water damage
    D. electrolysis

20. Many electric power tools, such as drills, have a third conductor in the line cord which should be connected to a grounded part of the power receptacle.
    The reason for this is to

    A. have a spare wire in case one power wire should break
    B. strengthen the power lead so that it cannot be easily damaged
    C. protect the user of the tool from electrical shocks
    D. allow use of the tool for extended periods of time without overheating

21. Employees are responsible for the good care, proper maintenance, and serviceable condition of the property issued or assigned for their use.
    As used above, *serviceable condition* means the property is in a state where it is

    A. capable of being repaired
    B. easily handled
    C. fit for use
    D. least expensive

22. A brush that has been used in shellac should be cleaned by washing it in

    A. water
    B. linseed oil
    C. lacquer thinner
    D. alcohol

23. Excessive moisture on a surface being painted would MOST likely result in

    A. alligatoring
    B. blistering
    C. cracking
    D. sagging

24. In order to reverse the direction of rotation of a series motor, the

    A. connections to the armature should be reversed
    B. connections to both the armature and the series field should be reversed
    C. connections of the motor to the power lines should be reversed
    D. series field should be placed in shunt with the armature

25. A megger is an instrument used to measure

    A. capacitance
    B. insulation resistance
    C. power
    D. illumination levels

26. The first aid treatment for chemical burns on the skin is

    A. treatment with ointment and then bandaging
    B. washing with large quantities of water and then treating as heat burns
    C. treatment with a neutralizing agent and no bandaging
    D. application of sodium bicarbonate and then bandaging

27. The chemical MOST frequently used to clean drains clogged with grease is   27.____

    A. muriatic acid   B. soda ash
    C. ammonia   D. caustic soda

28. When tapping a blind hole in a steel plate, the FIRST type of tap to use is a _____ tap.   28.____

    A. plug   B. taper   C. lead   D. bottoming

29. A common handshaving tool used in woodwork is a(n)   29.____

    A. trammel   B. router   C. auger   D. plane

30. *Dressing* a grinding wheel refers to   30.____

    A. making the wheel thinner
    B. replacing with a new wheel
    C. repairing a crack in the wheel
    D. making the wheel round

31. The maintainer who is MOST valuable is the one who   31.____

    A. offers to do the heavy lifting
    B. asks many questions about the work
    C. listens to instructions and carries them out
    D. makes many suggestions on work procedures

32. Of the following, turpentine is used for thinning   32.____

    A. latex paint   B. red lead paint
    C. calcimine   D. shellac

33. Of the following, the hacksaw blade BEST suited for cutting thin-walled tubing is one which has _____ teeth/inch.   33.____

    A. 14   B. 18   C. 24   D. 32

34. Because of its weather-resistant properties, a varnish commonly used on exterior surfaces is _____ varnish.   34.____

    A. spar   B. flat   C. rubbing   D. hard oil

35. A trip spring or spring cylinder on a snow plow assembly is a device that   35.____

    A. absorbs the shock of impact when the plow strikes an obstacle in the road
    B. provides for snap-action in the lowering of the plow blade
    C. allows for quick removal or attachment of the snow plow supporting frame
    D. detaches the plow blade and lets it hang free when the plow blade is dragged backwards

36. The term *preventative maintenance* is used to identify a plan whereby   36.____

    A. equipment is serviced according to a regular schedule
    B. equipment is serviced as soon as it fails
    C. equipment is replaced as soon as it becomes obsolete
    D. all equipment is replaced periodically

37. The ratio of air to gasoline in an automobile engine is controlled by the

   A. gas filter
   B. fuel pump
   C. carburetor
   D. intake manifold

38. *Energizer* is another name given to the

   A. automobile battery
   B. fluorescent fixture ballast
   C. battery charger
   D. generator shunt field

39. Wearshoes may be found on

   A. circuit breakers
   B. automobile brake systems
   C. snow plows
   D. door sills

40. When moving heavy equipment by means of pipe rollers, it is MOST important to

   A. use solid steel rollers
   B. use rollers with different diameters
   C. see that the trailing roller does not slip out from under the equipment
   D. use more than three rollers at all times

41. The one of the following storage areas that is BEST for the storage of paint is one which is

   A. unheated and not ventilated
   B. cool and ventilated
   C. sunny and ventilated
   D. warm and not ventilated

42. The leverage that can be obtained with a wrench is determined mainly by the

   A. material of which the wrench is made
   B. gripping surface of the jaw
   C. length of the handle
   D. thickness of the wrench

43. A star drill is used to bore holes in

   A. steel   B. concrete   C. wood   D. sheet metal

44. The one of the following actions of a maintainer that is MOST likely to contribute to a good working relationship between him and his assistant is for him to

   A. observe the same rules of conduct that he expects his assistant to observe
   B. freely give advice on his assistant's personal problems
   C. always be frank and outspoken to his assistant in pointing out his faults
   D. expect his assistant to perform with equal efficiency on any job assigned

45. Three common types of windows are

   A. batten, casement, and awning
   B. batten, casement, and double-hung
   C. batten, double-hung, and awning
   D. casement, double-hung, and awning

46. A staircase has twelve risers, each 6 3/4" high. The TOTAL rise of the staircase is

    A. $6'2\frac{1}{4}"$ B. 6'9"   C. 7'0"   D. 7'3 3/4"

47. A twenty-foot straight ladder placed at an angle against a wall should be at a distance from the wall equal to _____ feet.

    A. 3   B. 5   C. 7   D. 9

48. Reflective sheeting traffic signs that have become dirty should be wiped with kerosene or gasoline FOLLOWED by a

    A. wiping with a soft cloth soaked in thin oil
    B. hand rub with very fine sandpaper
    C. wash with detergent and a rinse with water
    D. coating of shellac applied with a brush

49. A temporary wooden fence carrying red flags and built around an opening in a pavement to warn oncoming traffic is known as a

    A. batter board   B. bulkhead
    C. bollard   D. barricade

50. *Four-ply belted* is used to describe the construction of

    A. belt-drive pulleys
    B. auto tires
    C. electrical wiring insulation
    D. seat belts

KEY (CORRECT ANSWERS)

1. A	11. A	21. C	31. C	41. B
2. D	12. A	22. D	32. B	42. C
3. D	13. D	23. B	33. D	43. B
4. B	14. B	24. A	34. A	44. A
5. D	15. C	25. B	35. A	45. D
6. C	16. C	26. B	36. A	46. B
7. B	17. B	27. D	37. C	47. B
8. C	18. B	28. B	38. A	48. C
9. C	19. B	29. D	39. C	49. D
10. C	20. C	30. D	40. C	50. B

TEST 2

DIRECTIONS: Each question or incomplete statement is followed by several suggested answers or completions. Select the one that BEST answers the question or completes the statement. *PRINT THE LETTER OF THE CORRECT ANSWER IN THE SPACE AT THE RIGHT.*

1. An oil bath filter is MOST often used on a(n)
    - A. air compressor
    - B. auto engine
    - C. electric generator
    - D. steam boiler

2. A 3-ohm resistor placed across a 12-volt battery will dissipate _____ watts.
    - A. 3
    - B. 4
    - C. 12
    - D. 48

3. Instead of using fuses, modern electric wiring uses
    - A. quick switches
    - B. circuit breakers
    - C. fusible links
    - D. lag blocks

4. The MOST common combination of gases used for welding is
    - A. carbon dioxide and acetylene
    - B. nitrogen and hydrogen
    - C. oxygen and acetylene
    - D. oxygen and hydrogen

5. If a wheel has turned through an angle of 180, then it has made _____ revolution(s).
    - A. 1/4
    - B. 1/2
    - C. 1/8
    - D. 18

6. Sewer gas is prevented from backing up through a plumbing fixture by a
    - A. water trap
    - B. return elbow
    - C. check valve
    - D. float valve

7. Putty that is too stiff is made workable by adding
    - A. gasoline
    - B. linseed oil
    - C. water
    - D. lacquer thinner

8. A vertical wood member in the wall of a wood frame house is known as a
    - A. A stringer
    - B. ridge member
    - C. stud
    - D. header

9. A 10-to-1 step-down transformer has an input of 1 ampere at 120 volts AC. If the losses are negligible, the output of the transformer is _____ volts.
    - A. 1 ampere at 12
    - B. .1 ampere at 1200
    - C. 10 amperes at 12
    - D. 10 amperes at 120

10. An oscilloscope is an instrument used in
    - A. measuring noise levels
    - B. displaying waveforms of electrical signals
    - C. indicating the concentrations of pollutants in air
    - D. photographing high-speed events

11. Assume that a brake pedal of a truck goes to the floorboard when depressed. The one of the following that could cause this condition is

    A. a leak in the hydraulic lines
    B. a clogged hydraulic line
    C. scored drums
    D. glazed linings

12. The universal joints of an automobile are located on the

    A. suspension springs   B. steering linkages
    C. wheel cylinders   D. drive shaft

13. The MAIN purpose of a flexible coupling is to connect two shafts which are

    A. of different diameters   B. of different shapes
    C. not in exact alignment   D. of different material

14. When using a standard measuring micrometer, starting with a zero reading, one complete counterclockwise revolution of the sleeve will give a reading of _____ inch.

    A. .001   B. .010   C. .025   D. .250

15. If a nut is to be tightened to an exact specified value of inch-lbs., the wrench to use is a _____ wrench.

    A. spanner   B. box   C. lock-jaw   D. torque

16. Common permanent type anti-freezes for automobile cooling systems are MAINLY

    A. alcohol   B. methanol
    C. ethylene glycol   D. trychloroethylene

17. Plexiglas is also called

    A. mylar   B. lucite   C. isinglass   D. PVC

18. Long, curved lines are BEST cut in 1/4" plexiglas with a _____ saw.

    A. rip   B. jig   C. keyhole   D. coping

19. The specific gravity of storage battery cells can be measured with a(n)

    A. odometer   B. hydrometer C. ammeter   D. dwell meter

20. A nail set is a tool used for

    A. straightening bent nails
    B. measuring nail sizes
    C. cutting nails to specified size
    D. driving a nail head into wood

21. To cut a number of 2" x 4" lengths of wood accurately at an angle of 45°, it is BEST to use a

    A. protractor B. mitre-box   C. triangle   D. square

22. The type of fastener MOST commonly used when bolting to concrete uses a(n)
    A. expansion shield B. U-bolt
    C. toggle bolt   D. turnbuckle

23. When an automobile engine does not start on a damp day, the trouble is MOST likely in the _____ system.
    A. ignition   B. cooling   C. fuel   D. lubricating

24. The battery of an automobile is prevented from discharging back through the alternator by the blocking action of the
    A. commutator   B. diodes   C. brushes   D. slip rings

25. The master cylinder in an automobile is actuated by the
    A. steering column   B. brake pedal
    C. clutch plate   D. cam shaft

26. The FINEST sandpaper from among the following is No.
    A. 3   B. 1   C. 2/0   D. 6/0

27. A screw whose head is buried below the surface of the wood that it is screwed into is said to be
    A. countersunk   B. scalloped
    C. expanded   D. flushed

28. The one of the following devices which is used to measure angles is the
    A. caliper   B. protractor
    C. marking gauge   D. divider

29. Before a new oil stone is used, it should be
    A. heated   B. soaked in oil
    C. coated with shellac D. washed with soapy water

30. Dies are used for
    A. threading the outside ends of metal pipes
    B. making sweated joints on lead pipes
    C. cutting nipples to exact lengths
    D. caulking cast-iron pipe joints

31. The energy stored by a storage battery is commonly given in
    A. volts   B. amperes
    C. ampere-hours   D. kilowatts

32. *Vapor lock* occurs in automobile
    A. gas tanks   B. crankcases
    C. transmissions D. carburetors

33. A woodworking tool used to bore odd-size holes for which there is no standard auger bit is a(n)

    A. single twist auger
    B. double twist auger
    C. expansive bit
    D. straight fluted drill

34. Soap is sometimes applied to wood screws in order to

    A. prevent rust
    B. make a tight fit
    C. make insertion easier
    D. prevent wood splitting

35. On a long run of copper tubing, the tubing is often bent in the shape of a horseshoe rather than being run in a straight line.
    The MAIN reason for this is to

    A. allow an excess that could be used in future repairs
    B. make it easier to install the tubing
    C. permit the tubing to expand and contract with changes in temperature
    D. eliminate the need for accurate measurements in cutting the tubing

36. Loss of seal water in a house water trap is prevented by the use of a

    A. drainage tee
    B. faucet
    C. hose bibb
    D. vent

37. BX is a designation for a type of

    A. flexible armored electric cable
    B. flexible gas line
    C. rigid conduit
    D. electrical insulation

38. *WYE-WYE* and *DELTA-WYE* are two

    A. types of DC motor windings
    B. arrangements of 3-phase transformer connections
    C. types of electrical splices
    D. shapes of commutator bars

39. Green lumber should NOT be used in the building of scaffolding because it

    A. will not hold nails well
    B. easily splits when nailed
    C. may warp on drying
    D. is too expensive

40. *Scotchlite* ready-made traffic sign faces with heat-activated adhesive backings are applied to backing blanks by use of a

    A. temperature-controlled oven
    B. vacuum applicator
    C. hot water bath
    D. heated roller assembly

41. *Scotchcal* is a(n)

    A. reflective sheeting
    B. epoxy protective paint
    C. fluorescent film
    D. high temperature lubricant

42. Wooden ladders should NOT be painted because the paint

    A. is inflammable
    B. may cover defects in the wood
    C. makes the rungs slippery
    D. may deteriorate the wood

43. To prevent ladders from slipping, the bottoms of the ladder side rails are OFTEN fitted with

    A. automatic locks   B. ladder shoes
    C. ladder hooks   D. stirrups

44. A bowline is

    A. the sag that a scaffold develops when men get on it
    B. a knot with a loop that does not run
    C. a temporary telephone wire strung during emergencies
    D. the reference line established in ditch excavations

45. A method sometimes used to prevent a pipe from buckling during a bending operation is to

    A. bend the pipe very quickly
    B. keep the seam of the pipe on the outside of the bend
    C. nick the pipe at the center of the bend
    D. pack the inside of the pipe with sand

46. A rectifier changes

    A. DC to AC
    B. AC to DC
    C. single-phase power to three-phase power
    D. battery power to three-phase power

47. Continuity in a de-energized electrical circuit may be checked with a(n)

    A. voltmeter   B. ohmmeter   C. neon tester   D. rheostat

48. Of the following crankcase oils, the one that should be used in sub-zero weather is SAE

    A. 10W   B. 20W   C. 20   D. 30

49. Caster in an automobile is an adjustment in the

    A. ignition system   B. drive-shaft
    C. rear differential   D. front suspension

50. If the spark plugs in an engine run too hot, the result is MOST likely that

    A. oil and carbon compounds will accumulate on the insulators
    B. the electrodes will wear rapidly
    C. the timing will be retarded
    D. the ignition coil may become damaged

KEY (CORRECT ANSWERS)

1. B	11. A	21. B	31. C	41. C
2. B	12. D	22. A	32. D	42. B
3. B	13. C	23. A	33. C	43. B
4. C	14. C	24. B	34. C	44. B
5. B	15. D	25. B	35. C	45. D
6. A	16. C	26. D	36. D	46. B
7. B	17. B	27. A	37. A	47. B
8. C	18. B	28. B	38. B	48. A
9. C	19. B	29. B	39. C	49. D
10. B	20. D	30. A	40. B	50. B

EXAMINATION SECTION
TEST 1

DIRECTIONS: Each question or incomplete statement is followed by several suggested answers or completions. Select the one that BEST answers the question or completes the statement. *PRINT THE LETTER OF THE CORRECT ANSWER IN THE SPACE AT THE RIGHT.*

1. If a nichrome wire 2 meters long has a resistance of 10 ohms, the resistance of another nichrome wire 1 meter long and with a cross-sectional area half that of the longer wire is, in ohms,

    A. 5   B. 10   C. 20   D. 40

    1.____

2. Two nichrome wires of exactly the same composition have the same weight, but one is 5 times as long as the other. If the resistance of the shorter wire is R, the resistance of the other is

    A. R   B. 5R   C. 25R   D. 50R

    2.____

3. A magnet pole has a strength of 400 units.
    The magnetic field intensity in air due to this pole and at a distance 4 cm from this pole is _____ oersteds.

    A. 25   B. 50   C. 100   D. 25π

    3.____

4. The number of revolutions per minute that a 6-pole alternator must make to produce a frequency of 60 cycles/sec is

    A. 1080   B. 1200   C. 2160   D. 21,600

    4.____

5. A voltmeter having a full scale deflection of 10 volts has an internal resistance of 1000 ohms.
    To convert this instrument to a voltmeter having a full scale deflection of 300 volts requires, in ohms, a multiplier of

    A. 3000   B. 6000   C. 9000   D. 12,000

    5.____

6. Which one of the following scientists is NOT directly connected with the invention and development of the transistor?

    A. John Bardeen   B. William B. Shockley
    C. Polykarp Kusch   D. Walter H. Brattain

    6.____

7. If there is a current of 0.1 ampere through a lamp for 100 seconds, the number of coulombs passing through in that time is

    A. 0.1   B. 1   C. 10   D. 100

    7.____

8. If the core of an electromagnet is made of 2 pieces of iron, each running the full length of the electromagnet, when a direct current is sent through the coil, the 2 core pieces will

    A. attract each other
    B. repel each other
    C. attract and repel alternately
    D. have no effect on each other

    8.____

9. If a 25-watt, 120-volt lamp and a 100-watt, 12-volt lamp are connected in a series to a 120-volt source,

   A. both lamps light normally
   B. neither lamp lights
   C. the 100-watt lamp is brighter
   D. the 25-watt lamp is brighter

10. A 30-watt, 120-volt resistor is connected to a 120-volt, 60-cycle source. The maximum current flow in the lamp, in amperes, is APPROXIMATELY

    A. 0.18   B. 0.25   C. 0.35   D. 0.4

11. A 0-20 milliampere meter has a resistance of 20 ohms. To convert this meter to a voltmeter with a range of 0-10 volts, one should connect a resistance of APPROXIMATELY _____ ohms in _____.

    A. 200; series
    C. 500; series
    B. 200; parallel
    D. 500; parallel

12. The current flow through a galvanometer is 10^{-5} milliamperes and produces a deflection of 1 scale division. If the resistance of the moving coil is 200 ohms, the voltage across the coil, in volts, is

    A. 2×10^{-3} B. 5×10^{-10} C. 5×10^{-5} D. 2×10^{-6}

13. A capacitor using a dielectric whose coefficient is 5 has a capacitance of A. An identical capacitor using a dielectric whose coefficient is 20 will have a capacitance equal to

    A. 2A   B. 4A   C. 10A   D. 100A

14. When resonance occurs in a circuit supplied with an alternating voltage, the

    A. impedance equals zero
    B. inductance equals the reciprocal of the capacitance
    C. capacitance equals the inductance
    D. inductive reactance equals the capacitive reactance

15. An electric heating coil of 6 ohms resistance is connected across a 120-volt line for 10 minutes.
    The energy liberated, in joules, in this period of time equals

    A. 7.2×10^3
    C. 25.8×10^4
    B. 14.4×10^5
    D. 43.2×10^4

16. If a triode has its plate current increased 20 milliamperes when the plate voltage is increased from 50 to 90 volts and the plate current is also increased 20 milliamperes when the grid potential changes 4 volts, the amplification factor of the tube is

    A. 1.8   B. 5.0   C. 10.0   D. 40.0

17. A charge of 30 coulombs passes through a wire in 3 seconds. The current flow in this wire, in amperes, equals

    A. 3.3   B. 10   C. 30   D. 90

18. The heat developed by 5 amperes flowing through a resistance of 4 ohms is

    A. 20 calories
    B. 24 calories per second
    C. 100 calories
    D. 4.8 calories per degree

19. 1 e.s.u. of potential difference equals

    A. 1 volt
    B. 300 joules/coulomb
    C. 10^8 e.m.u. of potential
    D. 4.187 volts

20. Two electrical condensers having capacitances of 6 and 12 microfarads, respectively, are connected in series. The TOTAL capacitance, in microfarads, of this combination is

    A. 2   B. 4   C. 9   D. 18

21. The voltage induced in a coil with an inductance of 0.25 henries when the current decreased uniformly from 2 amperes to zero amperes in 1/16 second is

    A. 4   B. 8   C. 16   D. 24

22. A transformer placed on DC is LIKELY to burn out because of the absence of

    A. a fuse
    B. voltage regulation
    C. hysteresis
    D. inductive reactance

23. If the effective AC voltage of a given circuit is 100, the maximum voltage is CLOSEST to which one of the following?

    A. 0   B. 71   C. 141   D. 173

24. One milliampere produces full scale deflection in a galvanometer whose internal resistance is 50 ohms.
    To convert this instrument into an ammeter whose full scale deflection is 1 amp, it should be shunted with a resistance, in ohms, CLOSEST to which one of the following?

    A. 0.005   B. 0.05   C. 0.5   D. 5.0

25. The results of the Millikan oil drop experiment lead to the conclusion that

    A. electric charges are negative
    B. electric charges are due to a transfer of electrons
    C. there is a fundamental unit of charge
    D. there are no isolated magnetic poles

26. A 60-watt, 120-volt incandescent lamp has a resistance, in ohms, of

    A. 0.5   B. 2.0   C. 60   D. 240

27. A 0-5 amp ammeter reads full scale when its 2-ohm movable coil has a voltage of 0.01 applied across it.
    The shunt has a resistance, in ohms, CLOSEST to which one of the following?

    A. 0.001   B. 0.002   C. 250   D. 500

28. The heat in kilocalories (1 kilocalorie = 4200 joules) developed by a 60 watt lamp in one hour is APPROXIMATELY

    A. 36   B. 50   C. 60   D. 95

29. Assume that a circuit consisting of a coil and a capacitor is adjusted to give resonance. If some turns are removed from the coil, then resonance can be restored by

    A. increasing the frequency
    B. decreasing the capacitance
    C. decreasing the frequency
    D. decreasing the inductance

30. A series AC circuit contains a resistance of 40 ohms, an inductive reactance of 100 ohms, and a capacitive reactance of 70 ohms.
    The impedance of this circuit is, in ohms,

    A. 50   B. 110   C. 150   D. 210

31. A series AC circuit contains a 20-ohm resistance, a 40-ohm resistance, a 60-ohm inductive reactance, and an 80-ohm capacitive reactance.
    The GREATEST amount of heat per second produced by any of these will be produced by the

    A. 20-ohm resistance
    B. 40-ohm resistance
    C. 60-ohm reactance
    D. 80-ohm reactance

32. If a sheet of glass is slipped between the plates of an air capacitor, the capacitance of the combination

    A. drops to zero
    B. is reduced to approximately one-half of the original value
    C. increases
    D. has a value which depends on the charge of the capacitor

33. The resistance of a piece of wire is 16 ohms.
    The resistance, in ohms, of a piece of the same wire twice as long and twice the diameter is

    A. 8   B. 16   C. 32   D. 64

34. A circuit containing resistance, capacitance, and inductance is in resonance when supplied with an alternating current of a given frequency.
    An increase in the frequency of this current will

    A. decrease the inductive reactance
    B. increase the capacitive reactance
    C. increase the total current in the circuit
    D. decrease the impedance

35. The heat developed by a 5 ampere current flowing through a resistance of 4 ohms is

    A. 20 calories
    B. 24 calories/sec
    C. 100 calories
    D. 4.8 calories per degree

36. A capacitor stores 50 joules of energy when charged by a 5000 volt source.
    The capacitance of the capacitor, in microfarads, is

    A. .02   B. .04   C. 2.0   D. 4.0

37. The amplification factor of a triode is represented BEST by which one of the following expressions?
    The

    A. change in grid voltage divided by the change in filament voltage
    B. plate current
    C. change in plate voltage divided by the change in grid voltage needed to produce that change in plate current
    D. change in plate voltage divided by the change in plate current needed to produce that change in grid voltage

38. Kirchhoff's Laws with regard to the current in an electrical circuit states that

    A. current is directly proportional to voltage
    B. the algebraic sum of the currents at a junction equals zero
    C. current is inversely proportional to electrical resistance
    D. the total current in a parallel circuit equals the sum of the currents in the individual parallel branches

39. A Fleming valve or diode performs which one of the following functions?

    A. Converts rectified DC to AC
    B. Converts AC to half-wave rectified DC
    C. Converts AC to smooth DC
    D. Steps up low voltage AC to high voltage AC

40. A capacitor discharges at a certain frequency through a circuit containing an inductance. If the capacitance is multiplied by four, the oscillation frequency is multiplied by

    A. $\frac{1}{4}$ B. $\frac{1}{2}$ C. 2   D. 4

41. A coil of 100 turns is wound on an iron core. The coil is connected to an AC source. Suitable connections are made to display applied voltage and circuit current on an oscilloscope.
    It is found that the current _____ the voltage by _____.

    A. leads; 90°
    B. lags behind; 90°
    C. leads; an acute angle
    D. lags behind; an acute angle

42. The mixing of an audio frequency electric current with a radio frequency carrier in a broadcasting station is known as

    A. oscillation
    B. modulation
    C. amplification
    D. rectification

43. An electron is accelerated through a potential difference of 20,000 volts. Its gain in kinetic energy is 20,000

    A. volts
    B. joules
    C. electron volts
    D. ergs

44. The radius of the circular path of a charged particle moving at right angles to a uniform magnetic field is DIRECTLY proportional to the

   A. momentum of the particle
   B. flux density
   C. charge on the particle
   D. wavelength of its radiation

45. The direction of an induced current is always such that the magnetic field belonging to it tends to oppose the change in the strength of the magnetic field belonging to the primary current.
   This law was FIRST enunciated by

   A. Ampere   B. Faraday   C. Henry   D. Lenz

46. A split ring commutator will be found on a

   A. synchronous motor
   B. AC generator
   C. DC motor
   D. induction-repulsion type of motor

47. A ballistic galvanometer is used MAINLY to measure which one of the following?

   A. Electric charge   B. Electric current
   C. EMF   D. Resistance

48. If a calibrated oscilloscope shows a sinusoidal current having a peak to peak value of 2.0 amperes, the effective value of the current as measured by an ammeter and expressed in amperes would be

   A. 0.50   B. 0.71   C. 1.0   D. 2.0

49. Of the following, the pair of functions of a vacuum tube that are MOST closely allied are

   A. rectification and amplification
   B. oscillation and rectification
   C. amplification and detection
   D. detection and rectification

50. If a thin sheet of metal is placed halfway between the two plates of a parallel-plate, air-dielectric capacitor, the capacitance is

   A. quadrupled
   B. doubled
   C. decreased to 1/2 of the original value
   D. decreased to 1/4

KEY (CORRECT ANSWERS)

1. B	11. C	21. B	31. B	41. D
2. C	12. D	22. D	32. C	42. B
3. A	13. B	23. C	33. A	43. C
4. B	14. D	24. B	34. B	44. A
5. C	15. B	25. C	35. B	45. D
6. C	16. C	26. D	36. D	46. C
7. C	17. B	27. B	37. C	47. A
8. B	18. B	28. B	38. B	48. B
9. D	19. B	29. A	39. B	49. D
10. C	20. B	30. A	40. B	50. C

TEST 2

DIRECTIONS: Each question or incomplete statement is followed by several suggested answers or completions. Select the one that BEST answers the question or completes the statement. *PRINT THE LETTER OF THE CORRECT ANSWER IN THE SPACE AT THE RIGHT.*

1. If a 1 mfd capacitor and a 2 mfd capacitor are connected in series across a 120-volt source, the potential difference across the 1 mfd capacitor is _____ volts.

    A. 30 B. 40 C. 60 D. 80

    1.___

2. If a battery having an EMF of 6 volts and internal resistance of 0.6 ohms is supplying a current of 0.5 amperes, the terminal voltage is _____ volts.

    A. 5.4 B. 5.5 C. 5.6 D. 5.7

    2.___

3. A capacitor C and inductor L are connected in series across an AC source. As the value of C is increased, the current in the circuit

    A. increases
    B. decreases
    C. remains constant
    D. may increase or decrease

    3.___

4. As the frequency of a generator is decreased, the impedance of a circuit

    A. increases
    B. decreases
    C. may increase or decrease
    D. does not change

    4.___

5. It is desired to determine the direction of electron flow in a vertical conductor carrying direct current.
   This may be done with the aid of a compass placed

    A. to the right of the wire
    B. to the left of the wire
    C. behind the wire
    D. in any of the above listed positions

    5.___

6. If the current flow in a circular coil consisting of a single turn of wire of 1 cm radius is 2 abamperes, it will produce a magnetic field intensity at the center of the coil equal, in oersteds, to

    A. π B. 2π C. 4π D. 8π

    6.___

7. Ampere's Law is concerned with

    A. the force on a wire carrying a current in a magnetic field
    B. electrochemical equivalents
    C. rms values
    D. unit magnetic poles

    7.___

8. A 60-watt, 120-volt and a 40-watt, 120-volt lamp are joined in series and connected to a 120-volt line.
   The current flow in the circuit, in amperes, is

    A. more than 0.5
    B. between 0.5 and 0.3
    C. 0.2
    D. less than 0.2

    8.___

132

9. The function of the grid in a three element vacuum tube is to

   A. aid electron flow at reduced cathode temperatures
   B. reduce the loss of heat from the cathode
   C. prevent secondary emission of electrons from the plate
   D. control the electron flow to the plate

10. Three capacitors of 4 mfd, 10 mfd, and 20 mfd are connected in parallel. The equivalent capacitance of this group equals, in mfd,

    A. 2.5   B. 17   C. 34   D. 800

11. Two 60-watt, 120-volt heaters are connected in series on a 120-volt DC line. The power consumption is now X times as great as it would be if they were connected in parallel. Assuming no change in resistance, X would be

    A. 1/4   B. 1/2   C. 2   D. 4

12. The current in an alternating current circuit is equal to the voltage divided by the

    A. impedance   B. capacitance
    C. reluctance   D. inductance

13. The core of a transformer is laminated largely for the purpose of

    A. reducing eddy currents
    B. aiding in heat dissipation
    C. increasing self-inductance
    D. increasing impedance

14. Kirchhoff's First Law is really a restatement of

    A. Lenz' Law
    B. Ohm's Law
    C. Faraday's Law of Electrolysis
    D. Law of Conservation of Energy

15. A condenser designed for use across a 220-volt AC line should have a peak inverse voltage rating of AT LEAST _____ volts.

    A. 110   B. 220   C. 250   D. 325

16. The voltage between the cathode and target of an x-ray tube is V volts. If e is the charge on the electron in e.s.u., then Ve has the dimensions of

    A. work   B. current   C. force   D. momentum

17. A transformer with 50 turns on the primary and 100 turns on the secondary is connected to a 6-volt battery.
    The voltage on the secondary will be

    A. zero
    B. equal to that on the primary
    C. twice the voltage on the primary
    D. half the voltage on the primary

18. When a 60 cycle source of e.m.f. is connected between the plate and the cathode of a diode, the current between the cathode and plate will

   A. reverse 60 times per second
   B. reverse 120 times per second
   C. flow continuously
   D. flow intermittently in the same direction

19. Inside a dry cell that is delivering current,

   A. electrons flow from + to -
   B. there is no resistance
   C. there is no current
   D. electrons flow from - to +

20. In a circuit containing an alternating source and a coil, increasing both the frequency of the source and the inductance of the coil (without changing the e.m.f.) will result in

   A. increased current
   B. decreased current
   C. same current
   D. increased or decreased current, depending on which factor is increased more

21. If the plate current of a triode electronic tube increases 10 milliamperes when the plate voltage is increased from 60 to 80 volts or when the grid potential changes 2 volts, the amplification factor of the tube is

   A. 5   B. 10   C. 20   D. 40

22. A series circuit with a capacitive reactance of 20 ohms, an inductive reactance of 50 ohms, and a resistance of 40 ohms has an overall impedance, in ohms, of

   A. 10   B. 50   C. 70   D. 110

23. Waves of 3 cm in length radiated by an electronic oscillator would have a frequency, in cycles/sec, of

   A. 10^6 B. 10^8 C. 10^{10} D. 10^{12}

24. If a student, in finding the resistance of a lamp on a 120-volt line, places the voltmeter in series with the lamp and the ammeter in parallel with the lamp, the

   A. ammeter will burn out
   B. voltmeter will burn out
   C. lamp will burn out
   D. lamp may not light

25. If a 120-volt, 60-cycle source is connected to a circuit containing resistance, inductive reactance, and capacitive reactance, each of 16 ohms, the current in the circuit is _____ amperes.

   A. 5   B. 7.5   C. 15   D. 30

26. If a nail is attracted to an electromagnet carrying direct current, and the current is quickly reversed, the nail will

   A. fall to the ground
   B. be repelled by the electromagnet
   C. heat up
   D. still be attracted

27. The volt is NOT a unit of

   A. charge per unit time
   B. e.m.f.
   C. work per unit charge
   D. potential difference

28. The energy used to carry unit charge around an electrical circuit is measured by the

   A. current
   B. potential difference
   C. power
   D. resistance of the circuit

29. Two 1 mfd capacitors are connected in parallel and the combination is then charged. If the capacitance, charge, and potential of each capacitor are C, Q, and V, respectively, the corresponding three values for the combination is which one of the following?

   A. C/2, 2Q, V
   B. 2C, 2Q, V
   C. 2C, Q, V
   D. 2C, 2Q, V/2

30. The resonant frequency f of an alternating e.m.f. in a circuit containing in series an inductance L, a capacitance C, and a resistance R, is given by the formula f =

   A. $2\pi\sqrt{LC}$
   B. $\frac{1}{2}\pi\sqrt{LC}$
   C. $\frac{1}{2\pi\sqrt{LC}}$
   D. $\frac{R}{2\pi\sqrt{LC}}$

31. In a series resonant circuit, the circuit impedance is ALWAYS

   A. equal to the inductive reactance
   B. greater than the capacitive reactance
   C. equal to the capacitive reactance
   D. equal to the resistance

32. Two resistances of 30 ohms and 20 ohms, respectively, are joined in parallel in an electric circuit.
The equivalent resistance, in ohms, of this parallel pair is

   A. 12   B. 25   C. 50   D. 600

33. A solenoid has an inductance of 0.32 henry.
Its reactance, in ohms, to an alternating current having a frequency of 1000 cycles/sec is

   A. 2010   B. 3125   C. 3200   D. 3310

34. If, with an impressed voltage of 240 volts and a current of 13 amp, a shunt-wound DC motor delivers 4 horsepower, its efficiency, in percent, is

   A. 80   B. 86   C. 90   D. 96

35. If the maximum value of an alternating voltage is 110, its value, in volts, at the 30° phase is

    A. 55   B. 78   C. 155   D. 220

36. A coil of 2.5 henries inductance would resonate with a 1 microfarad capacitance at a frequency, in cycles/sec, of

    A. 100   B. 1,000   C. 10,000   D. 100,000

37. When an alternating emf is supplied to a circuit consisting, in addition to the source, of wiring a 40 watt lamp and an 80 mf capacitor, the voltage in the circuit

    A. leads to current
    B. lags behind the current
    C. is in phase with the current
    D. becomes and remains zero after a few minutes

38. Of the following, the one which is incorporated in a DC generator but NOT in an AC generator is the

    A. slip rings   B. commutator
    C. series field   D. permanent magnets

39. When a capacitor C, an inductance L, and a resistance R are joined in series and an alternating emf is supplied to the circuit, the resonant frequency of this circuit can be decreased by doing which one of the following?

    A. Increasing L   B. Decreasing R
    C. Decreasing C   D. Decreasing L

40. Three 6 mfd capacitors are connected in parallel across a 120-volt AC line. The equivalent capacitance, in mfd, of this circuit is

    A. 2   B. 6   C. 18   D. 20

41. Assume that two capacitors, one of 3 microfarad capacitance and the other of 6 microfarad capacitance, are connected in series and charged to a difference of potential of 120 volts.
    The potential difference, in volts, across the 3 microfarad capacitor is

    A. 40   B. 80   C. 180   D. 360

42. Three resistors are connected to form the sides of a triangle ABC. The resistance of side AB is 40 ohms, of side BC 60 ohms, and of side CA 100 ohms.
    The effective resistance between points A and B, in ohms, is

    A. 32   B. 50   C. 64   D. 200

43. When a current of 2 amperes flows through a conductor of 2 ohms resistance for 3 seconds, the heat produced, in joules, is

    A. 12   B. 24   C. 36   D. 72

44. A length of wire, diameter 2 mils, has a resistance of 6 ohms. The same length of wire of the same material having a diameter of 4 mils has a resistance, in ohms, of

    A. 1.5   B. 3   C. 12   D. 24

45. The generalization that the algebraic sum of the currents at a junction in a circuit equals zero was postulated by

    A. Ohm   B. Kirchhoff   C. Onnes   D. Seebeck

46. It is desired to charge an electroscope negatively by induction. One of the steps that must be performed is to

    A. use a negatively charged rod
    B. remove positive charges
    C. remove electrons
    D. ground the electroscope

47. A series AC circuit contains an inductance L, a capacitance C, and a resistor R. The impedance of this circuit equals

    A. $R^2 + X_L + X_C$
    B. $\sqrt{R^2 + (X_L - X_C)^2}$
    C. $R^2 + \sqrt{X_L - X_C}$
    D. $R^2 - X_L - X^2_C$

48. In a selenium rectifier, current flow practically ceases when the

    A. selenium becomes negative
    B. selenium becomes positive
    C. accompanying alloy becomes negative
    D. applied voltage exceeds the critical value

49. An alternating current generator having 4 poles rotates at 60 revolutions per second. The frequency of the current produced, in cycles per second, is

    A. 60   B. 15   C. 120   D. 240

50. If an AC circuit contains resistance only, then current

    A. and voltage are in phase
    B. lags by 45°
    C. leads by 90°
    D. lags by 45° and voltage leads by 45°

KEY (CORRECT ANSWERS)

1. D	11. A	21. B	31. D	41. B
2. D	12. A	22. B	32. A	42. A
3. D	13. A	23. C	33. A	43. B
4. C	14. D	24. D	34. D	44. A
5. D	15. D	25. B	35. A	45. B
6. C	16. A	26. D	36. A	46. D
7. A	17. A	27. A	37. B	47. B
8. C	18. D	28. B	38. B	48. A
9. D	19. A	29. B	39. A	49. C
10. C	20. B	30. C	40. C	50. A

EXAMINATION SECTION
TEST 1

DIRECTIONS: Each question or incomplete statement is followed by several suggested answers or completions. Select the one that BEST answers the question or completes the statement. *PRINT THE LETTER OF THE CORRECT ANSWER IN THE SPACE AT THE RIGHT.*

1. Which of the following capacitors could be damaged by a reversal in polarity? A(n) _____ capacitor.
    A. ceramic
    B. paper
    C. mica
    D. electrolytic
    E. vacuum

2. If the current through a resistor is 6 amperes and the voltage drop across it is 100 volts, what is the approximate value of the resistor in ohm(s)?
    A. 1660   B. 166   C. 16.6   D. 1.66   E. 0.0166

3. What is the CORRECT use for an arbor press?
    A. Bending sheet metal
    B. Driving self-tapping screws
    C. Removing screws
    D. Removing "C" rings
    E. Removing bearings from shafts

4. Which one of the following is a tensioning device in bulk-belt-type conveyor systems? _____ take-up.
    A. Spring
    B. Power
    C. Hydraulic
    D. Fluid coupled
    E. Flexible coupled

5. When $X_L = X_C$ in a series circuit, what condition exists?
    A. The circuit impedance is increasing
    B. The circuit is at resonant frequency
    C. The circuit current is minimum
    D. The circuit has no e.m.f. at this time
    E. None of the above

6. Which of the following pieces of information is NOT normally found on a schematic diagram?
    A. Functional stage name
    B. Supply voltages
    C. Part symbols
    D. Part values
    E. Physical location of parts

7. When a single-phase induction motor drawing 24 amps at 120 VAC is reconnected to 240 VAC, what will be the amperage at 240 VAC? _____ amps.
    A. 6   B. 8   C. 12   D. 24   E. 36

8. Which one of the following meters measures the SMALLEST current?   8._____

   A. Kilometer B. Milliammeter C. Microvoltmeter
   D. Millivoltmeter E. Kilovoltmeter

9. If the current through a 1000-ohm resistor is 3 milliamperes, the voltage drop across the resistor is _____ volt(s).   9._____

   A. 1 B. 2.5 C. 3 D. 30 E. 300

10. The normally closed contacts of a relay are open when its solenoid is energized with VDC. The voltage at which the contacts re-close will be   10._____

    A. dependent upon the current through the contacts
    B. dependent upon the voltage applied to the contacts
    C. 24 VDC through the coil
    D. more than 24 VDC through the contacts
    E. less than 24 VDC through the coil

11. Electrical energy is converted to mechanical rotation by what component in the electric motor?   11._____

    A. Armature B. Commutator C. Field
    D. Start windings E. Stator

12. Ohm's Law expresses the basic relationship of   12._____

    A. current, voltage, and resistance
    B. current, voltage, and power
    C. current, power, and resistance
    D. resistance, impedance, and voltage
    E. resistance, power, and impedance

13. In parallel circuits, the voltage is *always*   13._____

    A. variable B. constant C. alternating
    D. fluctuating E. sporadic

14. Which one of the following is used as a voltage divider?   14._____

    A. Rotary converter B. Potentiometer C. Relay
    D. Circuit breaker E. Voltmeter

Question 15.

Question 15 is based on the following diagram.

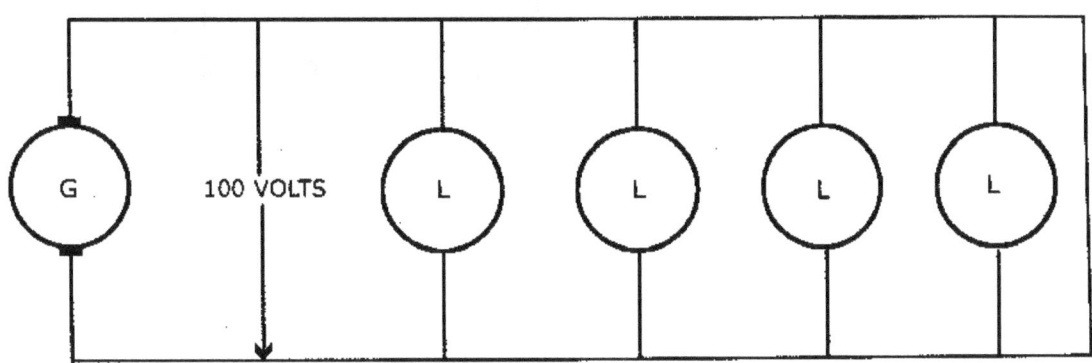

CURRENT IN EACH LAMP 1/2 AMPERE

15. What is the resistance of the entire circuit? _____ ohms. 15.____
    A. 15   B. 25   C. 35   D. 45   E. 50

16. Which one of the following tools is used to bring a bore to a specified tolerance? 16.____
    A. Tap   B. Reamer   C. Countersink
    D. Counterbore   E. Center drill

17. The primary function of a take-up pulley in a belt conveyor is to 17.____
    A. carry the belt on the return trip
    B. track the belt
    C. maintain the proper belt tension
    D. change the direction of the belt
    E. regulate the speed of the belt

Question 18.

Question 18 is based on the following diagram.

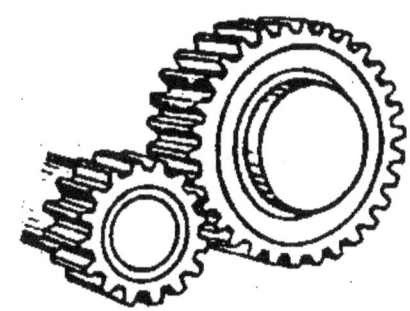

18. What is the name of the gears? 18.____
    A. Spur external   B. Spur internal   C. Helical
    D. Herringbone   D. Worm

Question 19.

Question 19 is based on the following diagram.

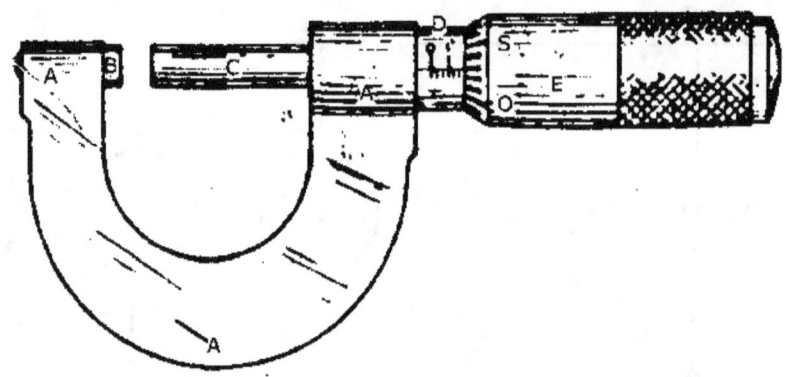

19. The part labeled D is the

    A. sleeve   B. thimble   C. frame
    D. anvil   E. pindle

19.____

Question 20.

Question 20 is based on the following symbol.

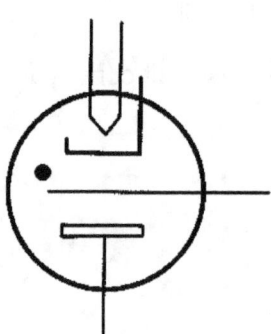

20. This symbol represents a _____ tube.

    A. thyratron vacuum   B. thyratron gas
    C. variable-mu vacuum   D. variable-mu gas
    E. vacuum photo

20.____

21. A diode can be substituted for which one of the following?

    A. Transformer   B. Relay   C. Rectifier
    D. Condenser   E. Rheostat

21.____

Question 22.

Question 22 is based on the following diagram.

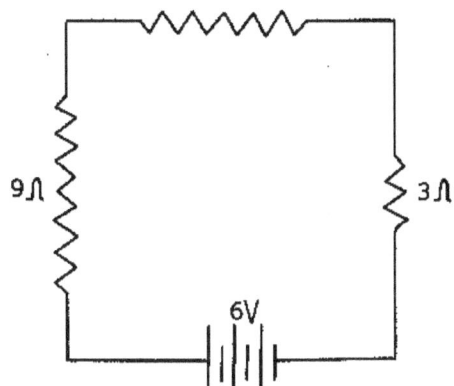

22. The rate of amperes flowing in the circuit is: 22._____

    A. .03 1/3   B. .18   C. .24
    D. .30 1/3   E. .33 1/3

23. The firing point in a thyratron tube is *most usually* controlled by the   23._____

    A. cathode   B. grid   C. plate
    D. heater   E. envelope

Questions 24-25.

Questions 24 and 25 shall be answered in accordance with the diagram below.

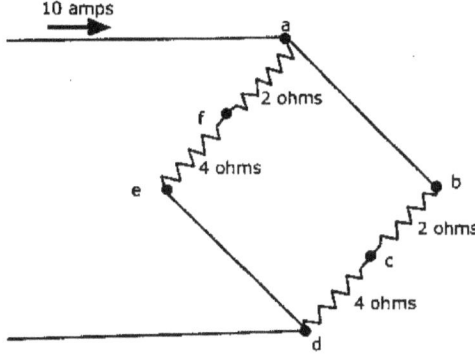

24. With reference to the above diagram, the voltage difference between points c and f is, *most nearly*, in volts,   24._____

    A. 40   B. 20   C. 10   D. 5   E. 0

25. With reference to the above diagram, the current flowing through the resistance c d is, *most nearly*, in amperes,   25._____

    A. 10   B. 5   C. 4   D. 2   E. 1

KEY (CORRECT ANSWERS)

1. D	6. E	11. A	16. B	21. C
2. C	7. C	12. A	17. C	22. E
3. E	8. B	13. B	18. A	23. B
4. A	9. C	14. B	19. A	24. E
5. B	10. E	15. E	20. B	25. B

EXAMINATION SECTION
TEST 1

DIRECTIONS: Each question or incomplete statement is followed by several suggested answers or completions. Select the one that BEST answers the question or completes the statement. *PRINT THE LETTER OF THE CORRECT ANSWER IN THE SPACE AT THE RIGHT.*

1. Two gears are meshed. The first gear has 20 teeth per inch and is rotating at 500 rpms. What is the speed of the second gear if it has 40 teeth per inch? _____ rpms. 1.____

   A. 500　　　B. 400　　　C. 250　　　D. 200

2. With two meshed gears, the first gear rotates at 100 rpms, the second gear rotates at 2000 rpms and has 10 teeth per inch.
   The first gear has _____ number of teeth per inch. 2.____

   A. 200　　　B. 100　　　C. 50　　　D. 150

3. Two pulleys are connected. The first pulley has a diameter of 5 inches; the second pulley has a diameter of 15 inches and rotates at 25 rpms.
   The speed of the first pulley is _____ rpms. 3.____

   A. 30　　　B. 75　　　C. 200　　　D. 400

4. Of two connected pulleys, the first has a radius of 10 inches and rotates at 50 rpms; the second rotates at 25 rpms.
   The diameter of the second pulley is _____ inches. 4.____

   A. 40　　　B. 30　　　C. 20　　　D. 10

5. Two pulleys are connected. The first pulley rotates at 75 rpms; the second pulley rotates at 100 rpms and has a diameter of 9 inches.
   The diameter of the first pulley is _____ inches. 5.____

   A. 10　　　B. 12　　　C. 15　　　D. 20

6. Of two connected pulleys, the first pulley has a radius of 12 inches and rotates at 60 rpms; the second pulley has a diameter of 16 inches.
   The speed of the second pulley is _____ rpms. 6.____

   A. 1000　　　B. 1020　　　C. 1040　　　D. 1080

7. If 16_{10} were converted to base 2, 8, and 16, the results would be _____ base 2, _____ base 8, and _____ base 16, respectively. 7.____

   A. 10000; 20; 10　　　　　B. 1000; 2000; 20
   C. 20000; 200; 20　　　　D. 2000; 100; 10

8. Converting CAF_{16} to base 10 and base 8, the results would be _____ base 10 and _____ base 8, respectively. 8.____

   A. 2437; 2567　　　　　B. 3247; 6257
   C. 4327; 5267　　　　　D. 3427; 2657

9. Converting 101011001_2 to base 8, 10, and 16, the results would be _____ base 8, _____ base 10, and _____ base 16, respectively.

   A. 135; 45; 59
   B. 567; 435; 259
   C. 315; 245; 135
   D. 531; 345; 159

10. If 136_8 were converted to base 2, 10, and 16, the results would be _____ base 2, _____ base 10, and _____ base 16, respectively.

    A. 001011110; 94, 5E
    B. 010100110; 92; 10E
    C. 00100000; 90; 15E
    D. 011001110; 96; 20E

11. It may be correctly stated that 1000 picofarads are equal to _____ microfarads.

    A. .0001   B. .001   C. .01   D. .1

12. If 5 megohms were converted to kohms, the result would be _____ kohms.

    A. 1000   B. 2000   C. 4000   D. 5000

13. 1 nanohenry would convert to _____ millihenries.

    A. .001   B. .0001   C. .00001   D. .0000001

14. If 7 milliamps were converted to microamps, the answer would be _____ microamps.

    A. 7000   B. 700   C. 70   D. 7

15. If two resistors are in parallel and are 100 ohms each, the total resistance is

    A. 100   B. 150   C. 50   D. 10

16. In reference to the circuit in Question 15, if the first resistor has 25 volts DC, (VDC) across it, the second resistor also has 25 VDC across it, and there are no other components in the circuit except for the power source, the total circuit voltage is _____ VDC.

    A. 25   B. 50   C. 250   D. 500

17. In reference to the circuit in Question 15, if the first resistor has 1 amp on it, and the second resistor also has 1 amp on it, the total circuit amperage is _____ amps.

    A. 1   B. 2   C. 3   D. 4

18. If two resistors are in series and are 100 ohms each, the total resistance is

    A. 50   B. 100   C. 150   D. 200

19. In reference to the circuit in Question 18, if the first resistor has 25 VDC across it and the second resistor also has 25 VDC across it, the total circuit voltage is

    A. 50   B. 100   C. 200   D. 500

20. In reference to the circuit in Question 18, if the first resistor has 1 amp across it and the second resistor also has 1 amp on it, the total circuit amperage is

    A. 1   B. 5   C. 10   D. 15

21. Where two resistors are in parallel, one is 100 ohms and the other is 300 ohms. The total resistance is _____ ohms.

    A. 25 B. 35 C. 55 D. 75

22. Three resistors in series are 25 ohms, 50 ohms, and 75 ohms, respectively. The total resistance is _____ ohms.

    A. 25 B. 50 C. 100 D. 150

23. Two inductors are in parallel; the first is 50 henries and the second is also 50 henries. The total inductance is _____ henries.

    A. 25 B. 50 C. 55 D. 60

24. Two inductors are in series and the first is 50 henries; the second is 50 henries. The total inductance is _____ henries.

    A. 25 B. 50 C. 75 D. 100

25. Where two inductors are in parallel, the first is 100 henries and the second is 200 henries. The total inductance is _____ henries.

    A. 50 B. 75 C. 65 D. 100

KEY (CORRECT ANSWERS)

1. C	6. D	11. B	16. A	21. D
2. A	7. A	12. D	17. B	22. D
3. B	8. B	13. D	18. D	23. A
4. A	9. D	14. A	19. A	24. D
5. B	10. A	15. C	20. A	25. B

TEST 2

DIRECTIONS: Each question or incomplete statement is followed by several suggested answers or completions. Select the one that BEST answers the question or completes the statement. *PRINT THE LETTER OF THE CORRECT ANSWER IN THE SPACE AT THE RIGHT.*

1. Two inductors are in series; the first inductor is 100 henries and the second is 200 henries.
   The total inductance is _____ henries.

   A. 200 B. 300 C. 400 D. 500

2. Two capacitors are in parallel; each capacitor is 30 farads.
   The total capacitance is _____ farads.

   A. 60 B. 80 C. 100 D. 200

3. Two capacitors are in series; each capacitor is 30 farads. The total capacitance is _____ farads.

   A. 10 B. 15 C. 20 D. 25

4. Two capacitors are in parallel; the first is 50 farads and the second is 100 farads.
   The total capacitance is _____ farads.

   A. 50 B. 100 C. 125 D. 150

5. Two capacitors are in series; the first is 50 farads and the second is 100 farads.
   The total capacitance is _____ farads.

   A. 33.333 B. 49.999 C. 13.333 D. 25.555

6. A resistor's color codes are orange, blue, yellow, and gold, in that order.
   The value of the resistor is _____ kohms ± _____ %.

   A. 200; 2 B. 300; 4 C. 360; 5 D. 400; 7

7. If a resistors color codes are red, black, and blue, the value of this resistor is _____ megohms ± _____ %.

   A. 20; 20 B. 40; 80 C. 30; 30 D. 50; 50

8. If a resistor's color codes are gray, green, black, and silver, the resistor's value is _____ ohms ± _____ %.

   A. 55; 5 B. 75; 15 C. 85; 10 D. 100; 25

9. One complete cycle of a sinewave takes 1000 microseconds. Its frequency is _____ hertz.

   A. 500 B. 1000 C. 2000 D. 5000

10. If one complete cycle of a squarewave takes 5 microseconds, its frequency is _____ khertz.

    A. 200 B. 500 C. 700 D. 1000

11. What is the PRT (pulse repetition time) of a 50 hertz (hz) sinewave? _____ milliseconds.   11._____

    A. 10   B. 20   C. 40   D. 60

12. The PRT of a 20 khz sawtooth signal is _____ megahertz.   12._____

    A. 50   B. 100   C. 200   D. 500

13. If a resistor measures 10 volts and 2 amps across it, the resistance is _____ ohms.   13._____

    A. 0   B. 2   C. 5   D. 10

14. If a 30 ohm resistor measures 10 volts, the power consumed by the resistor is _____ watts.   14._____

    A. 3000   B. 5000   C. 6500   D. 7000

15. If a 50 ohm resistor measures 4 amps across, the power consumed by it is _____ watts.   15._____

    A. 200   B. 400   C. 600   D. 800

16. If a 100 ohm resistor measures 25 volts across, the current on it is _____ amps.   16._____

    A. .15   B. .25   C. .55   D. .65

Questions 17-23.

DIRECTIONS: Questions 17 through 23 are to be answered on the basis of the following diagram.

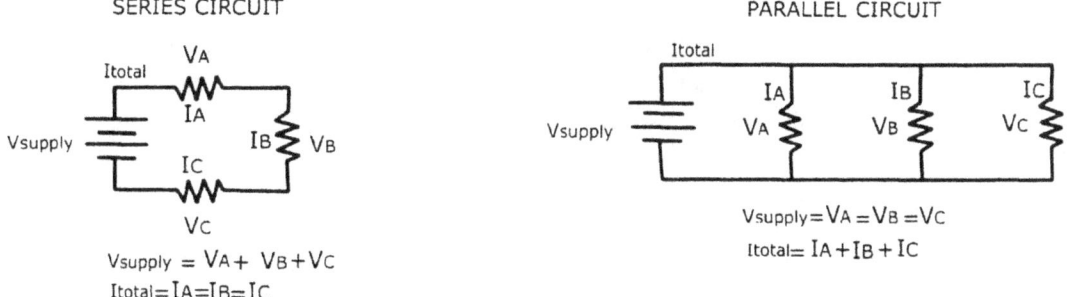

17. In the series circuit above, if Vsupply = 100 VDC, resistor A is 10 ohms, resistor B is 50 ohms, and resistor C is 5 ohms, the total circuit current is _____ amps.   17._____

    A. 1.538   B. 1.267   C. 1.358   D. 1.823

18. In the series circuit shown above, the current across each individual resistor is _____ amps.   18._____

    A. .5   B. 1.5   C. 2.5   D. 3.5

19. In the series circuit shown above, the total power drawn by the circuit is _____ watts. 19.___

   A. 140.25   B. 150.75   C. 153.38   D. 173.38

20. In the series circuit shown above, the power drawn from each individual resistor is _____, _____, and _____ watts, respectively. 20.___

   A. 23.65; 118.27; 11.827
   B. 17.567; 123.27; 11.27
   C. 18.627; 145.27; 12.27
   D. 21.735; 116.87; 11.83

21. In the parallel circuit shown above, if Vsupply = 100 VDC, resistor A is 10 ohms, resistor B is 50 ohms, and resistor C is 5 ohms, the total circuit current is _____ amps. 21.___

   A. 21   B. 27   C. 32   D. 45

22. In the parallel circuit shown above, the total power drawn by the circuit is _____ watts. 22.___

   A. 1200   B. 2300   C. 2700   D. 3200

23. In the parallel circuit above, the power drawn by each individual resistor is _____ watts, respectively. 23.___

   A. 100; 200; 2000
   B. 200; 400; 5000
   C. 300; 500; 750
   D. 450; 600; 1500

24. On an 0-scope display, one cycle of a signal takes up 4 1/2 divisions and the peak-to-peak amplitude of the signal takes up 3 3/4 divisions.
   With the volts/division knob set on 5 volts and the time/division knob set to 5 microseconds, the peak-to-peak amplitude and the frequency of the signal are _____ volts and _____ khz, respectively. 24.___

   A. 15.75; 100
   B. 22.5; 200
   C. 37.5; 350
   D. 45.75; 570

25. If a signal that has a peak-to-peak amplitude of 15 volts and a frequency of 5 megaherz is to be observed on an 0-scope with one complete cycle shown, the time/division knob and volts/division knob should be set on _____ microseconds and _____ volts per division, respectively. 25.___

   A. .02; 2   B. .05; 4   C. .07; 3.5   D. 10; 7.5

KEY (CORRECT ANSWERS)

1. B	6. C	11. B	16. B	21. C
2. A	7. A	12. A	17. A	22. D
3. B	8. C	13. C	18. B	23. A
4. D	9. B	14. A	19. C	24. B
5. A	10. A	15. D	20. A	25. A

EXAMINATION SECTION
TEST 1

DIRECTIONS: Each question or incomplete statement is followed by several suggested answers or completions. Select the one that BEST answers the question or completes the statement. *PRINT THE LETTER OF THE CORRECT ANSWER IN THE SPACE AT THE RIGHT.*

1. The gray code minimizes the possibility of ambiguity when changing state by:
    A. Changing state on leading or trailing pulse edges.
    B. Using a common clock to synchronize inputs.
    C. Changing only one bit at a time.
    D. Requiring coincidence between two or more samples.

2. Convert the decimal number 164 to hex.
    A. 104.   B. A4.   C. 10110100.   D. 5B.

3. A computer memory location is designated FO9Fh. The decimal equivalent is:
    A. 4367.   B. 1010101.   C. 10110100.   D. 61599.

4. Which of the following items is not an ASCII item?
    A. 8.   B. BS.   C. END.   D. A.

5. If the input lead to an operating TTL inverter became grounded, what would the output lead measure?
    A. +0 to +0.7 VDC.
    B. Ground.
    C. More than +5 VDC.
    D. Between +2.5 VDC and + 5VDC depending on load.

6. What is the range of supply voltage (VDD) to a CMOS logic IC?
    A. +4.5 to +5.5 VDC.   C. +5 to +25 VDC.
    B. -3 VDC to +10 VDC.   D. + 3 VDC to +15 VDC.

7. Using positive logic, a TTL IC will recognize the following voltages levels as valid "1" and "0" levels in an operational logic circuit:
    A. Binary 0 = +0.4 VDC, Binary 1 = +3.6 VDC.
    B. Binary 0 = 0.0 VDC, Binary 1 = +5.0 VDC.
    C. Binary 0 = +0.3 VDC, Binary 1 = +4.7 VDC.
    D. All of these.

8. If the output of a TTL gate measures 2.0VDC:
    A. There is a problem either in the gate or the loading.
    B. This is a normal high.
    C. This is a normal low.
    D. None of these.

9. A digital logic chip has a supply voltage of -5.2V. This chip belongs to which family?
    A. ECL   B. TTL   C. CMOS   D. RTL

10. Which of the following integrated circuit or semiconductors devices normally require special handling to avoid damage by static electricity?
    A. TTL   B. ECL   C. MOV   D. CMOS

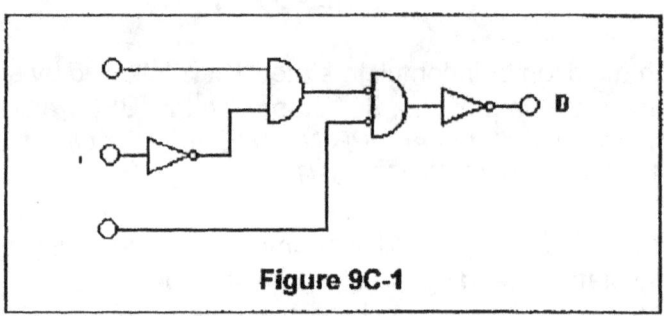

Figure 9C-1

11. On Figure 9C-1, the function D is described as:
    A. AB (-C).   B. C + (-A) B.   C. C + AB.   D. A + BC.

12. ECL achieves high speed due to:
    A. The use of gallium arsenide conductors.
    B. Construction in small geometries.
    C. The operating transistors being unsaturated.
    D. Operation in low noise negative supply region.

13. By DeMorgan's Theorem, (X + Y) =
    A. -X + -Y   B. (X + Y)   C. -(X + Y)   D. X Y

14. The logic family which typically has the largest fanout is:
    A. CMOS.   B. ECL.   C. TTL.   D. RTL.

15. In order of highest to lowest speed, the logic families are ranked:
    A. ECL, CMOS, Schottky TTL, Standard TTL.
    B. Schottky, Standard TTL, ECL, CMOS.
    C. CMOS, Standard TTL, Schottky TTL, ECL.
    D. ECL, Schottky TTL, Standard TTL, CMOS.

16. In a three bit binary ripple counter, the state following 111 will be:
    A. 110.   B. 000.   C. 001.   D. 111.

17. In a 4 bit BCD ripple counter the state following 1001 will be:
    A. 1111.   B. 1011.   C. 0000.   D. 1000.

18. Synchronous counters are distinguished from ripple in that:
    A. Logic inputs are applied in parallel.
    B. Counter feedback is synchronous.
    C. The clock is applied to all flip flops simultaneously.
    D. There is no ripple on synchronous counters.

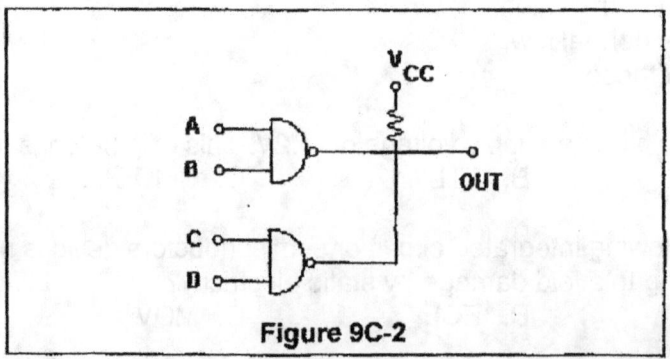

Figure 9C-2

19. The circuit shown on Figure 9C-2: 19._____
    A. Is a wired exclusive or.
    B. Is a wired or.
    C. Is used for high speed operation.
    D. Uses open collector gates.

20. What is the result of adding binary 110111 and 1001: 20._____
    A. 1000000.   B. 11111.   C. 100000.   D. 111111.

21. What is the binary result of multiplying hexadecimal 1C by 7? 21._____
    A. 11101100.   B. 11000100.   C. 11001100.   D. 11100100.

22. The value 123456 is based upon a number system which has a minimum radix of: 22._____
    A. 10.   B. 6.   C. 7.   D. 2.

23. A twos complement number is formed by the following method: 23._____
    A. Complement individual bits; then add 1.
    B. Add the number to all ones; then add 1.
    C. Subtract the number from all ones; then add 1.
    D. Add individual bits; then add 1.

24. Choose the correct solution to the following: 0101 + 0010 =19. 24._____
    A. 10111.   B. 1000.   C. 0111.   D. 01000.

Figure 9C-3

25. Refer to the waveforms shown on Figure 9C-3:20. 25._____
    With x and y as inputs to an "AND" gate, what is the output waveform?
    A. Waveform A   C. Waveform C
    B. Waveform B   D. Waveform D

26. Refer to the waveforms shown on Figure 9C-3: 26._____
    With x and y as inputs to an "OR" gate, what is the output waveform?
    A. Waveform D   C. Waveform B
    B. Waveform C   D. Waveform A

27. Refer to the waveforms shown on Diagram EL9C3C: With x and y as inputs to a 27._____
    "Exclusive OR" gate, what is the output waveform?
    A. Waveform A   C. Waveform C
    B. Waveform B   D. Waveform D

28. The standard serial output of a PC conforms to the following specification.
    A. 20 mA loop.
    B. RS232.@@
    C. NMEA0180.
    D. Centronics

29. Which of the following logic levels are in a normal ran for TxD and Rxd signals on an RS232 interface line?
    A. 2.5 V and +2.5 V.
    B. +0.20 V and +4.5 V.
    C. -10 V and +10 V.
    D. 10 V and 0 V.

30. What happens in a microprocessor system if electrical power input is interrupted?
    A.   Data stored in ROM is lost forever.
    B.   Data stored in ROM is lost, but can be restored by rebooting.
    C.   Data stored in RAM is lost.
    D.   Data stored in RAM is retained.

KEY (CORRECT ANSWERS)

1. C	11. B	21. B
2. B	12. C	22. C
3. D	13. D	23. A
4. C	14. A	24. B
5. B	15. D	25. B
6. D	16. A	26. D
7. D	17. C	27. C
8. A	18. C	28. B
9. A	19. D	29. C
10. D	20. A	30. C

TEST 2

DIRECTIONS: Each question or incomplete statement is followed by several suggested answers or completions. Select the one that BEST answers the question or completes the statement. *PRINT THE LETTER OF THE CORRECT ANSWER IN THE SPACE AT THE RIGHT.*

1. Complete the following sentence. A bit string manipulated by a computer in one operation is usually called:
   A. A bit.
   B. A word.
   C. A byte.
   D. A nibble.

2. In a microcomputer, the program counter contains:
   A. The address of the next instruction to be executed.
   B. Data.
   C. A sequential instruction set.
   D. An instruction set.

3. Choose the most correct statement.
   A. A RISC processor requires two or more clock cycles to execute a command.
   B. A RISC processor has fewer instructions available than an equivalent non-RISC processor.
   C. A RISC processor is inherently limited to a 32 bit architecture.
   D. RISC processors cannot implement a stack.

4. A one dimensional data structure in which values are entered and removed one item at a time at one end is called what?
   A. A ring counter.
   B. A FIFO.
   C. A stack pointer.
   D. A pushdown stack.

5. The output of an assembler is:
   A. Used only for solving floating point problems.
   B. A higher level language.
   C. Equivalent machine language instructions called object code.
   D. Not in executable machine language form.

6. What is the DOS command used to copy files from one drive to another?
   A. RD.
   B. COPY.
   C. DEL.
   D. FC.

7. What is the command used to determine the version of DOS that the computer is currently using?
   A. MEM.
   B. VER.
   C. VERIFY.
   D. CHKDSK.

8. All DOS file names may contain a maximum of how many characters?
   A. 6.
   B. 11.@@
   C. 10.
   D. 7.

157

9. Compilers are used with which type of code?.
    A. High level languages.
    B. Assembly languages.
    C. Machine languages.
    D. High level languages and assembly languages.

10. Choose the correct answer:11._____
    A. A bit is one binary digit.
    B. A nibble is 4 bits.
    C. A byte is 8 bits.
    D. All answers are correct.

11. An interpreter is used with which type of code?
    A. Object codes.
    B. Assembly languages.
    C. High level languages.
    D. Machine codes.

12. An internal short between the base and collector of a bipolar transistor might be indicated by which of the following?
    A. A weak signal at the collector, in phase with the input.
    B. No signal at the output.
    C. DC supply voltage on the collector.
    E. Little or no signal at the collector and a reversal of phase.

13. When attempting to test a bipolar silicon or germanium transistor, which of the following is likely to be correct if the test is conducted after the device has been removed from its circuit?
    A. If an ohmmeter is used without an external limiting resistor, excessive base current will destroy the device.
    B. If A PNP transistor is being tested, forward junction resistance will be greater than reverse resistance.
    C. Forward junction resistance should be less than reverse junction resistance.
    D. Circuit effects which cannot be accounted for, preclude the use of resistance measurements.

14. When replacing a diac which is used with a silicon controlled rectifier, which way must the diac be installed?
    A. The anode must be connected to the gate.
    B. Either way will work.
    C. The cathode must be connected to the gate.
    D. Either way, depending on the polarity of the SCR.

15. Which of the following statements about diac bidirectional trigger diodes is incorrect?
    A. A diac is a three layer device with two terminals.
    B. A diac switch functions in either direction.
    C. The breakover voltage is usually between 28 and 36 volts.
    D. Lamps and battery chargers are typical loads for a diac.

16. Which of the following statements correctly describes photo diode operation?
    A. Photodiodes generate light in response to incident photons.
    B. Reverse biased photodiodes are photoresistive.
    C. Efficiency is a measure of photons per electron.
    D. Dark current flows in response to black light.

17. Which of the following statements distinguish phototransistors from photodiodes.   17._____
    A. Phototransistors are faster than photodiodes.
    B. Photodiodes are more sensitive than phototransistors.
    C. Photodarlingtons are the fastest photoconductors
    D. None of these.

18. Photodiode reverse current is called: 18._____
    A. Dark current in the absence of light.
    B. Zener current if the diode is reverse biased.
    C. Photocurrent if the diode is forward biased.
    D. Dark current in very low illumination.

19. What is the life expectancy of a light emitting diode operated continuously under   19._____
    normal operating conditions?
    A. Up to 100 years.
    B. Light emitting diodes may last up to 20 years.
    C. Unlimited life expectancy.
    D. Approximately 87660 hours.

20. How may the polarity of the leads of an LED be identified prior to installation in a circuit?   20._____
    A. The cathode lead is usually longer than the anode lead.
    B. There may be a flat edge on the body near the anode.
    C. If the cathode can be seen, it is usually smaller.
    D. The ground lead is usually lighter in color.

21. In testing a GaAs light emitting diode within the manufacturer's operating parameters   21._____
    of voltage and current, it appears that no light is emitted. What explanation could be
    given:
    A. The LED is connected backwards.
    B. The LED may have run out of GaAs.
    C. The LED may be emitting invisible light.
    D. The LED is connected backwards and may be emitting invisible light.

22. What is the typical minimum bias voltage required for normal operation of a   22._____
    GaAsP light emitting diode?
    A. The LED will operate at 1.2 volts reverse bias.
    B. The LED will operate at 0.6 volts forward bias.
    C. The LED will operate at 2 volts reverse bias.
    D. The LED will operate at 1.2 volts forward bias.

23. Which of the following statements is not true of light emitting diodes?   23._____
    A. They can be manufactured to emit various wavelengths.
    B. They can operate at very high speed.
    C. They can be made to emit nearly pure white light.
    D. They are vulnerable to failure due to overcurrent.

24. What is the usual method of protecting a light emitting diode from damage that   24._____
    would result if the operating voltage became too high?
    A. A series current limiting resistor is used.
    B. A zener voltage regulator is used.
    C. A fast-blow fuse is used in series with the LED.
    D. The LED is attached to a heat sink.

25. Assuming that a light emitting diode has an internal resistance of 5 ohms, what value of series current limiting resistor should be used if the power supply voltage is 6 volts and the diode current is to be 0.05 Amperes at 1.6 Volts DC?
   A. 83 Ohms.
   B. b} 120 Ohms.
   C. 88 Ohms.
   D. 32 Ohms.

26. With regard to a 7-segment LED display, which statement is correct?
   A. Only one segment at a time can be illuminated.
   B. An external decoder/driver is usually used.
   C. They are often used as simple on-off indicators.
   D. Segments must be illuminated in sets of two.

27. Identify the statement below which is incorrect with respect to infrared light emitting diodes:
   A. Light from an IR LED is invisible.
   B. Photodiodes can be used with IR LEDs.
   C. Phototransistors can be used with IR LEDs.
   D. IR LEDs are often used in optical couplers but not in opto-isolators.

28. When a power MOSFET has 0V from gate to source the following is true:
   A. It is in pinch off.
   B. It is saturated.
   C. It is in a conducting region.
   D. It is drawing gate current.

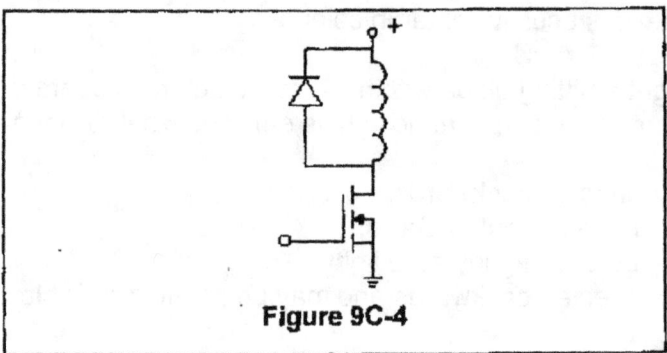

Figure 9C-4

29. The purpose of the diode in the circuit shown on Figure 9C-4 is to:
   A. Speed switching time.
   B. Protect the transistor.
   C. Increase current capacity.
   D. Compensate for thermal variations.

30. In the silicon transistor circuit below, you test the input and find that it is a 0.5V p-p sine wave centered about 4V. The output is a 1.5Vp-p sine wave centered about 7V. The most likely fact is that:
   A. The circuit is operating normally and is driving a high impedance.
   B. The circuit is operating normally and is heavily loaded.
   C. The transistor is bad.
   D. One of the circuit components is bad.

KEY (CORRECT ANSWERS)

1. B	11. C	21. C
2. A	12. C	22. D
3. B	13. C	23. C
4. D	14. B	24. A
5. C	15. D	25. A
6. B	16. B	26. B
7. B	17. D	27. D
8. B	18. A	28. A
9. D	19. C	29. B
10. D	20. A	30. A

EXAMINATION SECTION
TEST 1

DIRECTIONS: Each question or incomplete statement is followed by several suggested answers or completions. Select the one that BEST answers the question or completes the statement. *PRINT THE LETTER OF THE CORRECT ANSWER IN THE SPACE AT THE RIGHT.*

1. The majority of simple electronics circuits are based upon a logic

    A. A and a logic B state
    B. *on* and a logic *off* state
    C. 0 and a logic 1 state
    D. *go* and *no-go* state

    1.____

2. What voltage level exists in the 7400-series of 1C chips?

    A. -15 volts, ground, and +5 volts
    B. Ground, +5 volts, and +12 volts
    C. -12 volts, ground, and +5 volts
    D. +5 volts and ground

    2.____

3. A clock pulse is a transition

    A. from a logic 0 to a logic 1
    B. from a logic 1 to a logic 0
    C. from a logic 0 to a logic 1 and back to logic 0
    D. both A and B are correct

    3.____

4. The symbols shown to the right are those for a 2-input _____ gate and 2-input _____ gate.

    A. AND; NOR
    B. EXCLUSIVE-OR; NAND
    C. OR; NOR
    D. AND; NAND

    4.____

5. For which type of gate is the following definition CORRECT?
A binary circuit with two or more inputs and single output, in which the output is a logic 1 only when all inputs are logic 1, and the output is logic 0 if any one of the inputs is logic 0.

    A. AND gate   B. NAND gate   C. OR gate   D. NOR gate

    5.____

6. If the two inputs to a 2-input AND, NAND, OR, and NOR gate are both at logic 1, the outputs from the four gates are

    A. 1,1,0 and 0   B. 1,0,0 and 1
    C. 0,1,1 and 0   D. 1,0,1 and 0

    6.____

7. The term *to enable* a gate is the opposite of which of the following terms?

    A. To close a gate   B. To disable a gate
    C. To block a gate   D. All of the above

    7.____

8. A gate and a switch differ in which of the following ways?

    A. A gate is essentially a one-way device, whereas a switch is a two-way device.
    B. When a gate is closed, a signal can pass; when a switch is closed, a signal cannot pass.
    C. When a gate is open, a signal can pass; when a switch is closed, a signal cannot pass.
    D. A gate and a switch are identical in function.

9. A gating input of logic 0 to a 2-input NOR gate will allow what type of digital information to appear at the output of the gate?

    A. Logic 1 state B. Logic 0 state
    C. Unchanged input data D. Inverted input data

10. A gating input of logic 0 to a 2-input NAND gate will allow what type of digital information to appear at the output of the gate?

    A. Logic 1 state B. Logic 0 state
    C. Unchanged input data D. Inverted input data

11. The 7400, 7402, 7408, and 7432 IC chips each contain

    A. *only* a single gate B. four gates
    C. three gates D. two gates

12. A common-anode 7 segment display has the following inputs to its segments: A, D, E=1 and B, C, F, G = 0.
    What does the display read out?

    A. Nine B. Four C. Six D. Three
    E. None of these

13. A common cathode display has the following inputs to its segments: C,F.=0 and A,B,D,E,G=1.
    What does the display indicate?

    A. Nine B. Four C. Two D. Five

14. What is the difference between a 7490 and a 7493 counter?

    A. There is no difference.
    B. The 7490 is a decade counter, whereas the 7493 is a binary counter.
    C. The 7490 is a binary counter, whereas the 7493 is a decade counter.
    D. They have different pin configurations

15. The truth table to the right applies for the _____ gate.
    A. AND
    B. OR
    C. NAND
    D. NOR
    E. None of these

| IN | OUT |
AB	X
00	1
01	1
10	1
11	1

16. In the truth tables for a 2-input AND, NAND, OR, and NOR gate, the unique output state is, respectively,

    A. logic 1, logic 1, logic 0, logic 1
    B. logic 1, logic 0, logic 0, logic 1
    C. logic 0, logic 1, logic 1, logic 1
    D. logic 1, logic 1, logic 1, logic 1

17. When one inverts the output from an AND gate, he converts it into a(n) _____ gate.

    A. EXCLUSIVE-OR   B. NAND
    C. NOR   D. AND-OR-INVERT

18. If the two inputs to a 2-input AND gate and a 2-input NOR gate are left unconnected, the outputs from these two gates are, respectively,

    A. logic 1 and logic 0   B. logic 0 and logic 1
    C. logic 0 and logic 0   D. logic 1 and logic 1

19. The 7400, 7420, and 7430 IC chips have gates that have, respectively, the following numbers of inputs:

    A. two, three, five, and ten
    B. one, two, three, four
    C. two, three, four, eight
    D. two, three, four, six

20. The 7400, 7420, 7430 IC chips are all _____ gates.

    A. AND   B. NAND
    C. both AND and NAND   D. NOR

21. A four decade counter can count from

    A. 0001 to 10000   B. 0001 to 9999
    C. 0000 to 9999   D. 0000 to 100000

22. In a positive clock pulse, the transition from logic 1 to logic 0 occurs on the _____ edge.

    A. positive trailing   B. positive leading
    C. negative trailing   D. negative leading

23. The 74121-IC chip is a

    A. counter   B. flip-flop
    C. monostable multivibrator   D. programmable timer

24. When one debounces a SPDT switch, he

    A. makes sure that the switching action occurs quickly
    B. makes sure that the output from the switch can be controlled to produce a single clock pulse at a time
    C. turns the SPDT into, basically, a monostable multivibrator
    D. none of the above

25. When R=1 megohm and C=1 microfarad, the RC time constant has a value of

    A. 1 second   B. .000001 seconds
    C. .001 seconds   D. .000001 hz

4 (#1)

KEY (CORRECT ANSWERS)

1. C
2. D
3. C
4. A
5. A

6. D
7. D
8. A
9. D
10. A

11. B
12. E
13. C
14. B
15. E

16. B
17. B
18. A
19. C
20. B

21. C
22. C
23. C
24. B
25. A

TEST 2

DIRECTIONS: Each question or incomplete statement is followed by several suggested answers or completions. Select the one that BEST answers the question or completes the statement. *PRINT THE LETTER OF THE CORRECT ANSWER IN THE SPACE AT THE RIGHT.*

1. In HEXADECIMAL notation, the binary number DCBA = 1100 represents either _____ or the letter _____. 1.___

    A. eleven; B
    B. eleven; A
    C. twelve; C
    D. thirteen; D

2. The binary number, 11111, represents which of the following decimal numbers? 2.___

    A. 32   B. 16   C. 15   D. 3

3. A twelve-bit binary number can encode _____ decimal numbers. 3.___

    A. two thousand and forty-eight
    B. four thousand and ninety-six
    C. five hundred and twelve
    D. two hundred and fifty-six

4. The binary number, 1111, appears on the seven-segment LED display as a 4.___

    A. blank display
    B. decimal 15
    C. the letter F
    D. 0

5. The LARGEST binary number that can exist in binary-coded decimal (BCD) is 5.___

    A. 1000   B. 1111   C. 1001   D. 1010

6. The quantity, 0111 = DCBA, is in binary-coded decimal equal to decimal 6.___

    A. 7   B. 5   C. 9   D. 6

7. In which of the following choices are all of the IC chips either decoders or decoder-drivers? 7.___

    A. 7447, 7451, and 74150
    B. 7448, 7451, and 74160
    C. 7442, 7447, and 74154
    D. 7442, 7448, and 74150

8. Which of the following IC chips is a 4-line-to-10-line decoder? 8.___

    A. 7447   B. 7451   C. 74150   D. 7442

9. In a decade sequencer, one requires a 9.___

    A. 74150 chip and a decade counter such as the 7490
    B. 74150 chip and a binary counter such as the 7493
    C. 7451 chip and a decoder such as the 7442
    D. 7442 chip and a 7490 chip

10. A demultiplexer is similar to a 10.___

    A. shift register
    B. decoder
    C. device that can select one of a number of inputs and pass the logic level on to the output
    D. data selector

11. When connected in the proper way, the 74150 and 74154 chips can serve as a   11.____

    A. sequencer
    B. simultaneous decoder/driver
    C. multiplexer/demultiplexer circuit
    D. programmable sequencer

12. The current that passes through a light-emitting diode (LED) should generally NOT exceed   12.____

    A. one ampere   B. one milliampere
    C. 30 to 50 milliamperes   D. 300 milliampere

13. When the anode of a LED is connected to +5 volts and the cathode is connected to ground, the LED will   13.____

    A. remain unlit
    B. become lit, although only slightly
    C. light up immediately, but it may become unlit owing to the lack of a current-limiting resistor
    D. burn out

14. One can construct a simple logic probe from a   14.____

    A. light-emitting diode, capacitor, and battery
    B. LED, transistor, and battery
    C. LED and resistor
    D. LED and capacitor

15. When a logic probe is constructed from a LED and other components, a transistor is *usually* employed to   15.____

    A. make the LED light a bit more brighter
    B. conserve power
    C. *decrease* the current required to light the lamp monitor circuit
    D. *decrease* the voltage across the LED

16. A typical J-K flip-flop can have the following inputs: 16.____

    A. Strobe, enable, count, clear, and present
    B. Clock, preset, J, K, and clear
    C. Clock, count, J, K, and clear
    D. Clock, J, K, clear, preset, Q, and Q

17. A flip-flop is a   17.____

    A. three state device
    B. two state device
    C. one state device
    D. either a one state or a two state depending upon the logic state appearing at the strobe input

18. With the aid of a single gate, a 74126 gate with three-state output can be converted into a

    A. monostable multivibrator
    B. bi-stable memory element
    C. tri-stable memory element
    D. none of the above

19. When J = 0 and K = 1 in a J-K flip-flop,

    A. Q can go to or stay at logic 1, but cannot go to logic 0
    B. Q can go to or stay at logic 0, but cannot go to logic 1
    C. the flip-flop toggles
    D. Q remains at its logic state; the clock has no effect

20. When present at the inputs or outputs of logic devices, the small circle o represents

    A. that a positive clock pulse may be required to enable the device
    B. that a positive leading edge may be required to enable the device
    C. inversion
    D. a shorthand form for an AND gate

21. The preset and clear inputs to a flip-flop

    A. do not take precedence to the J-K inputs, but do take precedence to the clock input
    B. do not take precedence to the clock input, but do take precedence to the J-K inputs
    C. take precedence over all other inputs
    D. none of the above

22. A typical read-only memory (ROM) IC chip has

    A. memory cell select inputs, memory enable input, read/write select input, data inputs, and data outputs
    B. data inputs, data outputs, memory enable input, and memory cell select inputs
    C. memory enable input, memory cell select inputs, and data outputs
    D. data inputs, data outputs, read/write select inputs, memory cell select input, and clock input

23. A typical random access memory (RAM) IC chip has

    A. memory cell select inputs, memory enable input, read/write select input, data inputs, and data outputs
    B. data inputs, data outputs, and memory cell select inputs
    C. data outputs, memory cell select inputs, and memory enable input
    D. data inputs, data outputs, read/write select input, memory cell select input, and clock input

24. Shift registers can

    A. convert serial data into parallel data
    B. convert parallel data into serial data
    C. store both serial and parallel data
    D. do all of the above, depending, of course, upon the nature of the specific shift register used

25. The 74194 shift register can
    A. parallel load
    B. shift right
    C. shift left
    D. all of the above

KEY (CORRECT ANSWERS)

1.	C	11.	C
2.	D	12.	C
3.	B	13.	C
4.	C	14.	C
5.	B	15.	C
6.	A	16.	B
7.	C	17.	B
8.	D	18.	D
9.	D	19.	B
10.	C	20.	C

21. C
22. C
23. D
24. D
25. D

www.ingramcontent.com/pod-product-compliance
Lightning Source LLC
Chambersburg PA
CBHW080933020526
44116CB00033B/2369